Date Due

APR 24 '89			
MAY 10 1991			

BRODART, INC.   Cat. No. 23 233   Printed in U.S.A.

The Triumph
of the Eucharist
Tapestries Designed by Rubens

Studies in Baroque Art History

Ann Sutherland Harris

Chair for Academic Affairs
Metropolitan Museum of Art

The Triumph
of the Eucharist

Tapestries Designed by Rubens

by
Charles Scribner, III

UMI RESEARCH PRESS
Ann Arbor, Michigan

Produced and distributed by
UMI Research Press
an imprint of
University Microfilms International
Ann Arbor, Michigan 48106

Library of Congress Cataloging in Publication Data

Scribner, Charles.
The Triumph of the Eucharist: Tapestries
Designed by Rubens.

(Studies in Baroque Art History ; no. 1)
Revision of thesis (Ph.D.)—Princeton University, 1977.
Bibliography: p.
Includes index.
1. Rubens, Peter Paul, Sir, 1577-1640. Triumph of the
Eucharist. 2. Tapestry—Flanders—History—17th century.
3. Counter-Reformation in art.   I. Title. II. Series.

NK3055.A3R82 1982   746.392'4   81-23080
ISBN 0-8357-1288-5   AACR2

For Ritchie,
my parents,
and C. S. IV.

Contents

List of Figures

Following page 144

Preface

I was first introduced a decade ago to Rubens's *Triumph of the Eucharist* in Emile Mâle's *L'art religieux après le Concile de Trente*. Although Mâle's discussion was necessarily brief, the importance which he attached to the tapestry cycle as a monument of post-Tridentine art was evident: "Tel est ce beau poème de l'Eucharistie, où Rubens a mis son genie et où l'Espagne a mis sa foi profonde et ses espérances. Ni l'Italie ni la France ne pourraient montrer, au XVIIe siècle, une oeuvre aussi grandement conçue" (p. 86).

A survey of the literature at that time revealed, however, that while there had been a few articles on the tapestries and one slim exhibition catalogue there was no monograph on the cycle that treated systematically its preparatory stages, iconography, and overall significance within the artist's vast oeuvre. In addition to Mâle's claim, the fact that the Eucharist cycle represents not only Rubens's largest tapestry commission but also his largest extant program of ecclesiastical decoration suggested that a detailed study was warranted. Fortunately, unlike the other tapestry cycles (indeed, unlike *all* Rubens's large cycles except for the Whitehall ceiling paintings), the Eucharist tapestries still remain in their original surroundings, the Convent of the Descalzas Reales in Madrid.

In the fall of 1972 I traveled to Madrid to study the tapestries, which had been placed on permanent exhibit a few years earlier. During my visit to the convent I was struck by their size and magnificence. At the same time, I felt the important of determining their original location and decorative function. The tapestries are displayed in a gallery, a converted dormitory, the walls of which are not quite high enough to permit them to hang freely (the lower borders are rolled onto the floor). Where did the artist and his patron, the Infanta Isabella, intend the series to hang? The answer, I was certain, was essential to a proper understanding of Rubens's cycle.

The present study passed through two preliminary stages. The first was my undergraduate thesis, submitted to the Department of Art and Archaeology, Princeton University, in April 1973. The second was a paper on the architecture of the tapestries and their reconstruction, presented at the Annual Meeting of the College Art Association in January 1975 and later published as an article in *The Art Bulletin* (December 1975). Finally, the manuscript was submitted as my doctoral dissertation for Princeton University in the fall of 1976.

Since 1977 two important books relating to the Eucharist tapestries have appeared. The first is Nora de Poorter's volume for the *Corpus Rubenianum Ludwig Burchard*, published in the fall of 1978. It offers, like its companion volumes, a comprehensive, fully illustrated *catalogue raisonné* with a lengthy introduction, a compendium of related documents, and other useful background information. Since it is in agreement with most of my findings I have simply used the notes to identify those few areas of disagreement, which have already been summarized in my review for *The Burlington Magazine* (November, 1980). In addition, I have added notes directing the reader to Ms. de Poorter's volume for additional source material wherever it might be helpful.

The second, more recent, publication is Julius S. Held's monumental *catalogue raisonné* of Rubens's oil sketches (*The Oil Sketches of Peter Paul Rubens*, Princeton, 1980). No amount of additional notes could adequately underscore the importance and usefulness of Professor Held's work. Wherever feasible, I have amended certain notes to refer to Held's book. Every future work of Rubens scholarship will be in his debt, as mine has been.

Throughout its extended "gestation period," this book has benefited from the generous contributions of several scholars. My first thanks are to John Rupert Martin. Professor Martin first interested me in Rubens and continually encouraged, criticized, and improved this present study from its inception. In addition, his own contributions to Rubens scholarship, especially his monographs on the Jesuit ceiling paintings and the *Pompa Introitus Ferdinandi*, provided ideal models for the full treatment of a cycle by Rubens.

I am equally grateful for the subsequent interest, encouragement, and guidance given by Professor Julius S. Held. In addition to his many questions, criticisms, and suggestions for my study of the Eucharist tapestries, Professor Held generously shared with me the fruits of his extensive study of Rubens's oil sketches prior to the publication of his definitive *catalogue raisonné*. The experience has been as exciting as it has been instructive, and it is a pleasure to acknowledge so large a debt.

My thanks also to the following scholars for their help: Egbert Haverkamp Begemann, David R. Coffin, Horton M. Davies, Thomas L. Glen, Robert A. Koch, Irving Lavin, Anne-Marie Logan, Micheline Moisan, and Fr. Charles Weiser. My special thanks to Jacques Barzun and my father, Charles Scribner, Jr., for their encouraging words and for their invaluable lessons in clear writing. They are masters of the art.

New York
October 1981

Part I

A Royal Commission

1

The Early Cycles

Among his major commissions for monumental decorative programs, Rubens designed four great tapestry cycles. The subjects ranged from ancient history (the *Decius Mus* and *Constantine* tapestries) and mythology (the *Achilles* series) to the Catholic Faith (the *Eucharist* cycle), but all shared important characteristics. Each narrative cycle was treated in a distinctly epic fasion in which the pictorial conception rivaled the sumptuousness and sheer grandeur of the tapestry medium, and each involved several preparatory stages of design. In this respect the tapestry cycles represent a collaborative effort involving Rubens himself, his assistants and the tapestry weavers. They offer an ideal area in which to study Rubens as both painter and orchestrator of a vast undertaking, a dual role in which he was to be equaled only by his Italian counterpart of the High Baroque, Gian Lorenzo Bernini.

Given the scale and complexity of such projects, it was natural that Rubens's first commission to design a tapestry program should have come well after he had established himself in Antwerp as court painter to the Archdukes Albert and Isabella and had assembled a large studio of pupils, collaborators, and assistants, the most notable of whom was Anthony van Dyck. The commission was for a cycle of tapestries illustrating the life and death of the legendary Roman counsul Decius Mus.[1]

The Decius Mus Series

The contract for Rubens's first tapestry series was drawn up in late 1616 between a prominent Genoese merchant, Franco Cattaneo, and two Antwerp tapestry dealers, Jan Raes and Frans Sweerts.[2] Rubens was to design the panels and to pass judgment on the finished pieces. The cycle was to be woven *twice*, with slightly different dimensions owing to the varying size and shape of the two rooms in which the tapestries were destined to hang. One set comprised seven panels and two overdoors; the other, seven panels and one overdoor hanging. The fact that from the start the commission involved two "editions," presumably for two different patrons, explains why Rubens referred to this cycle in a letter to Sir Dudley Carleton on 7 May 1618, as having been commissioned by "certain Genoese gentlemen": "*ho fatto alcuni cartoni molto superbi a requisitione d'alcuni Gentilhuomini Genuesi li quali adesso si mettono in opere.*"[3]

It has been suggested, initially by Max Rooses,[4] that one of the patrons was Nicolo Pallavicini, a friend of the artist from the time of his sojourn in Italy (1600–1608) and later the godfather of Rubens's second son, Nicolaas, who was baptized on 23 March 1618—while this very cycle was being executed by the tapestry weavers.

The circumstances of Rubens's first tapestry commission—and his first commission for a large decorative program—marked a new departure for the young Antwerp artist. No longer was the relationship between artist and patron a personal and private one. In the past Rubens's commissions, whether for altarpieces, portraits, or secular paintings, had involved an essentially simple agreement between him and his patron whereby he was expected to deliver the painting, following certain specifications, at a given time and for a stated price. The two great commissions for Antwerp altarpieces of *The Raising of the Cross* and *The Descent from the Cross* may serve as prominent examples.[5]

In the contract for the Decius cycle, however, the relationship became more complex. First of all, Rubens was not a party to the contract itself, although he surely was involved in drawing up the terms and in determining the nature (and probably the subject) of the cycle. There was now an intermediary between Rubens and the patrons: the tapestry merchants. But one cannot conclude that Rubens was therefore merely employed by the workshop to design one of their commissions. The contract specified that he should judge whether the manufacturers were entitled to an increase in payment. So Rubens's responsibilities extended beyond designing the cycle to evaluating the final execution of the tapestries. His close association with tapestry workshops was to continue over a decade, and it was to extend to the artist's personal life: Rubens's second wife, the young Helène Fourment, was the daughter of a tapestry dealer, Daniel Fourment. In fact it is likely that he designed his last tapestry cycle (The *Achilles* series) for Fourment. But Rubens already had tapestries in his blood, so to speak. He was descended on his mother's side from a tapestry manufacturer, Hendrick Pype (or Pypelinckx), who died in 1580.[6]

The fact that Rubens's commission involved two sets of weavings should discourage any attempt to interpret the subject, Decius Mus, and the narrative of this cycle as allusions to a particular patron. The story is taken from Livy (VIII: 6, 9, 10) and tells of Decius's deliberate sacrifice of his life to save the Roman army. Rubens, adhering closely to the text, divided the narrative in the following manner:

1. The adlocution: Decius relates his dream to his men.
2. The interpretation of the victim: Decius learns that he is fated to die for the Roman army.
3. Decius is consecrated to the gods of the Underworld.
4. Decius dismisses his lictors.
5. Decius is killed in battle.
6. The funeral of Decius.

In addition to these six primary episodes, Rubens added an allegorical tapestry of the goddess Roma crowned by Victory and a decorative panel of Trophies.

The choice of this little-known subject for Rubens's first major cycle is significant. Never before had this story been illustrated by a cycle of paintings or tapestries. Rubens's choice—if indeed we may credit that choice to him—testifies to his genuine and scholarly interest in the ancient Latin authors and in classical antiquity in general. That interest had been nurtured during his years in Italy, where he was able to study ancient monuments, inscriptions, and collections of antiquities such as the famous Farnese collection assembled by Fulvio Orsini. His studies culminated in a project to illustrate his brother Philip's book on classical philology, the *Electorum Libri Duo* (1608), which represents his first known series of book engravings.[7]

The story of Decius Mus offered the artist more than an opportunity to express his love of classical antiquity, to combine authentic objects and dress with motifs from ancient sculpture, and to bring the characters back to life in an epic yet naturalistic way. It also provided an example of Roman *virtus* and *pietas*, the willingness of Decius to submit himself to the will of the gods and to offer himself to them as a sacrifice for his people. Rubens was undoubtedly attracted to this theme by its stoical and almost proto-Christian implications. As a young man Rubens had been close to the circle of the neo-stoic philosopher, Justus Lipsius: Rubens's *Four Philosophers* portrait, now in the Pitti Palace in Florence (*K.d.K.* 45) attests to his deep emotional ties with that group. More important to a full understanding of the Decius cycle is the simple fact that for Rubens there was no conflict, indeed no real separation, between the highest ideals and values of ancient Rome and the Christian faith of New Rome, to which the artist subscribed unreservedly. Rome was still Rome, and Rubens's sense of its continuity finds the closest parallel in the traditional dialogue between the Old and New Testaments. A Christian humanist, he interpreted many of the ancient authors and classical subjects as prefiguring Christian ideals. We shall see later how important the tradition of Old Testament typologies was to his religious art. In the Decius Mus cycle the typological concept was extended to include classical antiquity in a broader and less defined but no less valid fashion. The historical point of transition from pagan to Christian Rome was appropriately to be chosen as the subject of his next cycle of tapestries, the Constantine series.

Before leaving the Decius tapestries we may consider briefly the various stages in which Rubens designed the cycle. Since the series had been commissioned and therefore was undoubtedly discussed by the artist and his patrons—in this case, their representative, Franco Cattaneo—one might reasonably assume that Rubens first made a series of drawings or even rough oil sketches (*bozzetti*) to show to his patron and perhaps also to the tapestry manufacturers. If so, none of these "first thoughts" has survived. In fact only one chalk drawing related to this commission exists: an anatomical study of arms for the figure of the soldier who kills Decius in battle.[8] But such a study ordinarily finds its place relatively late in the various preliminary stages, when Rubens corrected a pose, gesture, or even whole figure by drawing from a live model. In this case the drawing should be placed between Rubens's oil sketch (*modello*) for *The Death of Decius* and the final cartoon from which the tapestry weavers worked.

The earliest and most important stage that has been preserved for this cycle is the series of modelli which Rubens painted as models for his studio assistants to enlarge each composition into tapestry-sized paintings or cartoons. Only four original modelli have survived;[9] several other episodes, however, are represented by contemporary copies. The best-known and most revealing modello is the oil sketch of *The Adlocution of Decius* in the National Gallery in Washington. The varying degree of "finish" conveys a sense of the process by which Rubens painted such an oil sketch. If we compare it with the final stage, the cartoon for this subject (Liechtenstein Collection, Vaduz), we note how little the general composition was altered in its expansion while several changes and modifications were made in details. For example, the eagle hovering over Decius has been omitted completely, Decius's facial features have been altered, and the rather sketchy armor has now been carefully articulated for the benefit of the tapestry weavers.

One important aspect that distinguishes a tapestry modello from a preparatory sketch for another kind of commission (an altarpiece, for example) is the fact that it reverses the intended composition. Owing to the usual method of tapestry weaving, the modello and its subsequent enlargement must be painted in mirror image of the tapestry. Consequently, figures in tapestry modelli and cartoons appear left-handed and movement ordinarily is from right to left—the opposite of what we would expect. This fact raises an important question about the so-called cartoons, which in the case of the Decius cycle are preserved *in toto*.

Traditionally, cartoons for tapestry weavers were painted in tempera on paper, the most famous example being Raphael's cartoons for his series of *The Lives of the Apostles* for the Sistine Chapel.[10] These cartoons, now in the Victoria and Albert Museum in London, were still in the Netherlands in Rubens's time and must surely have exerted a strong influence on him and on other artists working in the tapestry medium. At the very least, they offered a lofty standard which a young artist such as Rubens, having been recently exposed to the giants of the Italian Renaissance in their native country, would strive to equal and, if possible, to excel. On the other hand, their condition at this time must already have suffered considerably—tempera on paper is no medium for preserving masterpieces. Therefore, it is possible that Rubens's choice of oil on canvas for his first tapestry cartoons was a deliberate effort to give them a better afterlife (that is, beyond their original function in the tapestry workshop) than the Raphael cartoons had enjoyed. Today the Decius cartoons hang as a set of monumental paintings in their own right, and it is likely that Rubens had this end in mind from the very start.

Unfortunately Rubens's intentions for these large canvases, which according to later documents were executed chiefly by the young Van Dyck,[11] must remain a matter of speculation. We have no clue as to whether they remained in the tapestry workshop for the subsequent reweavings of the series—there were several—or whether they passed immediately to a patron or purchaser. However, the possibility that Rubens hoped to sell additional sets of these tapestries is supported by a letter to Carleton, written two weeks after Rubens's first mention of the commission. On 26 May 1618 he wrote to Carleton: "I will send Your Excellency all the measurements of my cartoons of the history of Decius Mus, the Roman Consul who sacrificed himself for the victory of the Roman people; but I must write to Brussels for the exact figures, since I have consigned everything to the master of the factory."[12]

There can be little doubt that the artist was here referring to the Liechtenstein canvases. The original Genoese commission evidently did not preclude Rubens's arranging for an additional set of the same cycle for another patron. Therefore it is all the more probable that he intended the cartoons on canvas, magnificent as they were, to remain for sometime in the hands of the tapestry manufacturers.

The Constantine Tapestries

Rubens's second tapestry series followed his first by approximately five years and is first mentioned in a letter from Nicholas-Claude Fabri de Peiresc to Rubens, dated 24 November 1622. This cycle was devoted to the life of the Emperor Constantine, the first Christian emperor of Rome. It comprised twelve episodes designed by Rubens to be woven by the tapestry workshops of Marc de Comans and François de la Planche in Paris. For each of the twelve panels, the artist painted a modello in oil on panel. (A thirteenth, allegorical, modello for *The Triumph of Rome* was dropped from the cycle and replaced by *The Death of Constantine*.[13])

The circumstances of this commission have been the subject of considerable speculation and debate among scholars. Most have assumed that the series was commissioned by King Louis XIII since the tapestries were, in fact, woven for him and inspected by him. He eventually gave them to Cardinal Francesco Barberini, who took the seven completed tapestries to Rome to hang in the Barberini Palace, where they were later augmented by a series of six panels designed by Pietro da Cortona. There the tapestries remained until they crossed the Atlantic to hang in the Philadelphia Museum of Art as a gift of the Kress Foundation.

Nevertheless, Dubon, Haverkamp Begemann, and Held reject the hypothesis that the cycle originated with a commission given by the French king to Rubens. The existing documentary evidence has most recently and most convincingly been interpreted by Held as indicating that the cycle was actually designed "on speculation," as a joint venture for Rubens and the Parisian tapestry manufacturers.[14] Evidently they had hoped to sell the series to King Louis, and their hopes were fulfilled. To some degree, then, the cycle may be said to have been conceived and designed with a specific patron in mind. But in no way was it a personal commission. In fact, it was necessary for Rubens's correspondent and friend Peiresc to explain the various episodes to the King and his advisors.

These unusual circumstances of the commission inevitably affect our interpretation and understanding of its subject, the life of Constantine. The story of the first Christian emperor provided a fitting—and flattering—theme with which the young King Louis might adorn his palace walls. Its visual ancestor, the magnificent cycle of frescoes in the Sala di Costantino in the Vatican Stanze, designed by Raphael and executed by Giulio Romano, undoubtedly made the subject all the more appropriate for a Catholic monarch who was seeking to bring peace and unity to his religiously divided realm. Rubens was undoubtedly aware that the King—for that matter, any young king with lofty aspirations—would see himself reflected in such a cycle glorifying a secular, Christian ruler ("on earth as it is in heaven"). But John Coolidge's notion that the tapestries are interwoven with strands of political allegory, propaganda, and specific allusions to King Henry IV, Louis XIII, and his mother, Maria de' Medici, must be rejected.[15] Coolidge even went so far as to interpret the whole cycle as a political allegory criticizing Maria de' Medici's years of regency, and he interpreted individual scenes as deliberate references to contemporary historical events. For example, the tapestry of Constantine overseeing the plans for Constantinople was seen as an allusion to King Louis's reimbursing the Huguenots for their destroyed meetinghouse.[16] One might well question such a line of interpretation on the basis of the sheer lack of visual support within Rubens's tapestries. The fact that the original idea for the cycle was not the King's at all, but must be attributed wholly to Rubens and the tapestry dealers, makes any such allegorical reading doubly improbable. After all, the King might have shown no interest in the cycle, in which case another purchaser would have been sought, perhaps even his mother. There is, in fact, some evidence—admittedly slim—that Rubens later intended to design tapestries for the chambers adjoining the long galleries which he was decorating for Maria de' Medici.[17]

The Constantine series provides a second type of venture into tapestry design for Rubens, a joint undertaking between the painter and the tapestry merchants. Unlike the preceding series, the preparatory work for this cycle did not include a series of large permanent paintings to serve as cartoons. Instead the cartoons were painted in tempera on paper by assistants and perhaps, as Held has suggested,[18] under the direction of Jacob Jordaens, who was especially skilled in this medium. The change in procedure possibly reflects Rubens's characteristic sense of economy. Since the project was, from the start, designed on speculation it would have been an extraordinary commitment (financial as well as artistic) to plan and execute the cartoons, now numbering twelve rather than eight, as monumental finished paintings. Thus Rubens adapted his procedure to the peculiar circumstances of the project. Only two drawings survive that can be connected with this cycle, and there are no preliminary oil sketches or bozzetti. Since the latter usually served as demonstration pieces to submit to a patron, their absence here can be similarly explained by the fact that Rubens had no assured patron with whom to deal.

In general, Rubens's first two tapestry cycles may be viewed as having much in common and as relatively straightforward undertakings. Each involved a narrative of Roman history, illustrated in a series of episodes designed and presumably selected by Rubens. In each case, the process of design was limited to an autograph modello by the master and a subsequent enlarged repetition by his studio assistants (Van Dyck and perhaps Jordaens). Furthermore, Rubens's designs included only the figural scenes; the decorative borders were apparently designed in the tapestry workshops, which was standard procedure. However, the possibility of some collaboration on his part should not be ruled out entirely.

Although the Decius series was commissioned by a patron, Rubens's primary relationship was with the tapestry weavers and not with Franco Cattaneo. There is no mention in the documents of Cattaneo's having to approve Rubens's sketches, the cartoons, or even the final tapestries. Rather, the artist himself was left in charge of the commission, even to the point of passing judgment on the final payments to be made to the weavers for their work. Thus Rubens's activity on the Decius tapestries, in close collaboration with the weavers, prepared him for his second undertaking which was a collaborative venture from the beginning and owed even less to the considerations of a patron. In this respect, these two secular cycles differ sharply from Rubens's grandest religious program of decoration at this time (ca. 1620), the commission for the thirty-nine ceiling paintings for the Jesuit Church in Antwerp. This vast project for decorating the ceilings of two aisles and two galleries with paintings recalls the Venetian *soffitti* of Titian, Tintoretto, and Veronese and represents a new departure for Rubens as designer and coordinator of decorative programs.

The Jesuit Ceiling Paintings

The commission followed a couple of years after the completion of the Decius cycle. Fortunately the original contract between Rubens and the Jesuit fathers has been preserved, and so it is possible to organize the visual material according to the various conditions which the artist had to fulfill: bozzetti, modelli, drawings, and copies (or recordings) by later artists of the final paintings, which were destroyed by fire in 1718. This cycle has been treated systematically by John Rupert Martin.[19] Even the most summary review of the series, particularly with respect to Rubens's function as both designer and coordinator, reveals not only a telling contrast to the two neighboring tapestry series (which closely preceded and followed the Jesuit commission) but also an illuminating and almost necessary antecedent for his third and largest tapestry commission, the Eucharist cycle, which was also to be his most extensive surviving program of church decoration after the ceiling paintings perished.

The contract which Rubens signed on 29 March 1620 with Jacobus Tirinus, the Superior of the Jesuit house, required Rubens himself to paint small sketches (*teekeninge*) from which Van Dyck and other assistants would execute the large canvases. Rubens could either give these sketches to the church or keep them for himself, in which case he was obliged to substitute an original altarpiece for a side chapel of the church.[20] He chose the latter alternative, which gives some indication of the value the artist placed on his preliminary designs.

During the course of designing this vast cycle Rubens painted far more oil sketches than the contract required. Some were the result of changes in the iconographic program, which Martin has traced in detail. But most of the additional sketches owe their existence to the fact that for almost every subject, Rubens painted a preliminary *grisaille* (or *bozzetto*) before the more finished and full-color modello. Thus unlike the two tapestry cycles, the Jesuit ceiling project was prepared by two stages of oil sketches. In this respect it recalls Rubens's procedure for designing his major altarpieces, beginning with the project for the Chiesa Nuova in Rome (1606–8). For his most important commission in Rome, Rubens painted first a preliminary sketch, which served as a demonstration piece for his patrons, and then several detailed modelli through which the various components of the altarpiece evolved into their final forms.[21] The fact that Rubens adopted a similar procedure for the Jesuit ceiling paintings is indicative of the close collaboration, as in the Chiesa Nuova, between painter and patron. The series of grisailles—and, in a few cases, drawings—served not only as a means for working out the first ideas for each subject but, more important, as a preliminary draft for the Jesuit fathers to approve and, in some cases, modify. Such a procedure was particularly well suited to a large complex cycle in which the patron played an active role in determining the iconography, and it is not surprising that Rubens adopted it once again when designing his next monumental cycle of paintings, the Medici cycle.

The Medici Cycle

As a large narrative cycle of paintings devoted to a historical ruler (in this case a living, though eclipsed, heroine), the Medici cycle may be seen as an outgrowth and expansion of the first two tapestry cycles. Here, too, the subject was an epic one—although in view of Maria's rather dull life that epic was necessarily more fiction than fact, a credit to Rubens's fertile imagination. The biographical narrative, now comprising twenty-six episodes, or just over twice as many scenes as in the recent Constantine cycle, was similarly prepared by oil sketches (modelli) which were enlarged by Rubens's studio assistants.[22] In this case the large canvases were to be the final works, and here the similarity with tapestry cartoons ends since, unlike the latter, the Medici canvases were retouched extensively by Rubens himself and hence became autograph works. The other chief departure from Rubens's prior two historical cycles is in the introduction of allegorical figures. Ranging from Olympian deities to personifications of evil forces, they serve to elevate the Queen Mother's rather unglorious life to a mythical plane on which mortals mingle freely—and often casually—with the gods. Rubens's true achievement was not only his diplomatic treatment of the politically sensitive subject but his new creation of "living allegory."

The successful, almost magical, transformation of conventional and previously wooden personifications into lively and psychologically active participants in the epic drama recalls Rubens's similar transformation of the allegorical title page—heretofore a rather dry and artificial composite of inscriptions, symbols, and personifications—into a sculptural and naturalistic unity wherein the allegory is brought to life. An especially striking example is the title page for the *Politico-Christianus* by Carolus Scribanius, the rector of the Jesuit Church in Antwerp, published in 1624 by the Plantin-Moretus press. Held has suggested that this title page may have had some influence—if only as background imagery—on Bernini's tomb of Pope Urban VIII in St. Peter's.[23]

The close similarity in treatment of the allegorical figure of *Caritas* in the two works makes Held's hypothesis an attractive one. At the least, it underscores the fact that the expressive naturalism characteristic of Bernini's sculptures was already anticipated "in miniature" by Rubens's designs for engraved title pages. During the decade of the 1620s, when Bernini was beginning to receive his first papal commissions, Rubens himself translated the living allegory of the title pages into a full-color, monumental, and characteristically Baroque context, first in the Medici cycle and (shortly thereafter) in his third tapestry cycle, *The Triumph of the Eucharist*, where that translation is more ambitious and more literal. As we shall presently see, he drew from the title pages not only the conception of fully integrated allegory and symbols but also the use of architectural structure and, in some cases, the introduction of inscriptions (or "titles").

Yet the title page *per se* played only a limited role in the evolution of Rubens's most complex cycle of tapestries and program of decoration. The Eucharist cycle fused several elements from practically every field of the artist's prior activity: the two tapestry cycles, the Jesuit ceiling commission, the Medici cycle, altarpieces, allegorical paintings (which include the title pages), and even portraiture. In addition, Rubens drew upon—and transformed into his personal High Baroque idiom—several sources of monumental church decoration to which he had been exposed during his sojourn in Italy two decades earlier. But the whole was inevitably greater than the sum of its parts, and the Eucharist cycle represents not only Rubens's grandest commission in tapestry and ecclesiastic decoration but also his most comprehensive expression of the Catholic Faith. As a fully orchestrated decorative program it was to be surpassed only once, and then only temporarily, by another of the artist's creations: his elaborate decorations for the *Pompa Introitus Ferdinandi*, which in a truly Berninesque manner combined painting, sculpture, and architecture in a Baroque totality.[24] These perishable monuments, however magnificent, survived only in a commemorative volume illustrated with engravings, whereas the Eucharist tapestries, which anticipated that late work, remain today at their original location, the Convent of the Descalzas Reales in Madrid. They offer a unique opportunity to study what may be called Rubens's High Baroque idiom of Counter-Reformation art.

2

The Eucharist Cycle

Rubens's third tapestry cycle, usually entitled *The Triumph of the Eucharist*, comprises at least sixteen and possibly as many as twenty separate tapestries. The documentary evidence is slight: no contract has been preserved or has yet come to light. The commission is not mentioned in any of Rubens's surviving letters; nor is it named in any of the few documents which appear to concern it. Nevertheless, it is generally—and justifiably—agreed among scholars, beginning with Rooses, that the series was commissioned by Rubens's royal patron, the Infanta Isabella, Governor of the Spanish Netherlands.[1] Rubens had been appointed court painter to her and her husband, the Archduke Albert, in 1609, and he continued to serve in this post after the latter's death in 1621. During the ensuing decade Rubens undertook several diplomatic missions for the Infanta and became her trusted and able diplomat. For his efforts in this field he was to be ennobled by King Philip IV of Spain and knighted by King Charles I of England. The treaty of peace which Rubens successfully prepared between these two kingdoms was undoubtedly the most important assignment and achievement in his diplomatic career; and his significant contribution in this area is reflected in the memorable tribute paid him by his longtime friend, General Ambrogio Spinola: "Of all his talents," Spinola said, "painting is the least."[2]

Indeed, with the exception of some official portraits and altarpieces, most of Rubens's work for the Infanta was found outside the realm of art. For this reason the Eucharist cycle assumes a significant place in the fruitful but unconventional painter-patron relationship between Rubens and the Infanta. It stands as the one great cycle he designed for her and thus represents a fitting counterpart to two major commissions which closely preceded and followed it respectively: the Medici cycle, designed for the Queen Mother of France, and the Whitehall ceiling designed for the King of England. However, whereas those two commissions were intended to be kept and publicly displayed by their royal patrons as self-glorifying monuments, the Infanta intended her commission to be a gift for her favorite (and secluded) convent in Madrid, the *Convento de las Señoras Religiosas Descalzas Reales*. The work was conceived to glorify not herself but rather her Catholic faith. These unusual circumstances of the Infanta's commission pay her greater tribute than any self-serving cycle might have done. Yet Rubens was to find a way to include his patroness in the cycle and (a decade later) to recall her commission in a public monument, the Infanta's funerary stage for the *Pompa Introitus Ferdinandi*.

The Convent of the Descalzas Reales had been founded by Doña Juana of Austria, the daughter of the Emperor Charles V, and hence Isabella's aunt (the Infanta was a daughter of Charles's son Philip II).[3] It became a favorite retreat for female members of the Spanish royal family, and the Infanta herself spent eight months there as a child. Her continued association with these "Poor Clares" (or Discalced Franciscans)[4] is revealed by the fact that after her husband's death in 1621 she wore the habit of a tertiary in their order for the rest of her life. She appears so dressed in her portrait by Rubens painted in 1625 (now in the Norton Simon Collection, Fig. 1),[5] of which there are several replicas and which may, as we shall see, have been closely connected with the commission for the Eucharist tapestries. That this was intended to be an official, rather than private, portrait is indicated not only by its many copies and variants but also by the fact that it was engraved for publication by Paulus Pontius.

The subject chosen for the Infanta's extravagant gift of tapestries to the convent was a logical one. The nuns of the Descalzas Reales had a special devotion to the Eucharist and each year they held two major processions of the Blessed Sacrament within the walls of their convent: one on the octave of the Feast of Corpus Christi; the other on Good Friday. To hold a Eucharist procession on Good Friday was most unusual and required a special papal dispensation.[6] (During Good Friday no Mass may be celebrated in any church, and the sacrament is reserved at a side altar, having been removed from the high altar the night before.)

Traditionally the nuns borrowed tapestries from the royal collections to adorn the stark walls of the convent for these triumphal celebrations and processions, according to Elias Tormo, who wrote the comprehensive monograph on the Descalzas Reales, which includes a volume on the Eucharist tapestries.[7] In commissioning Rubens to design this cycle, therefore, the Infanta sought to provide the nuns with a permanent and iconographically suitable set of hangings for these solemn occasions.

The paucity of documentary evidence surrounding this cycle leaves the actual circumstances of the commission and its precise dating a matter of conjecture. The credit for piecing together the few references in a convincing way must go to Max Rooses.[8] No significant new documents have been published since his volume of 1886, and his interpretation of them remains valid.

The earliest known document connected with the tapestries is a letter dated 21 May 1627 from Philippe Chifflet, the Infanta's court chaplain at Brussels, to the papal nuncio to Brussels, J. F. Guidi di Bagno. Chifflet writes that Rubens intends to travel to Rome in September of that year but, before doing so, has to finish several paintings for the Infanta:

> Rubens faict conte de partir pour Rome environ ce temps là, après qu'il aura parachevé plusieurs tableaux qu'il a entrepris pour S.A.[9]

Rooses, followed by subsequent scholars, understood these paintings to refer to the cartoons for the Eucharist cycle. One must, as Held has cautioned,[10] admit the possibility that Chifflet refers to other works, but the subsequent evidence virtually confirms their identification with the Eucharist cycle.

A brief note in a manuscript in the Chifflet collection, now preserved in the library of Besançon, records that in January of 1628 Rubens was given some pearls by the Infanta as an expression of her thanks for the tapestry designs: "En janvier 1628 furent donnés à Pierre-Paul Rubens plusieurs perles, à bon compte des patrons de tapisserie pour les cordelières de Madrid."[11]

For some unknown reason, the artist had been unable to carry out his plans to travel to Rome. (Unfortunately he was never to make the trip or to witness firsthand the flowering of the High Baroque there under the direction of his Italian counterpart and artistic kinsman, Gian Lorenzo Bernini.)

Another note by Chifflet records that Rubens received thirty thousand florins for the tapestry cartoons and that the tapestries themselves were valued at one hundred thousand florins.[12] Since it is undated we do not know when that payment was made or, more important, when the tapestries were completed by the weavers and appraised. But a *terminus ante quem* is provided by the final document, a letter from Chifflet to Guidi di Bagno dated 21 July 1628. Chifflet reports that two days earlier the Infanta ordered two wagons loaded with tapestries, canvases, maps, and some paintings to depart for Spain:

> S.A. a faict partir dès deux jours en çà deux chariots qu'elle faict passer en Espagne chargez de tapisseries, de toiles et de chartes geographiques et de quelques peintures.[13]

Held has observed that if this shipment contained most—and maybe all—of the Eucharist tapestries, then the date of the original commission must be pushed as far back as possible to allow for the very long process of weaving such a large cycle as this one.[14] Rooses believed that most of Rubens's preparatory work had probably been carried out between August 1625 and February 1626, when the artist was residing in Brussels and was therefore in close proximity to the tapestry workshops which were to execute his designs.[15] Perhaps even more pertinent to the evolution of this cycle is the fact that during these same months Rubens could keep in close touch with his patroness, the Infanta Isabella, and her theological advisors at the court in Brussels. Both the iconographic complexity of the cycle and the existence of distinct preparatory stages (sketches) indicate the strong probability of close collaboration between patron and painter on this project. Rooses's dating therefore becomes all the more persuasive.

V. H. Elbern, who organized the first exhibition in Cologne (1954–55) of works connected with the cycle and who wrote the first comprehensive *catalogue raisonné*, offered the intriguing suggestion that the commission itself originated during the few days that the Infanta spent in Antwerp in July of 1625 on her way back to Brussels from Breda.[16] She had gone to Breda to celebrate the surrender of the Dutch forces to the Marquis of Spinola on June 5th. (The surrender was to be commemorated a decade later by Velasquez in his famous painting for Philip IV, now in the Prado.) Two letters written by Rubens at this time reflect how eager he was to meet with her on her return trip,[17] and we know from still another Chifflet document[18] that while in Antwerp Isabella visited the artist's studio and sat for the portrait mentioned earlier. Elbern's hypothesis is not only convenient in practical terms but is also particularly attractive in the light of the cycle's emphasis on the victorious and militant aspects of the Catholic Faith, personified by *Ecclesia triumphans* and reflected in the cycle's usual title: *The Triumph of the Eucharist*.[19] The surrender at Breda was one of Spain's rare victories in her tragic and prolonged war in the Netherlands. At the time, it was viewed as a turning point, a sign that Spain would eventually triumph over the rebel forces. The Infanta would surely have considered this event an appropriate cause for giving thanks to God. And, in view of the religious implications of the struggle—the Catholic south against the Protestant north—how better to express the thanks than by commissioning a tapestry cycle proclaiming the power and triumph of the Eucharist? It is tempting to think that the cycle might first have taken shape while the Infanta sat for her portrait and had discussed the recent victory with the painter-diplomat.

It has been suggested that the commission may also reflect the influence of the allegorical poem, *Triumphos Divinos*, by the Spanish epic poet and dramatist Lope de Vega, which was published that same year.[20] (This question of a literary source will be considered at a later point, in Part II.) Finally, when we recall that the word "Eucharist" in its derivation from the Greek means "thanksgiving," the historical circumstances surrounding the Infanta's commission and her choice of subject for the cycle appear still further intertwined and suggest that the tapestries reflect, in addition to the traditional devotions and celebrations of the nuns at the Descalzas Reales, the faith and hope of the Spanish cause.

The Program

The actual number of tapestries designed for this cycle and their intended order within it have been the subjects of considerable question and disagreement among scholars. Most of them, beginning with Rooses and including, among others, Oldenbourg, Evers, and Haverkamp Begemann, have set the total number of tapestries at fifteen.[21] This figure is based upon a letter (first published by Rooses) written in 1648 by King Philip IV of Spain, in which he ordered fifteen large canvases, along with several smaller ones, to be sent to him from the Royal Palace in Brussels to Madrid.[22] Rooses assumed—probably correctly—that these fifteen large canvases referred to the full-size cartoons for the Eucharist cycle. The smaller ones evidently referred to the modelli even though these were, in fact, painted on panel, not canvas. Several of the cartoons and modelli, as we shall see, were sent to Spain in response to the King's request. Nevertheless, a survey of the tapestries themselves, which are still preserved in the Descalzas Reales and which have recently been placed on public view, reveals that the number fifteen was incorrect. The present study, moreover, will point out some of the problems involved in attempting to determine the exact number.

In general, the Eucharist cycle can be divided into two groups of hangings. The main series comprises eleven large narrative panels, each of which illustrates a separate religious subject on a feigned tapestry hanging with an illusionistic architectural setting of framing columns, i.e., a tapestry within a tapestry. These architectural framings are divided into two distinct orders : Doric, with fluted and banded columns; and Composite, with twisted or Solomonic columns. The fact that these tapestries are all roughly the same height, differing only in width, further encourages treating them as a unified series, something every scholar discussing the cycle has done. Yet no two writers have ever agreed on their order. If, as Held has demonstrated,[23] we take Rooses's order and number each piece accordingly from one to eleven, the next account—Tormo's—would run:

5, 2, 3, 1, 8, 6, 4, 7, 9, 10, 11; Puyvelde's numbering would read: 5, 2, 3, 1, 4, 8, 7, 6, 9, 10, 11; Elbern's would read: 6, 8, 7, 9, 1, 4, 10, 11, 2, 5, 3; and, most recently, Müller Hofstede's proposed sequence[24] would be numbered: 6, 8, 7, 9, 10, 11, 1, 4, 2, 5, 3. Tormo, who published the first comprehensive study of the cycle, referred to this group as "processional tapestries," since he believed they were intended to be hung along the walls of the clositer as backdrops for the convent's two Eucharistic processions.[25] Other scholars have, in turn, retained this convenient appellation and it will similarly be used in this discussion, although it will become evident that the term derives from a basic misconception of these tapestries' original function and location. The question of their intended location and arrangement will be treated in Part III of this study, following the iconographic survey and study of the individual pieces.

Although the series of eleven pieces forms a conceptual unity—each represents an illusionistic hanging within architecture—it may be subdivided not only into two groups of distinct architectural orders but also into convenient iconographic groupings. Elbern was the first to recognize four such groups: the first comprises the four Old Testament prefigurations of the Eucharist; the second is made up of two allegorical victories of the Eucharist over its historical foes, paganism and heresy; the third includes two gatherings of Eucharistic heralds and defenders; and finally the last contains a triumphal procession of three chariots.[26]

This division and arrangement was adopted with one variation by E. Müller-Bochat, who examined Rubens's cycle within the rich tradition of Petrarchan triumphal imagery in literature and the visual arts. He placed Elbern's third group last since he saw the Eucharistic announcers and defenders as an entourage following the three triumphal chariots.[27] This arrangement was later accepted by Held as the most satisfactory.[28] Müller Hofstede, on the other hand, preferred to place that entourage between the Old Testament typologies and the allegorical victories.[29]

Since Müller-Bochat's arrangement presents a thoroughly reasonable, as well as simple, iconographic progression, it has been retained for the following iconographic study, but with one minor modification: the Old Testament typological subjects will be described according to their Biblical sequence so that instead of appearing first, as in Müller-Bochat's account, *The Sacrifice of the Old Covenant* will come last in its group. This arrangement is here adopted only as a convenient means of presenting the various subjects within an iconographic study. In no way is it intended to imply a physical arrangement of the tapestries. Although, as we will be shown, the program for hanging the tapestries is intimately related to the iconographic program, the problem of the tapestries' intended location and arrangement is not simply a matter of determining an iconographically logical sequence. Therefore it will be studied as a separate issue.

In addition to the series of eleven narrative tapestries there is a second group of five much narrower pieces which together form a single composition: the Eucharist adored by angels and earthly rulers of church and state. This group is related to the larger series but is also self-contained and conceptually distinct. It was to hang around the high altar of the convent chapel as part of the decorations for the Eucharistic processions.[30] These tapestries include the same architectural framings of the larger tapestries but not the device of feigned tapestries hanging therein. The credit for identifying the five pieces as parts of one large composition goes to Rooses, who did so on the basis of a loose copy (variant) of an oil sketch, which confirms his hypothesis.[31] Subsequently, scholars writing about this group have tended to treat the altar group as independent from the main processional series. Accordingly, this group will be discussed after the first eleven panels. Nevertheless, it will become clear that they should not have been treated virtually as a second tapestry series. In the final analysis, Rooses was closer to the truth in treating them as a subdivided final composition in the long procession of subjects within the Eucharist cycle.[32]

Finally, there are four additional (and smaller) tapestries within the convent of the Descalzas Reales, and their relationship to the main cycle remains problematic. Tormo included two of them (and, by implication, a "lost" third) in his hypothetical reconstruction of the group surrounding the high altar.[33] The smaller two, he believed, neither belonged in this cycle nor were designed by Rubens,[34] but rather by one of his pupils. More recently, however, Held has identified preliminary oil sketches for them by Rubens, so each piece must be considered afresh. This group will consequently be treated last.

The Preparatory Stages

Before beginning a survey of the series piece by piece, we will consider briefly the various preparatory stages through which each composition passed before it was finally woven into a tapestry. No rough pen-and-ink sketches have been discovered for this series. In fact, no preparatory drawings at all have been convincingly identified. The absence of drawings, however, should not appear too surprising, for by this time Rubens rarely depended upon life studies for his large projects: there exists only one life drawing for the Decius cycle, one for the Medici cycle,[35] and none for the Jesuit ceiling or the Constantine series. The few relatively finished drawings for the Jesuit ceiling are connected with compositions for which we have no extant bozzetto, which suggests that the bozzetto as a preparatory device virtually precluded such a chalk drawing. In the Eucharist cycle this appears to be the case also. We may assume that Rubens made some very sketchy notes of compositions, jottings that he saw no reason to preserve once the composition was established. But there is really no reason to posit any lost drawings of a more finished nature for this cycle. Fortunately enough preparatory material survives to convey a clear idea of Rubens's standard procedure for designing each component of this large series.

The Bozzetti

The first stage for each composition is a small oil sketch or bozzetto. Nine such sketches have so far been discovered for the eleven processional tapestries: seven are preserved in the Fitzwilliam Museum in Cambridge,[36] two in the Musée Bonnat in Bayonne.[37] There is documentary evidence, moreover, that the two missing sketches once existed, for they appear to be described in the seventeenth-century inventory of the Antwerp painter and collector, Victor Wolfvoet.[38] One composite bozzetto exists for the five altar tapestries (Art Institute, Chicago).[39] And so we may safely say that Rubens's first procedure of design seems to have been consistent throughout the cycle.

These preliminary bozzetti, painted in oil on panel, have usually been referred to as grisailles, and indeed the very economical use of color might suggest such a term. But if we compare them with true grisailles by Rubens, such as those for title page engravings, we immediately recognize the inapplicability of the term to the Eucharistic sketches. Since they contain a range of colors, even if applied sparingly, they should simply be considered bozzetti. Their apparent function, as presentation pieces, accounts for the introduction of colors into such modest sketches.

Unlike the subsequent stages—the modelli and cartoons—the bozzetti for the processional tapestries are all in the same sense as the final tapestries: they are not painted in mirror image as is every sketch for the previous two tapestry cycles. This exceptional fact misled Ludwig Burchard to conclude that the panels in the Fitzwilliam Museum represent later copies painted from Rubens's modelli and reversed for engravings.[40] But their sketchy quality, small size, and the many compositional differences between them and the later stages of design (including, of course, the finished tapestries) quickly rule out such a theory. Engravings for each of the tapestries do exist and reveal their origins in the modelli, not in these bozzetti.

Tormo suggested that the "correct" sense of the bozzetti was for the convenience of the Infanta and her advisors;[41] that the sketches represent not so much Rubens's private experiments with compositional ideas as a complete series of presentational sketches to be shown to his patron for discussion and approval. This interpretation of the sketches would explain not only the representation of the intended sense of each composition but also the inclusion of color. It also accounts for their surprisingly finished quality. Although they reveal the economical "shorthand" of a preliminary sketch, they are sufficiently carefully executed that one has no trouble reading them. Iconographically as well as conceptually, they establish the first fixed program for the cycle. As we shall discover in Part III, Rubens had determined at this point not only the subject and basic composition for each tapestry but also its physical location. The bozzetti were truly meant to "fit together" and each was carefully designed with the others in mind. They reveal a uniformity of shapes and scale that distinguishes them from the bozzetti designed for Rubens's other projects.

Whether these sketches reflect Rubens's own iconographic inventions or a program that he was given by the Infanta and her advisors must remain a matter of speculation. However, this author believes that while the program may well have been outlined in very broad terms by his patron, Rubens himself was responsible for the iconographic details and for the unifying concept (*concetto*) of this cycle (which, as we shall discover, depends equally upon the use of illusionistic architecture and the unprecedented device of a tapestry within a tapestry). Only an imagination as fertile as Rubens's could have been responsible for such an original development and exploitation of the tapestry medium, which had heretofore been a rather conservative mode of decoration. As in the case of the Jesuit ceiling, however, Rubens surely discussed various aspects of the program with his patron and her advisors. He may also have called upon his Jesuit friends in Antwerp for ideas and advice in points of theology and iconography. A more difficult question is the identity of the Infanta's principal advisor for the program, if she had one at all. In view of his authorship of the only documentary material on this project, it is tempting to conclude that the court chaplain, Philippe Chifflet, took an active part in the discussions between the Infanta and Rubens. This must remain pure hypothesis, pending the discovery of any new documentary evidence, but Chifflet's position at court and his evident knowledge of this commission, including such specific details as payments and appraisals, make the hypothesis a reasonable and perhaps even compelling one.

The Modelli

The second and in many ways most important preparatory stage is represented by the more finished oil sketch or modello. Several times larger than the corresponding bozzetto, the modello is fully colored and sufficiently detailed for it to have served as a model for the studio assistants to enlarge into the cartoon without much intervention on the master's part. The original modello has been preserved for each of the eleven processional pieces and for three of the five altar tapestries (as well as for each of the four questionable additional panels). Hence the modelli offer a remarkably complete picture of the entire cycle at this stage. In every case the composition has been reversed to take into account the process of weaving. Inasmuch as they are entirely by Rubens's own hand these sketches assume a prominent place in our study of the cycle as a whole, for they alone offer a detailed insight into Rubens's personal formulation and evolution of each scene. Special attention was clearly paid to such details as relative dimensions, architectural features, and the perspective and lighting of the architecture. The final tapestries closely follow the modelli in all these specific areas (in a reverse sense, of course). In view of the careful articulation of the architectural enframings, then, one can truly speak of the modelli as blueprints; and it is in this respect that they are distinguished from their counterparts in the two earlier tapestry cycles and that they anticipate Rubens's models (*patroons*) for the *Pompa Introitus Ferdinandi*.

As paintings in their own right, the modelli are equally impressive in their animated brushwork and rich color. After they had fulfilled their original purpose as tapestry models, it appears that several—and perhaps all—of them were hung in the Infanta's Royal Palace in Brussels, from which some were later removed and transported to Spain by order of the King.[42] Another reflection of the high esteem in which they were held in Rubens's day is provided by their many copies and adaptations both by artists in Rubens's circle as well as by later artists, a fact that has created some confusion in establishing the identity of the originals. It was also from the modelli, finally, that the reproductive engravings were made.

The Cartoons

The final stage—the tapestry cartoon—was painted, as in the previous cycles, almost entirely by Rubens's assistants. Here and there one may detect some finishing or correcting passages by the master, but in general the cartoons represent a studio production. As in the Decius cycle, the Eucharist cartoons were painted in oil on canvas and their dimensions correspond to those of the tapestries themselves. The fact that they were painted in oil on canvas and not in the more usual tempera on paper, as in the Constantine series, led Elbern to conclude that "they are not in the strict sense of the word 'cartoons,' which could then be viewed as traced designs of the sort that are made in the tapestry-weaving mill from the picture prototype."[43] He preferred to call them simply "canvases" (*Leinwände*). Nevertheless, since their primary purpose was to serve as cartoons or full-size models for the tapestry weavers to translate into their woven medium, there is no reason why the term *cartoon* should not be retained. Elbern's comment, however, does raise the interesting question of any possible further intention for these large paintings apart from their purely functional role in the process of weaving the tapestries. We are again confronted by the same question that was posed by the similar cartoons for the Decius cycle. Were they intended from the start to hang as independent and finished works of art in their own right? There is some (admittedly slight) documentary evidence that may suggest an affirmative answer.

We know from King Philip's letter of 1648 that the cartoons at this time hung in the Royal Palace in Brussels.[44] His request for all of them—or, at least, for fifteen—was, it appears, only partially fulfilled: six were sent to Spain, together with several of the modelli (of which six remain there today, in the Prado). The six cartoons were then presented, probably by the King himself, to the Dominican church at Loeches. There they were displayed in the transept of the church, as A. Ponz described them in the memoirs of his travels during 1770. The other cartoons remained in the Royal Palace in Brussels, where they were described in several seventeenth and eighteenth-century accounts. At least four of them were destroyed in the palace fire of 1731.

In 1808 Napoleon's invading army carried off the canvases in the Loeches church. Two of them were taken to France, where they were bought for the Chambre des Pairs; today they belong to the Louvre and are deposited in the museum in Valenciennes. The other four canvases were bought by the Danish ambassador to Madrid (M. Bourke) and were shipped to England and purchased by the Duke of Westminster, in whose collection they remained until they were acquired for the Ringling Museum in Sarasota, Florida, where they hang today and have recently been joined by a newly discovered (i.e., seventh) cartoon, from an English collection.[46]

These brief histories of the canvases suggest that from the seventeenth century they were treated and appreciated as independent paintings. Although they do not equal Rubens's own modelli, the surviving cartoons offer impressive compositions of great monumentality and striking color. It is, therefore, all the more tempting to assume that Rubens intended them to have a life apart from the tapestries for which they were designed. In fact, it is entirely possible that they were executed in oil on canvas at the request of the Infanta herself. Since she would probably never have the chance to see the tapestries hung in the Madrid convent, Isabella may have wanted to keep the cartoons as decorative paintings for her own palace. But their original and primary function is betrayed by the fact of their reversal. Had they been commissioned separately, as a full-scale memento for the Infanta, *after* the tapestries were woven and donated to the convent, Rubens certainly would not have retained the reversals of the cartoons and left all his figures permanently left-handed.

The Tapestries

The final stage, the translation of Rubens's cartoons into tapestries, was the most painstaking and time-consuming of all, especially for a cycle as vast and elaborate as this one. The precise amount of time taken in the weaving is not know, but on the basis of Chifflet's few references to the project we may make an approximation. In late May of 1627 Rubens apparently had not yet finished several of the cartoons, according to Chifflet's letter of 21 May 1627 to Guidi di Bagno. So we may assume summer 1627 as a *terminus post quem* for the completion of the cartoons and the commencement of the tapestry weaving, with one important qualification: it is probable that by this time at least some of the cartoons were already in the workshops and were being woven into tapestries. We should not necessarily assume that all the cartoons were sent to the weavers at the same time; more likely, they were delivered as they were completed. Since Rubens was not given the gift of pearls for his cartoons until January of 1628 it is also possible that the last ones were not finished until the end of 1627. By this time the process of weaving must have been well advanced, for we have a *terminus ante quem* for the tapestries' completion: 19 July 1628—the date of their shipment to Spain, according to Chifflet's second letter to Guidi di Bagno of 21 July 1628.

It would appear, then, that the tapestries were woven in about a year: from the summer of 1627 to the summer of 1628. If so, the weaving of so large a series was accomplished in an unusually short period of time. An inspection of the Madrid tapestries confirms this view and suggests, moreover, that the Infanta wanted the series finished as quickly as possible, for the tapestries bear the insignia of several Brussels workshops. According to Tormo, the tapestries were contracted to Jan Raes and his workshop. He, in turn, gave roughly a third of the commission to Jacques Geubels, with whom he had worked for many years. The insignia of Jacques Fobert and Jean Vervoert also appear on some of the pieces, thereby indicating that the cycle was shared among several workshops. A detailed study of the various pieces in the context of the different Flemish tapestry workshops, practices, and techniques might throw some additional light on the actual process of weaving the Eucharist tapestries.[47] Such an inquiry is beyond the scope of the present study; in general, however, it seems that the unusual practice of sharing this commission among several weavers reflects both the enormous size of the cycle and the apparent haste which the Infanta required for its execution and delivery. If we recall that the commission probably originated in July of 1625 and that Rubens's preparatory work was still not completed two years later, we can understand why the Infanta might have wished to speed up the final stage. How much direct contact Rubens had with the workshops is difficult to estimate. It was probably slight, for by this time he was deeply engaged in his diplomatic missions for the Infanta. By now his experience with tapestry manufacture and his personal knowledge of the weavers was such that he probably did not feel required to spend much time personally overseeing the final translation of his designs.

The original set of tapestries in Madrid represents the only complete and accurate weaving of the cycle. Several additional reweavings of individual tapestries were subsequently undertaken by various workshops, which testifies to the popularity of Rubens's designs. One additional set of Eucharist tapestries is preserved in the Cologne Cathedral and was the focus of an exhibition devoted to the Eucharist cycle in 1954–55. This set of eight pieces is discussed in detail by Elbern in his study and catalogue of the cycle for that exhibition.[48] The Cologne group, for all its magnificence and monumentality, is cruder in execution than the Madrid set, undoubtedly because the weavers did not have the benefit of either Rubens's large cartoons or his original modelli. They evidently worked from copies, possibly from engravings. Although these will not be given special attention in our study, the published engravings of the processional tapestries are significant as an indication of the widespread dissemination of Rubens's compositions. Tormo suggested that Rubens himself commissioned and paid for the engravings since he knew that the tapestries would be forever secluded in the cloistered convent.[49] The prints offer still one more reflection of the importance that the artist attached to his cycle.

Unlike the previous two tapestry series, then, the Eucharist cycle exists in a unique edition that was designed not only for a specific patron but also for a certain setting. Any analysis of the series, even a purely iconographic one, must be based on the Madrid set of tapestries as well as on Rubens's preparatory oil sketches and the cartoons. The following iconographic study will therefore treat the final tapestry as the definitive composition, but will also take into account every known preparatory sketch and cartoon. Only in those cases of questionable attribution—that is, where additional paintings and drawings have been seriously considered Rubens's own work—will copies be examined. Since the material is not presented as a *catalogue raisonné*, questions of style, iconography, formal motifs, and even connoisseurship will be considered as they arise; they are as intertwined as the tapestries themselves. The organizing principle or approach will be essentially a narrative one, for the Eucharist cycle is, in the final analysis, a colossal religious epic composed by an artist whom Winckelmann (anticipating Burckhardt by a century) aptly compared to Homer in his "inexhaustible fertility" of imagination.[50] The scope of Rubens's subject—nothing less than a sacramental history of salvation—and the literary richness of his imagery remind us that the seventeenth century produced the last great flowering of the epic tradition. And if we seek a contemporary literary counterpart to Rubens, a poet with an equally vast treasure of images and an equally high purpose, we have only to substitute for Homer the English Protestant John Milton. Both Milton and Rubens created epic statements of their faiths and doctrines. Both took old—and specifically classical—forms and breathed new life into them.

Part II

The Sacramental Epic

3

The Prefigurations

By the seventeenth century the rich tradition of medieval symbolism and allegory in religious art had been partially eclipsed by the rediscovery of classical antiquity during the Italian Renaissance and, more immediately, by the new interest in naturalism heralded by the Carracci and Caravaggio around the turn of the century. Whereas in the Middle Ages artists invariably sought to allegorize each detail of a Biblical or devotional subject, the Baroque artist often exploited such traditional subjects as opportunities to paint landscape or genre. Although Rubens was exceptional inasmuch as he achieved a rare synthesis of traditional, medieval iconography and heroic, Baroque forms of expression, his oeuvre of Biblical subjects nevertheless contains examples apparently stripped of any theological gloss. One monumental example is his *Daniel in the Lions' Den* (National Gallery, Washington), in which the famous episode from the Book of Daniel was selected chiefly as an excuse to fill the vast canvas with wild animals.

Yet, as Emile Mâle has shown in his seminal work on Counter-Reformation iconography,[1] the elaborate concordances between the Old and New Testaments which had dominated medieval art by no means disappeared in the wake of classical revivals and the new naturalism. There was a concerted effort among the religious orders of the Counter-Reformation to revive the waning tradition of Old Testament prefigurations in religious iconology.[2] A leading role in this revival was assumed by the most crusading of the newly formed orders, the Jesuits. Rubens himself played a crucial part, for the most ambitious and extensive outgrowth of the revival of Biblical concordances was the cycle of ceiling paintings for the newly constructed Jesuit Church in Antwerp, Rubens's first major commission of church decoration.

The upper galleries of the church were decorated with ceiling paintings which, in the words of the Jesuit father Michael Grisius in 1622, represent "the mysteries of our salvation in parallel fashion from the Old and New Testament. . . ."[3] (The lower aisles were decorated with male and female saints.) In his thorough iconographic analysis of the program, J. R. Martin observes that one of its most striking aspects "is its traditional—not to say medieval—character." He further points out that "in this pairing of type and antitype we may recognize the symbolic method made popular in the fourteenth and fifteenth centuries by two illustrated books, the *Biblia pauperum* and the *Speculum humanae salvationis*. That is not to say, of course, that the programme of the Jesuit cycle was simply adapted from one or the other of these late medieval compendia, but only that it exemplifies a similar principle of anagogical imagery."[4]

Thus *The Fall of the Rebel Angels* prefigured (and was paired with) *The Nativity*; *Solomon and Sheba* prefigured *The Adoration of the Magi*; *The Sacrifice of Isaac* was the prototype for *The Crucifixion*; and so forth. In the Jesuit ceiling cycle, the presentation of the Old Testament prefigurations was a didactic one. Each Old Testament prefiguration not only alluded iconographically to its New Testament counterpart, but was *physically paired* with the latter so that the program of the ceilings was a straightforward one which unfolded as the worshipper proceeded down each side. Such an approach was, of course, completely in keeping with the didactic aims and methods of the Jesuits.

In the Eucharist cycle, Rubens's incorporation of Old Testament prefigurations may be seen as a natural offshoot of his undertaking for the Jesuits a few years earlier. The first subject of the group, *Abraham and Melchizedek*, owes, as will become evident, a compositional as well as iconographic debt to its counterpart in the Jesuit program. There are, nevertheless, some important distinctions to be drawn between the role of such prefigurations in the Jesuit ceiling and in the Eucharist cycle. In the latter they form an iconographic group of four, rather than an alternating pattern (of nine separate compositions) throughout the cycle. But, more important, in the Eucharist cycle Rubens discarded the idea of pairing each Old Testament subject with its New Testament counterpart. In the Eucharist cycle there are, strictly speaking, no New Testament subjects at all, no Biblical pairs for the Old Testament prefigurations of the Eucharist. Rubens substituted allegorical subjects to represent the fulfillment of those prefigurations. And, finally, the simple linear sequence of alternating types following a straight Biblical narrative was abandoned in the Eucharist cycle in favor of a more complex structure for which the illusionistic architecture provided an appropriate metaphor as well as visual framework; the iconographic unity ultimately depended not so much upon an anagogical principle, as in the Jesuit cycle, as upon a dominant theme shared by each component of the program: the Eucharist. Consequently, the prefigurations are to be understood as prototypes not for specific New Testament subjects but rather for the sacrament in general.

Mâle has noted that most Old Testament prefigurations in seventeenth century religious art were centered upon either the sacraments or the Virgin and thus were selected for an explicitly Counter-Reformational purpose;[5] the familiar Old Testament prototypes were used as Biblical precedents which, if interpreted correctly, clearly bolstered those Catholic doctrines which had come under the most severe attack by Protestants. In the Jesuit ceiling, in which approximately half of the prefigurations concern the Virgin, the Counter-Reformational implications are strongly asserted, as Martin has observed in his discussion of the cycle's iconography.[6] We would expect no less from the Jesuits, whose order was "cofounded" by Christ and the Virgin.

In his selection and use of prefigurations for the Eucharist, Rubens had two important traditions from which to draw. One was Flemish, the other Roman. One was modest in scale and materials, while the other was monumental. The first tradition, and one with which Rubens would likely have been familiar at a very early age, was deeply rooted in Flemish art: the triptych or polyptych—in this case, the altarpiece devoted to the Eucharist. One prominent and accessible example is Dirk Bouts's altarpiece of *The Last Supper* (1464–67) in St. Peter's Church in Louvain. The central field is given to Bouts's famous *Last Supper*; each of the flanking wing panels is devoted to an Old Testament prefiguration of the Eucharist. The fact that three of Bouts's four subjects reappear in Rubens's Old Testament group suggests that the former may well have been one of the chief northern sources for the latter.[7]

Rubens's interest in early Netherlandish triptychs has been observed by several scholars. Perhaps their influence upon his work is nowhere better documented than in his own triptych altarpieces painted during the decade 1610–20. Not only did Rubens create the last major revival of the triptych form, but he also revived the use of "disguised symbolism" which Erwin Panofsky was first to recognize in the work of the early Flemish masters, (including Van Eyck, Van der Weyden, Bouts, and Van der Goes, among others).[8] In a recent dissertation on Rubens and the Counter-Reformation, Thomas Glen has demonstrated the great extent to which Rubens retained the traditional vocabulary of disguised symbolism and reintroduced it into the context of his classical, heroic, and fully Baroque style.[9] To a large degree, then, the four prefigurations in the Eucharist cycle may be viewed as Rubens's adaptation and transformation of the northern sacrament triptych to a new medium and full-blown program of chapel decoration. But Rubens fused this northern heritage with an equally vital Roman tradition: the monumental decoration for sacramental chapels, in which Old Testament prefigurations play a comparable role, but do so with greater emphasis.

In the Basilica of St. John Lateran in Rome, Pope Clement VIII erected a magnificent altar of the Blessed Sacrament in the north transept. The project was important for two reasons: because of its location in the Lateran, the cathedral of Rome and the mother of all churches throughout the world; and because it was to serve as a kind of monumental reliquary housing a board of the table on which Christ was said to have celebrated the Last Supper—or the first Eucharist. This altar, which would later have a profound influence upon Bernini's baldacchino and sacrament chapel in St. Peter's,[10] had been constructed by the time of Rubens's arrival in Rome in 1601 and would surely have been known to him by the time he left the city in 1608. It may have provided a source for the Eucharist tapestries comparable to its significance for Bernini's baldacchino, as will be shown in Part III.

The altar's decoration included four prominent statues of Old Testament figures, each accompanied by a bas-relief illustrating a prefiguration of the Eucharist: Melchizedek offers bread and wine to Abraham; Moses strikes the rock to provide drink for the Israelites; Elijah receives bread and water from an angel in the desert; and Aaron carries the sacrificial loaves of bread to the altar of the Most High. As in Bouts's altarpiece, there are four prefigurations, of which three of the chief protagonists (Melchizedek, Moses, and Elijah) reappear in Rubens's group, and the fourth (Aaron) is closely related to Rubens's fourth subject.

The emphasis upon such prefigurations to buttress the Catholic doctrines of the Eucharist was maintained in subsequent projects for decorating the sacrament chapels of Roman basilicas. Lanfranco included similar subjects in his paintings (now destroyed) for the sacrament chapel of San Paolo fuori le Mura; and at the entrance of the corresponding chapel in St. Peter's are mosaics designed by Pietro da Cortona, also illustrating Old Testament prototypes.[11] In each case, beginning with Pope Clement's commission, the choice and context of the prefigurations involved a decidedly Counter-Reformational intent, expressed with all the clarity and conviction required of official religious art by the Council of Trent.

Rubens's first iconographic group of tapestries is thus related not only to early Flemish antecedents such as the Bouts altarpiece, but also to a living and weighty iconographic tradition in the official Catholic art of Rome itself. Working within both traditions, Rubens managed to infuse the typologies with a dramatic power and monumentality entirely of his own creation.

Abraham and Melchizedek

The first of the four Old Testament prefigurations of the Eucharist (Fig. 4) depicts the encounter between the Patriarch Abraham and the Priest-King

Melchizedek, as described in Genesis (XIV, 17–24): Abraham on his return from his victory over Kedorlaomer was met in the valley of Shaveh by Melchizedek, "priest of God most high" and King of Salem (the future site of Jerusalem). There Melchizedek—the name may be translated as "king of righteousness"—gave Abraham and his men bread and wine in return for which Abraham offered him a tithe of all the booty.

A later reference to the event is found in Psalm 110 ("You are a priest forever in the succession of Melchizedek"), which St. Paul reinterpreted as a prefiguration of Christ. In his double identity as priest and king, Melchizedek is seen by St. Paul as "like the Son of God" (Hebrews, VII, 3). For medieval scholastics the subject provided two primary symbolic interpretations: 1) as a prefiguration of the Three Kings' offering to the Christ child in the tithe given by Abraham, and 2) as a prefiguration of the Eucharist. For Calvin and other Protestant reformers, however, the bread and wine were no longer to be understood as signifying the Eucharist, but were merely "to feed the men who were on their way returning from battle."[12] Against such sacramental denials the Counter-Reformation reaffirmed a Eucharistic interpretation of the sacrifice of Melchizedek as the offering of bread and wine described in the canon of the Mass: "*sanctum sacrificium, immaculatam hostiam*." As such, Rubens's composition offers a distinctly Catholic rendering of the Old Testament subject, in which the sacramental elements (bread and wine) are intrinsically related to the theme of sacrifice in the Mass, a doctrine which had been denied by Protestantism and had subsequently been defended by the Council of Trent.

In medieval art Abraham was usually depicted as a knight in armor, receiving the gifts from Melchizedek, who was dressed as a high priest. Comparing the tapestry with such earlier representations as the panel from Bouts's altarpiece of *The Last Supper* it is clear that Rubens retained the basic iconography but, at the same time, charged it with unprecedented epic grandeur characteristic of his own style and, more generally, of the Counter-Reformation's revival of medieval subjects in religious art.

Like the ten other tapestries of the cycle, *Abraham and Melchizedek* presents a tapestry within a tapestry and underscores the illusion by showing three putti in the act of hanging the tapestry within its architectural framework of Doric columns (one freestanding at the left, two others partially covered at the right), a highly ornamented entablature at the top, and a stone base on which is placed a small decorative pedestal. This architectural setting is festively decorated with garlands of fruit which are arranged by a putto directly over the heads of Abraham and Melchizedek. The gold highlighting in the capitals, bases, and flutings of the columns and in the relief work, together with the festive hangings (the garlands and, of course, the tapestry itself, whose elaborate borders are conveniently displayed by the putto in the process of hanging it), combine in a rich sumptuous effect that is matched by an equally theatrical composition.

In the center of the "stage" Abraham, dressed in Roman armor, rushes up the front steps of Melchizedek's palace to receive the loaves from the Priest-King, who is magnificently arrayed in blue and white vestments and covered by a gold cloak held by a young acolyte. Behind Abraham also stand his soldiers (six are here visible) and at the right a young boy holding his horse. Behind Melchizedek servants busy themselves with the task of providing the loaves for distribution by the young acolytes or attendants. At the bottom, two partially nude servants emerge from below—exactly from where is not certain—carrying large metal vases filled with wine. The entire scene thus includes seventeen figures caught up in the drama and excitement of the main encounter. The use of classical detail—in the armor, helmets, and vases—and monumental architecture of steps, rusticated columns, and arches conveys an epic quality not to be found in any previous examples of the subject by other artists. In this respect it owes at least as much to the Decius and Constantine cycles.

Rubens had treated the subject at least twice before. The earliest example (Museum, Caen, *K.d.K.* 110) is dated around 1615 and offers several interesting points of comparison: here one finds a similar use of Roman—instead of medieval—armor, classical architecture, and muscular, seminude servants (one carrying a basket of bread and another crouched over a large vase of wine). However, all the figures are placed on one level. The second example, the ceiling painting for the Jesuit church in Antwerp (now destroyed, but for which an oil sketch is preserved in the Louvre, Paris, *K.d.K.* 211), is closer to the tapestry in several respects.[13] The two central figures are no longer on the same plane: Melchizedek stands a few steps above the Patriarch. The architectural backdrop of rusticated columns, recalling the garden portico designed by Rubens for his own house in Antwerp, is now set behind Melchizedek so that it divides the composition roughly in half. The figures are more animated than before, as in the tapestry, and the sacramental significance of the event is stressed by a clear gap between the two principal figures which effectively isolates the loaves and vase of wine directly beneath them.

In the tapestry the centrality of the sacred elements is further emphasized by a triangular placement of the two main figures, the apex of which is located just above the bread and wine. One can trace the central vertical axis through the upright vase, the loaves, and the rearmost pilaster, which conveniently breaks off and thereby remains within the triangular area. As in the Jesuit ceiling painting, the use of architectural elements is more in keeping with fanciful stage scenery than any recognizable structure, and the placement of the two figures recalls Rubens's earlier paintings, *The Reconciliation of Jacob and Esau* (Schloss Schlessheim, *K.d.K.* 290) and *St. Ambrose and the Emperor Theodosius* (1618–19, Kunsthistorisches Museum, Vienna, *K.d.K.* 191). In the latter, a close compositional similarity is paralleled by an important iconographic relationship: the relative location of the main figures emphasizes the preeminence of ecclesiastical over secular power. Both the Roman Emperor and the Patriarch must show deference to God's Priest.

It is therefore noteworthy that in the artist's first oil study for the tapestry, the bozzetto (Fitzwilliam Museum, Cambridge, Fig. 2), the iconographic use of steps had not yet been introduced. Both Abraham and Melchizedek stand on level ground, and since his helmet has not yet been removed (as it would be in the tapestry), Abraham stands higher than the Priest-King. In this respect the bozzetto looks back to the early Caen canvas rather than to the more recent Jesuit painting. It also reveals several substantial differences from the final conception, more so than in any other tapestry of this cycle. *Abraham and Melchizedek* thus provides a particularly vivid example of the artistic development from bozzetto to final cartoon. Since all the preparatory stages are still extant the evolution can be traced without a break.

In the bozzetto it is clear that Rubens originally intended the tapestry to be square: one can still discern the ruled lines of the square central area around which a more traditional tapestry border was conceived, with the two twisting columns flanking the composition. The composition is far simpler than in the final tapestry: here one finds no young acolytes, no servants carrying basket and vases, nor even the boy with Abraham's horse. More significant, it appears that Rubens may not yet have conceived the elaborate tapestry-device which was to distinguish this cycle from his other three when he began this sketch. The sweeping white lines at the top, as Held has observed, are "clearly an afterthought": on closer inspection one can see the tips of the spears showing through (even in the photograph). Hence the absence of putti and, more important, of an illusionistic architectural setting. Held further noted that this pentimento provides "internal evidence that one of the basic devices of the series was evolved by Rubens only during his work on the small oil sketches,"[14] which therefore may explain why, so far, no preliminary drawings for the cycle have been discovered. He also suggested that the pentimento (not to be found in other bozzetti) indicates that Rubens very likely began work on the series with this very sketch, an assumption which would also help to explain the wide gap between the first and final studies for this tapestry.

The next preparatory stage, originally intended as the finished modello, is represented by the oil panel in the Prado, Madrid (mistitled *La Presentacion del Diezmo*, Fig. 3). The panel was originally square like the bozzetto: the two additional columns, along with the upper and lower architectural borders, were added later in an attempt to create a uniform set of the six Prado modelli. Not only are these portions clearly inferior in brushwork, but one can actually see that a different grain of wood (of Southern Mediterranean origin, according to Puyvelde[15]), was used in the enlargement. As a finished model for the large cartoon, the composition has been reversed from the bozzetto. There are, moreover, now several additions and alterations. Steps have been added to elevate Melchizedek over Abraham. The horse and boy have been introduced at the left, crowded behind Abraham, and the servant carrying the basket of bread on his neck has been added at the right. This figure, which probably derives from the *Farnese Atlas* (now in Naples), appears throughout several of the artist's earlier works, beginning with *The Adoration of the Magi* of 1610 (Prado, Madrid, *K.d.K.* 26) and including *Abraham and Melchizedek* in Caen and two paintings for the Jesuit church in Antwerp: *Solomon and the Queen of Sheba* and *Abraham and Melchizedek*.[16]

Similarly the horse and boy had by this time become a common motif in Rubens's art. The pair derives from Titian's *Adoration of the Magi* (Prado, Madrid) and first appears in the Decius Mus cycle in *Decius Consecrated to the Infernal Gods* (Liechtenstein Collection, Vaduz, *K.d.K.* 144) and again in *The Triumph of Rome* (Mauritshuis, The Hague, *K.d.K.* 233), originally designed for the Constantine series. Rubens was later to include it in his enlargement of the 1610 *Adoration of the Magi* during his visit to Madrid in 1628. Thus the motif finally returned to its source. Characteristically, Rubens appears to have given an iconographic meaning to the motif that is consistent with its origins.[17] In each case he includes it in an event of momentous religious significance involving the preeminence of the religious over the secular order: Decius humbly receives the consecration of the *Pontifex Maximus*, captives and warriors surround their enthroned ruler (Roma, symbolizing Catholicism), Abraham reverently receives the sacramental elements from the Priest-King, and finally the Three Kings (now joined by the artist himself, whose portrait is included in the painting's addition) pay homage to the Christ child. In each scene the boy, dutifully holding his master's horse, witnesses the event with appropriate intensity and awe and offers a leitmotif of religious adoration.

In the middle of the feigned tapestry a putto hangs from the garland of fruit, and at the bottom, in front of two large, richly embellished vases, rests a decorative pedestal. On either side, the base is decorated with a frieze showing two geese eating from hanging vines, a motif with clear Eucharistic significance. The feigned tapestry is far more explicitly indicated as hanging within an actual architectural setting which is now described with the use of perspective. The viewer approaches the scene from the lower left: note the *di-sotto-in-su* view of the steps and the angle from which the columns are to be seen. Even the underside of the ceiling, adorned with relief work, is described in detail. The precise use of light and shadow further stresses the contrast between the two levels of reality—between the tapestry design and its architectural setting. The Solomonic columns are lit from the left, and thus the putto casts a shadow against the feigned tapestry. Within the latter the chief source of light is the sun, which is obscured by clouds and located between the foreheads of Abraham and Melchizedek so as to indicate a psychological tension between them at the climactic moment of the Eucharistic meeting.

In general the brushwork is more highly finished than one might expect in an oil sketch, especially in the faces, the polished armor, and the gold vases. All the more surprising, therefore, are the substantial differences between this modello and the final cartoon (Ringling Museum, Sarasota, Fig. 4). Between these two final stages the artist changed the overall shape of the tapestry, the orders of the flanking columns, and the number of putti, as well as several internal compositional details. One notices, for example, the introduction of additional acolytes, foreground servants, and soldiers, as well as changes in the background architecture, such as the additional broken arch between the two figures.

Fortunately the discrepancies between the Prado modello and the cartoon, which was painted almost entirely by Rubens's assistants, can be bridged by a second, highly finished oil study entirely by the master's hand: *Abraham and Melchizedek* in the National Gallery, Washington (Fig. 5). A brief comparison between this panel and the cartoon confirms that it was Rubens's final modello. It includes all the additional elements which were then faithfully repeated in the workshop cartoon. There are, however, a few unusual details which, in turn, offer further confirmation of its place between the former modello and the cartoon. The stooped figure at the right, holding the basket of loaves, is here (as in the Prado panel) shown in profile. In the cartoon, however, his face has been turned, and like his colleague below he stares out toward the viewer. There is also a slight difference in the placement of the two vases: in the cartoon they overlap, revealing no space between them, but in both the tapestry itself and the Washington modello there is daylight between them. Since the tapestry weavers presumably copied the cartoon as faithfully as possible, one can only assume that this area of the canvas was later damaged and retouched. The cartoon does appear to have been restored in several places: the foremost spear no longer continues to the neck of the vase, as it does in both tapestry and modello; and an entire vertical strip of canvas has been replaced at the left (hence the awkward putto, in the upper left corner, whose head is inclined in the wrong direction). The upper right-hand corner was also removed and replaced by a new piece, probably as a result of the cartoon's previous location within an arch in the apse of the Dominican church at Loeches, where it remained until the early nineteenth century.[18] Therefore the comparison of modello and cartoon should not be pressed too far.

In addition to its overall quality there is one piece of compelling evidence for the modello's originality (as opposed to its being a later replica) in the pentimento between the two vase carriers: here an image of a similar vase (neck and handle) as well as the faint head of a man appears beneath the white robes of Melchizedek. Evidently at the outset of painting the panel Rubens had not yet determined the relative positions of the two additional servants. It is both significant and quite natural that neither of the two questionable replicas of this modello reveal such a pentimento.

One very faithful, if rather academic, copy is preserved in the John-son Collection, Philadelphia. Only Puyvelde has claimed it as an original, *along with* the Washington modello, speculating that after painting the latter for his workshop to enlarge to full-size cartoon the artist then pro-ceeded to paint an exact replica for his patron, to be hung in her apart-ment.[19] But even the briefest comparison of the two refutes this fanciful theory; the Philadelphia panel cannot possibly have been painted by the master himself. The two servants at the right reveal little understanding of anatomy, and the exaggerated musculature of the left man's back ap-pears merely as a mound of lumps. A second copy (private coll., U.S.A.) had been attributed to Rubens by Erik Larsen.[20] He apparently knew of the Washington modello (referring to it as the "Lord Northbrook" ver-sion) but selected the former as the original modello by the master, though admitting some collaboration in minor passages. Again, a comparison between the two disproves the attribution. One need only compare the two faces of Melchizedek or the servants at the bottom.

Although clearly inferior in quality, these two copies are of some interest inasmuch as they were clearly based on the Washington modello and not on the final cartoon, as the profiles of the bread carrier indicate. Moreover, their very existence along with several other variants reveals the extent to which the modello was appreciated and copied in its day as a finished composition and not merely as a preparatory stage for a larger work. A copy of the bozzetto was painted by Victor Wolfvoet (Maurits-huis, The Hague), in which the artist excluded the architectural framing. In addition to the oil copies, engravings were made of the modello. One, executed by Jacques Neeffs, includes an inscription from St. Paul (Hebrews, VII, 1–2): "*Abrahae a Regum Caede Regresso Melchisedech Obviavit et Benedixit Cui Decimas Omnium Divisit.*"[21] In this otherwise faithful reproduction the engraver badly misunderstood the architectural setting, as indeed did later tapestry weavers who reproduced the original. Whereas Rubens was very specific in creating an illusionistic setting for his feigned tapestry, later copyists apparently saw the device as no more than a decorative frame.

Two questions remain to be answered. The first is why the Washington modello is so highly finished (much more so than any of the other modelli for the cycle). One simple and attractive hypothesis, offered by John Walker, is that Rubens wanted to show this particular modello to the Infanta as an example of what the finished tapestries would look like;[22] hence the liberal use of gold highlighting. The second and far more basic question is why Rubens took the trouble of painting two finished modelli for the one tapestry. It cannot be simply that the artist found certain compositional elements of the Prado version unsatisfactory (for example, the cramped placement of Abraham's horse and Melchizedek's page next to the columns). For although such a theory might account for his widening the composition it fails to explain the complete change in the architectural setting, the orders of the columns and their arrangement. Why, for instance, is this the only composition with one freestanding column balanced by two covered ones? Puyvelde suggested that the change was a result of the tapestry weavers' finding the Solomonic columns "*trop lourdes*,"[23] but it is most unlikely that Rubens would have left such a fundamental change to the taste of the weavers. In fact, he did not. The problem of the two modelli is intimately connected with the significance of Rubens's illusionistic architecture, and its solution requires an analysis of the latter, which will be taken up in Part III.

Moses and the Discovery of Manna

The second tapestry in the series of Old Testament prefigurations illustrates Moses and the Israelites gathering *manna* (Fig. 6). The subject, taken from Exodus (XVI, 13–36), represents the second miraculous feeding of the Israelites by God during their journey through the Sinai desert (the first was the rain of quails). The mysterious manna (a translation of the Hebrew "What is it?"—the question the Israelites asked each other upon seeing the substance for the first time) is alternately described as "fine flakes, fine as hoar frost" and as "white, like coriander seed" and tasting "like a wafer made with honey." The circumstances of the feeding—the heavenly source, the unknown food, and Moses's pronouncement ("That is the bread which the Lord has given you to eat")—suggested to early Christian commentators an obvious prefiguration of the Eucharist. This interpretation was further supported by the reference in St. John's Gospel (VI, 28–51), in which Christ himself reinterprets the Old Testament miracle: "I am the bread of life. Your forefathers ate the manna in the desert and they are dead. . . . I am that living bread which has come down from heaven; if anyone eats this bread he shall live forever."

The reception of the manna was thus understood by theologians as symbolizing several aspects of the sacrament: 1) as a food given by God which man could not provide for himself, thus as the product of divine grace; 2) as "daily bread"—the Israelites fed on it for forty years—thus the sacrament of communion; 3) as spiritually increasing faith, as in the above passage in St. John; and 4) as a Eucharistic banquet (referring to the Apocalypse, II, 17).[24] For artists the subject offered three possible representations: the actual rain of manna, its collection by the Israelites, and the distribution into urns of gold. Of these, the first two scenes were the most commonly depicted. Rubens, with characteristic inventiveness, fused them in a single composition.

In early Christian art the Israelites were often shown collecting the manna with hands covered out of respect for the sacredness of the food. At other times they are shown catching it in urns or baskets, as in this tapestry. Like *Abraham and Melchizedek*, the scene was often construed as a typological counterpart to *Christ Giving Communion to His Apostles* and toward the end of the Middle Ages was a favorite subject for the decoration of monastic refectories. The equation between manna and the sacrament was at times made more explicit by depicting the food as actual Hosts.

In designing his tapestry, therefore, Rubens had a long iconographic history on which to base his composition which, as in the previous case, remains within the established medieval tradition. This tapestry is considerably narrower than *Abraham and Melchizedek* and in general reveals a simpler and more tightly organized, though equally dramatic, composition. The feigned tapestry hangs between two Solomonic columns on a cord strung through a gold ring in the center; no putti are here shown in the process of arranging it. At the base it is draped over the stonework which is decorated with a Eucharistic scroll relief, thus creating an effective contrast of texture: masonry juxtaposed with elaborate tapestry border. In addition to the flanking columns, the composition is framed internally by two dominating figures.

At the left stands Moses, looking up to the sky, his left hand raised toward the raining manna in exultation while his right hand, in which he holds a rod, points to the ground. At the right, balancing the composition, stands a woman with her back to the viewer. With one hand she holds a child; the other is raised to steady the basket of manna on her head. This figure recalls a similar woman carrying a vase in Raphael's fresco *The Fire in the Borgo* (Stanze, Vatican), which Rubens undoubtedly knew from his early years in Rome. Between these two figures a partially nude man crouches over a sack of manna, recalling the muscular servants of the previous tapestry, as the woman above him who bends under the weight of her filled basket resembles the bread carrier in the latter. She, however, is about to be relieved of her burden as the man in front of her reaches forward to take it. In the background a young girl leans forward, holding out her skirts to catch the falling seeds. The contrapuntal gestures, particularly Moses's own, provide a sense of excitement and movement in these figures who are closely grouped almost as if in a circular dance.

Detached from the more mundane task of collecting the daily food, Moses offers a psychological contrast to the other figures and is shown in communion with God. He looks heavenward with all the intensity and emotional fervor of the favorite Baroque image of the saint in ecstasy. This figure may be derived from a similar composition by Giulio Romano, of which Rubens made a drawing during his sojourn in Italy (Louvre, Paris).[25] Giulio's Moses, though it resembles the tapestry figure in stance, profile, and drapery, is far more relaxed and static. Rubens's introduction of the ecstatic pose is consistent both with his High Baroque style and with the triumphal spirit of the Counter-Reformation. The figure was later to reappear in the unusual oil study *Moses, Aaron, and Miriam Celebrating the Crossing of the Red Sea* for which the final composition, if ever executed, has evidently been lost. This sketch, attributed by Michael Jaffé to Rubens but surely painted by one of his followers,[26] represents Moses invoking God, again in thanksgiving (Exodus, XV, 1–21). In composing the scene, for which no previous illustration is known, the artist apparently turned to Rubens's early drawing after Giulio Romano for the grouping of the figures, but the pose—the upward gesture of Moses—is clearly derived from the more recent *Manna* tapestry. In the latter, then, Rubens combined two iconographic possibilities (the raining and the gathering into baskets) and to these added a dramatic expression of thanksgiving in the figure of Moses, which was later to be incorporated in a similar context.

All three preparatory stages for the tapestry are extant. The bozzetto (Musée Bonnat, Bayonne, Fig. 7), as in the case of *Abraham and Melchizedek*, incorporates only faint references to the tapestry-device. Here, too, one can discern the original ruled lines of the central composition, and the white strokes of the tapestry folds may again represent an afterthought. For example, the tapestry does not overlap the base line, as it does in later preparatory stages. One Solomonic column is indicated at the right, carefully constructed: the source of light (upper right) and the angle of view (from the left) are the same as those of the tapestry. But no corresponding column on the left is visible: the treatment of this area is extremely vague and sketchy. At the bottom are faint indications of the vine-scroll motif.

Between the bozzetto and the modello (County Museum, Los Angeles, Fig. 8) Moses is moved closer to the picture plane and thus assumes a more prominent place within the group. His gesture has also been modified, since the raised hand is no longer clutching the rod. The woman on her knees, the foremost figure in the bozzetto (recalling a similar figure in the drawing after Giulio), has been replaced by the crouching male. Her companion who bends forward to place manna into the basket has also been dropped from the composition and is replaced by the girl holding out her skirts. The transition from bozzetto to modello entails a tightening of the composition and an increased monumentality in the major figures, who have been enlarged to fill more of the tapestry space. Rubens also heightens the sense of drama through his use of contrasting movements and gestures.

The modello presents an interesting contrast with its *Abraham and Melchizedek* counterpart (National Gallery, Washington). For although it represents the artist's final formulation of the composition (as comparison with the full-scale cartoon indicates), it could never be mistaken for a finished painting. Unlike the Washington modello, this panel is easily identifiable as a preliminary sketch and is impressive for its lively, rapid execution and great economy of brushwork, recalling Roger de Piles's observation that Rubens "painted quite as much as he drew."[27] The architectural setting, moreover, is remarkably vague—especially the left column—compared with the former modello, but this may be due in part to damage from overcleaning.[28]

The cartoon (Ringling Museum, Sarasota, Fig. 9) reflects very few changes from the modello. The columns, along with the rest of the architectural setting, are now considerably more elaborate and detailed. The head of the old man emerging from behind the right column is also more fully described. The relatively dry and mechanical portrayal of the figures indicates that the canvas was almost entirely the work of assistants. Perhaps, however, the master's brush can be detected in the figure of the young girl spreading her skirts, the only figure whose full face is shown. Around her left forearm there appears to have been some reworking during the execution of the cartoon: part of Moses's drapery was painted out, allowing more of her arm to be visible. And, compared with the modello, her head has been tilted slightly to the left. The passage may thus provide an example of Rubens's last-minute correction of the composition before it was sent off to the tapestry weavers.

As in *Abraham and Melchizedek* the preparatory studies for this tapestry remained accessible to Rubens's studio and followers and were copied. A copy of the bozzetto by V. Wolfvoet (Mauritshuis, The Hague) in oil on copper reveals, as in the previous case, the omission of all architectural trappings. No engraving of the composition, however, is known.[29]

Elijah and the Angel

The prophet Elijah is commonly associated in art with two miraculous feedings, each of which has been interpreted as a Eucharistic prefiguration. The first (I Kings, XVII, 1–7) is his feeding at the brook of Kerith by ravens who brought him bread and meat each morning and evening, as the Lord had promised. The second and more sacramental represents a miracle which, like the rain of manna, occurred in the wilderness (I Kings, XIX, 4–8).

After a day's journey, fleeing from Jezebel, Elijah came to a juniper tree and in despair prayed for death. While he slept, an angel appeared, woke him, and presented him with bread and a pitcher of water. A second time the angel came, woke him, and told him to rise and eat. Elijah obeyed the voice and, "sustained by this food, he went on for forty days and forty nights to Horeb, the Mount of God."

Like the two previous tapestry subjects this scene can be found on altarpieces dedicated to the Blessed Sacrament; it appears on a cover panel of the triptych by Ambrosius Franken I (Koninklijk Museum voor Schone Kunsten, Antwerp), as well as in *The Last Supper* polyptych by Bouts (St. Peter's, Louvain). It was not, however, a standard prefiguration but appears to derive from St. Thomas Aquinas's liturgy for the Office of Corpus Christi,[30] the Feast for which Rubens's cycle was designed.

Traditionally, artists almost always depicted Elijah either lying down, sometimes asleep, or seated beneath the tree. In his tapestry (Fig. 10), however, Rubens shows him standing to receive the two prefigured elements of the Mass (the *vas aquae* here represented as a beautiful crystal chalice). He has chosen to depict not the familiar scene of Elijah's awakening but his responding to the angel's command, "rise and eat." In this way he maintains a compositional continuity with the two preceding tapestries. Just as Abraham and Moses stand, reaching out, to receive their sacred food, so Elijah is shown in profile, looking intently at the agent of divine grace. Thus it is the obedient reception of the sacrament (as well as its fortifying power) which is here staged as an heroic and dramatic encounter. In this respect Rubens's iconography is distinctly Counter-Reformational.

In its dimensions, architectural setting (the tapestry hangs from a central ring between two narrowly spaced Solomonic columns), and compositional details, such as draping the tapestry border over part of the base vine-scroll reliefs, the tapestry presents an obvious companion piece for *Moses and the Manna*. In each case the figures almost entirely fill the feigned tapestry area. At the left stands Elijah; the angel approaches from the right, rushing forward with the loaf of bread and chalice. One wing remains outstretched, and his drapery is spread out in cascades of folds. Behind Elijah looms the trunk of a tree, but it is certainly not a juniper. The ground around him is covered with foliage, and in the lower right-hand corner one catches a glimpse of background landscape. As in *Moses and the Manna*, the composition is simple and tightly organized. Like Abraham and Moses, Elijah is presented as a bearded, athletic Old Testament hero, the exaggerated musculature perhaps indicating that the image is not to be understood as a living person but rather an artistic representation, thus stressing the double-tapestry illusion.

Turning to the bozzetto (Musée Bonnat, Bayonne, Fig. 11), one finds that the composition underwent only minor alterations from its original conception. Here the figures are smaller and fill less of the tapestry area than in the final composition, but their relative positions remain the same. Some background landscape has already been indicated (note the group of trees at the bottom right), but there is less foliage at the left behind the prophet. The tapestry-device, moreover, appears somewhat undefined: the left column is clearly indicated (lit from the left, to be seen from the right side), but there is no corresponding right-hand column (in *Moses and the Manna* there was no left column). In the base, however, there is evidence of an intended vine-scroll motif, so it appears that Rubens already had in mind a definite architectural setting at this stage. In the sky a bird is shown carrying a ring-shaped object in its beak. What it was meant to symbolize is not clear; perhaps Rubens intended to recall the first miraculous feeding by the ravens.

In the modello (Musée Bonnat, Bayonne, Fig. 12) the bird has disappeared.[31] In fact, very little of the sky is visible at all, owing to the increased foliage and the enlargement of the two figures. They have also been moved closer together so that Elijah is shown just about to take hold of the glass. Both columns are now clearly defined, as in the tapestry-device, draped over the front pediment. Both figures are described in full, and the angel is particulary striking in its gesture, stance, and the billowing drapery. The intensity of its expression is equally arresting. But in the cartoon (Louvre, Paris), as in the final tapestry, much of the spontaneity and drama has been lost. The angel's head, reduced in size, has been softened and idealized. Similarly, Elijah is no longer the old and worn figure of the modello. The intensity of his glare has been diluted during the rather mechanical translation and enlargement to full-size canvas by the workshop assistants. Here one looks in vain for any trace of the master's brush, perhaps a result of the modello's relatively finished state. The tapestry weavers, however, succeeded in retaining much of the excitement of the encounter in their superb reproduction of the animated drapery. The composition was engraved twice: by Coenrad Lauwers after the modello and by Willem Paneells, who omitted the architectural setting.

The Sacrifice of the Old Covenant

Unlike the three preceding tapestries the fourth, and final, Old Testament prefiguration, *The Sacrifice of the Old Covenant* (Fig. 13), is a most unusual subject in art and not one of the standard typologies of the Eucharist. The actual Biblical source for this scene—if any—remains to be established with certainty.

Smith identified the subject as the processional transfer of the Ark of the Covenant from the house of Obed-Edom to Jerusalem, at the end of which King David offered sacrifices to God, blessed the people, and distributed food among them (II Samuel VI, 12–19; and I Chronicles, XV, 25–XVI, 3).[32] Most commonly illustrated is David dancing before the Ark on its way through the gates of the city. If Smith is correct, then Rubens evidently chose to represent—possibly for the first time in art—a later moment in the narrative: the sacrifice of the lambs being performed as the Ark is carried into the *tabernaculum*, the sanctuary which David had prepared for it. In keeping with this interpretation, the composition was recently entitled *King David Sacrificing Before the Ark*,[33] in which case one must read the celebrant as David himself. But inasmuch as the figure is an elderly, bearded man and is dressed as a high priest, we must rule out the identification, for David was still a young man at the time. Far more troublesome is the fact that the youthful King is nowhere to be found in this scene.

Another possible subject for this tapestry is the procession of the Ark into the newly constructed Temple of Solomon, a ritual which was similarly accompanied by sacrifices (I Kings, VIII, 1–66; and II Chronicles, V, 1–VII, 10). In this case, one might identify the celebrant as Solomon, although here again there are problems: the celebrant bears no attributes of a king and the "temple" lacks the most obvious feature which would identify it as Solomon's: the Solomonic column.[34]

Rooses entitled this tapestry simply *The Sacrifice of the Old Law*, and such a generalized interpretation seems preferable to insisting that the scene illustrates a specific Biblical passage.[35] While the correct Biblical source remains open to question, the significance of this tapestry is clear: it prefigures both the sacrifice of the Mass and the several independent devotions to the sacrament, especially Eucharistic processions, which flourished during the Counter-Reformation.

At the right, a high priest stands with his left hand raised in a gesture of invocation, his right hand holding a knife with which he is about to slit the throat of the sacrificial lamb placed on top of the ornate altar adorned with sphinxes. He wears the vestments prescribed for Aaron, the first high priest of the Old Testament (Exodus, XXXIX, 1–31), in particular the breastplate of precious stones, but he cannot be identified as Aaron himself if the scene represents one of the transports of the Ark that occurred many generations later, in King David's or King Solomon's reign.[36] Nevertheless, as Aaron's successor, the high priest is closely associated with his prototype—just as every pope recalls St. Peter—and this fact, as we shall see, may have an important bearing on Rubens's possible sources for this subject.

In front of the altar stand three young Levites. One reaches forward, holding a vase in which to collect the blood of the sacrificial lamb. Behind him two others carry candles and lead a procession of people up the steps toward the sacrifices. The faithful, in turn, climb the steps, carrying their offerings of lambs. At the lower left-hand corner a family group has just come into view, recalling the similar placement of the two servants in *Abraham and Melchizedek*. At the right stands a table decorated with a carved griffin upon which are placed loaves of bread arranged in two piles of six in accordance with Mosaic law (Leviticus, XXIV, 1–10). In the background four priests carry the Ark towards the tabernaculum, of which an apse and curtain (perhaps the Veil of the Tabernacle) are visible behind the celebrant. A portico is indicated by two rows of columns (those in the rear, Corinthian), but, as in *Abraham and Melchizedek*, the architectural relationship between the steps, columns, and arches is unclear. Combined more as a stage backdrop than a logical structure, they recall a similar use of architectural elements in the Constantine tapestries (for example, *St. Helena with the True Cross*) and in the Medici cycle (*Henry IV Departing for Germany*, K.d.K. 251). The absence of twisted "Solomonic" columns, so commonly associated with the Temple of Jerusalem, may indicate that this edifice is not Solomon's famous Temple but one of its predecessors: either the Tabernacle which David erected or even the first Tabernacle established by Moses and Aaron (Exodus, XL, 1–33). If this *is* Solomon's Temple, Rubens may simply have chosen to omit the columns from the exterior portico since, as we shall see in Part III, there was a tradition that they belong properly to the *interior* of the Temple.[37]

The Ark, carried solemnly on the priests' shoulders, is richly decorated, topped by two cherubim bent over to guard the sacred contents, according to the Biblical description (Exodus, XXV, 10–22): "They shall be made with wings outspread and pointing upward and shall screen the cover with their wings." Elbern has suggested that Rubens designed the Ark from a description in the monumental and lavishly illustrated reconstruction of the Temple of Jerusalem by the Spanish Jesuit J.B. Vallalpando. Although Elbern was unable to find evidence that Rubens had ever seen this three-volume treatise, published in 1956–1604 in Rome, an itemized list of payments to Balthasar Moretus reveals that Rubens actually owned a copy, having purchased it in 1615.[38]

Surrounding the Ark, a crowd of people surge toward the tabernacle; in the rear one can make out men "blowing on horns and trumpets" (I Chronicles, XV, 28).

The *trompe-l'oeil* tapestry is hung in place between two Doric columns by four putti who also string a garland across the top. In the center hangs a cartouche inscribed with the Hebrew letters for *Jaweh*, the Old Testament name for God ("I Am Who I Am"). In front of the tapestry— in the viewer's own space—rests an ornamental pedestal on which is placed a burning lamp flanked by two cornucopia, one filled with grapes, the other with wheat. These emblematic "footnotes" refer to the Old Testament sacrifices in the tapestry above and emphasize the scene's typological significance: the wheat and grapes symbolize the two elements of the Mass, the New Testament sacrifice, and the lamp refers not only to the "lamp outside the Veil of the Tokens in the Tabernacle of the Presence" (Leviticus, XXIV, 1–4), which Aaron was commanded to "keep trim regularly from dusk to dawn," but also to the corresponding lamp that is kept burning beside every Christian tabernacle. Similarly, the inscription on the cartouche refers not only to the "God of Abraham, Isaac, and Jacob," who commanded these sacrificial offerings, but also to the same God of the New Covenant, who instituted the sacrifice of the Mass. Yet the tapestry does more than correlate the Old and New Testament sacrifices: it also prefigures the doctrine of the Real Presence in the sacrament: throughout the Old Testament the Ark was the actual dwelling place of God ("Make me a sanctuary, and I will dwell among them," Exodus, XXV, 9) and is therefore the forerunner of the Christian tabernacles and monstrances which house the sacrament.

The Ark provided an effective symbol for the art of the Counter-Reformation. In reply to Protestant denials of the doctrine of the Real Presence of Christ in the Eucharist, artists were commissioned to illustrate several appropriate Old Testament passages concerning the Ark as confirmation of that doctrine by typological analogy. For instance, in the cupola outside the chapel of the Blessed Sacrament in St. Peter's, Rome, one finds not only such traditional prefigurations as *Aaron Gathering Manna for the Ark*, but also such unusual subjects as *Uzzah Struck Dead for Touching the Ark* and *The Idol of Dagon Falling at the Passing of the Ark*.[39] These represent in vivid terms the physical reality of God's Presence in the sacrament, as prefigured in the Ark, and thereby emphasize the respect with which one must approach it, an implicit condemnation of Protestant sacrilege. In the Eucharist cycle the themes of power and punishment are deferred to later, more allegorical, tapestries. This final prefiguration introduces the themes of triumph and celebration, and of all the Old Testament subjects it is the most liturgical. The spectacle not only alludes to the cycle's general theme of triumph and of thanksgiving but also prefigures the comparable splendor of Baroque Catholic liturgy. Thus it presents compositionally as well as iconographically a fitting climax for the Old Testament group.

Unfortunately both the bozzetto and the cartoon have been lost, so we cannot fully trace the evolution of this composition. The modello, however, does exist, and has recently crossed the Atlantic to this country where it is now preserved in a private collection (Coll. William A. Coolidge, Topsfield, Mass., Fig. 13). A comparison between this panel and the final tapestry reveals that little was altered between the modello and the cartoon. This superb oil sketch is relatively finished and detailed. There are only a few pentimenti, and these involve the placement of the Doric columns. In the base of the left column it appears that Rubens was still working out the angle of view when he began the modello (the viewer is to see it from the left side). On the right the woman's arm and shoulder curiously overlap the column. Several minor details were added in the cartoon, as in previous cases: for example, the Hebrew inscription and the ornate tapestry border which is wrapped around the right column. But several of the more decorative aspects—the garland, the cartouche, and the lamp stand—have already been indicated in the modello with great precision. Painted entirely by the master's hand, the sketch presents a striking example of his animated brushwork in a lively, pulsating composition. He exploits to its fullest degree the inherent tension between the repeated, stable architectural forms both within and outside the feigned tapestry and the energetic, surging mass of figures, which are only barely contained within their stage setting.

A pen-and-ink drawing (private collection, Holland) was published by N. Beets as a preparatory study by Rubens from the modello. Elbern included it as such in his catalogue of the Cologne tapestries, and Michael Jaffé, in his review of the latter, accepted its authenticity, citing it as "an important pen drawing" by the master.[40] On comparison with the modello, however, the drawing betrays itself as a copy *after* the oil study, and nowhere—Beets's careful analysis to the contrary—can one find evidence of Rubens's own hand. Furthermore, such a detailed drawing has no logical place within the various preparatory stages for the tapestry; the attribution must therefore be ruled out completely.

The modello was engraved by A. Lommelin. Basan, who had seen an example of this extremely rare print identified its subject as the sacrifice of Samuel after the recovery of the Ark from the Philistines.[41] Thus we are offered one more alternative identification (I Samuel VII, 1–9). In its favor is the fact that the Prophet Samuel performed the burnt offering of "a suckling lamb." However, he was not a high priest, and it is difficult to interpret the impressive architectural structure as the "house of Abinadab." Furthermore, Samuel's offering was an invocation to be spared from an impending attack by the Philistines, not a joyous and triumphal thanksgiving such as we find in Rubens's tapestry, whose proper identification therefore remains open to further speculation.

The four preceding tapestries form, as we have seen, an iconographic unit within the Eucharist cycle. At the very least they share a common typological significance, since each illustrates an Old Testament prefiguration of the Eucharist. But their particular selection and combination raise the question of a possible deeper unity and, along with it, the question of Rubens's use of his most likely sources.

Considering the prefigurations as a group, Elbern made the interesting observation that three of Rubens's four subjects traditionally belong to the iconography of *The Last Supper*, citing Bouts's altarpiece as an example that Rubens and his advisors were likely to have known. In fact, Elbern suggested that the typological connection between the group of four Old Testament scenes and *The Last Supper* may have originated with this altarpiece, noting that the scene of *Elijah and the Angel* was unusual in this context.[42]

In view of the close iconographic association between Rubens's group of prefigurations and Bouts's polyptych, it is all the more puzzling that Rubens chose as his fourth subject not the traditional Passover sacrifice, but a highly unusual replacement. (Réau, accordingly, mistook Rubens's fourth tapestry for a representation of the Passover.[43] The Passover meal is directly related—Biblically, theologically, and iconographically—to the

Last Supper, and its absence underscores the fact that nowhere in Rubens's cycle are we to find a representation of *The Last Supper*,[44] the central subject of both the altarpiece by Bouts and the Lateran sacrament altar. In fact, there is no actual sacrament of communion represented in any of the tapestries. No one—historical or allegorical—is shown actually partaking of the sacrament, either in a prefigured form (the Passover meal) or at its institution (the Last Supper). To be sure, the theme of *sacrifice*, so much a part of the iconology of both the Last Supper and the Passover meal, has been retained in Rubens's fourth prefiguration: the ritual sacrifice of the lamb on the altar recalls the Passover sacrifice as it prefigures Christ, the true Paschal lamb, who is simultaneously lamb and priest in his own sacrifice.

More important, Rubens's substitution of this obscure and perhaps even unprecedented subject for the traditional Passover provides a key to a recurrent theme throughout the entire cycle: the concept of Eucharistic devotion *apart from* the celebration of the Mass, the liturgical act of sacrifice. The idea of incorporating into this last subject prefigurations of both the priesthood and the offerings of bread and wine may have been suggested by the fourth Old Testament subject in the Lateran sacrament altar: *The High Priest Aaron Placing Loaves of Bread on the Altar of The Most High*. In Rubens's tapestry we find the loaves of bread placed prominently in the foreground, along with the altar and, behind it, Aaron's successor. So Rubens's choice of subject enabled him to combine aspects of Bouts's *Passover* with elements of the Lateran relief into one grand prefiguration of the Eucharist. But the subject chosen offered still more in the way of Eucharistic imagery, for it included the Ark of the Covenant, a triumphal procession, and the Tabernacle of The Most High.

The transport of the Ark, of course, immediately suggests the Eucharistic processions of the Counter Reformation—specifically those of the Descalzas Reales for which the tapestry cycle was commissioned. Hence, the circumstances of Rubens's commission may, in the final analysis, explain his choice of subject for the final prefiguration. The key element is the Ark, the container of God's actual and physical, though invisible, Presence. Throughout the four prefigurations, God appears only once, and in a significant manner, i.e., in the form of the Ark. Nowhere do we find a figural representation of Him. Similarly Christ's presence throughout the entire cycle is confined to the sacrament; nowhere does Rubens represent or allude to his human form. In this way, the prefigurations—and, as we shall see, all the tapestries—are thematically focused on the unique identity of the Eucharist to the exclusion of any other representation of Christ: that is, He may here be found *only in the Eucharist*. For all its apparent simplicity, this total—indeed exclusive—identification of Christ with the Eucharist underscores the profoundly sacramental, and thoroughly Catholic, theology behind Rubens's program and imagery.[45]

Elbern has claimed that Rubens's tapestries indicate a great change in liturgy from the time of Bouts's altarpiece, which, in turn, explains the exclusion of a Communion scene (or the Last Supper) from its program. That change, rooted in the Eucharistic mysticism of the Middle Ages and intensified during the Counter-Reformation, involved a gradual process through which the Eucharist became independent of the Mass and developed its own liturgy, a new Eucharistic cult.[46] Rubens's fourth subject thus assumes a special significance beyond its obvious role as a general prototype for the sacrament. Just as its triumphal imagery prefigures the later allegorical triumphs of the sacrament and reflects the triumphalism of this Counter-Reformational cycle, so, too, does the Ark signify the Catholic emphasis upon the Real Presence. Finally, as we shall discover in Part III, even the idea of the Tabernacle in this scene is related to the *concetto* of the cycle as a whole and provides an additional reason why Rubens chose this subject as the final—and most comprehensive—prefiguration of the Eucharist.

Taken together, the four Old Testament tapestries reflect both the endurance of medieval tradition in the use of established typologies and its thorough transformation into a new idiom. All four present, as it were, a dramatic prologue for the subsequent allegorical scenes of victories and triumphs, in which the Eucharist becomes still further removed from the altar, becomes still less identified with its natural substance, and—in the true sense of an apotheosis—is transfigured into a resplendent image of divinity.

4

The Victories

Following the group of Old Testament prefigurations of the Eucharist, the pair of Eucharistic *Victories* takes us into the realm of history—or, as is so often the case with Rubens, of historical allegory. No longer drawn from the Bible or standard compendia such as the *Speculum humanae salvationis* and the *Biblia pauperum*, these subjects depend upon less easily identifiable sources and owe their primary debt to Rubens's own historical and allegorical imagination. Both tapestries are large, are of similar dimensions, and are framed by Solomonic columns so that they might be clearly understood as a visual as well as iconographic pair. Chronologically, the pair alludes to the two major challenges faced by orthodox Christianity in its Eucharistic doctrine: the early challenge of paganism and the successive threats of heresy and dissension. The first scene—*The Victory over Pagan Sacrifices*—looks back to the early Christian period; while the second—*The Victory of Truth over Heresy*—looks not only to the past but also forward to the allegorical triumphs and, more generally, to the ultimate victory of Catholic doctrine over Protestant negations. In this respect, the two victories may be seen to bridge the Biblical prefigurations and the purely allegorical triumphs of the Eucharist.

The Victory over Pagan Sacrifices

The Victory over Pagan Sacrifices (Fig. 14) represents in the foreground a traditional Roman sacrifice of a bull suddenly interrupted by a miraculous apparition of the Eucharist. In the upper left-hand corner appears a young, angelic herald with nude torso, surrounded by a heavenly burst of light. In his left hand he holds a golden chalice; in his right, lightning bolts. The appearance of the beautiful yet terrifying figure in the sky has thrown the Romans into utter confusion, and the scene recalls a similar episode in the Medici cycle (*The Council of the Gods*, K.d.K. 254), in which Apollo (Belvedere) routs personifications of evil from Mount Olympus. At the right, the kneeling *Cultrarius* continues to hold the bull's horns as he looks up in terror at the apparition. Beside him the partially nude *Popa* leans over the bull, still holding his sacrificial axe in one hand while raising the other in a defensive gesture. Close behind him press two other men cowering in fear, the old hooded priest with a long white beard and behind him a younger priest. Directly beneath the apparition a Negro servant holding a torch turns violently away from the vision and is about to flee (only the back of his head is visible). In the foreground the disarray is even greater: a musician (his lyre just visible to the right of the column) has fallen to the ground, his back to the viewer, while the young *Camillus* holding a flute grabs the sacrificial altar, knocking it over. At the musician's feet lie several other sacrificial objects: the empty *patera*, a box of incense, and the large vase from which wine spills over the ledge.

In the background a parallel event takes place. Two priests are about to pour libations upon a fire before the statue of Jupiter (crowned with laurel and holding a staff, his eagle beside him). At that moment four figures fleeing from the apparition (two with torches) rush into the temple and interrupt the sacrifice. In the middle ground, bridging the two scenes, a young man and a woman kneel halfway up the flight of steps; she gestures in surprise while her companion folds his hands in prayer. As in *The Sacrifice of the Old Covenant*, various architectural elements—rows of columns, steps, arches, and niches—are used to break up the picture space into areas outside and within the temple. Once again, however, the setting is not wholly rational, but more in keeping with stage scenery. If not in the architectural trappings, at least in his description of antique objects (the sacrificial furnishings) Rubens sought to be archaeologically accurate. The toppling altar inscribed to Jupiter, the patera, and the vase of libations all indicate the artist's deeply rooted interest in classical antiquity and recall similar details in the Constantine tapestries. *The Marriage of Constantine* included a similar altar along with sacrificial bull, Popa, Cultrarius, and youthful attendants. The same group is also found in the Decius Mus cycle, in *The Interpretation of the Victim* (Liechtenstein Coll., Vaduz, *K.d.K.* 143). All three tapestries, in turn, look back to Raphael's Sistine Chapel tapestry, *The Sacrifice at Lystra* (Vatican), which Rubens had seen in Rome.

The central figure of the cowering Popa was adopted from the artist's earlier oil sketch for *The Expulsion of Adam and Eve from Paradise*, originally intended for the Jesuit ceiling but later dropped from the program. (This sketch was in turn based on a woodcut by Tobias Stimmer.)[1] Comparing the oil sketch (National Gallery, Prague) with the tapestry, one finds that Adam's gesture and facial expression have been repeated and given a similar meaning. In the tapestry modello (Prado, Madrid, Fig. 15) the figure is reversed; but the bozzetto, now lost, may well have revealed a figure identical to and in the same sense as Adam. An equally interesting parallel can be seen between the angel at the gate of Eden and the Eucharistic herald in the tapestry. The idealized, youthful figure, the swirling drapery, lightning bolts (or "flaming sword"), and the outstretched gesture are common to both. Here, then, is an example of Rubens's turning back to an earlier and unused composition as the basis for a later work for which there was no iconographical precedent. The angel, in this context, is particularly significant since the allegorical herald is given no specific identification and suggests no obvious Biblical or emblematic prototype. But both angel and herald share a common ancestor: the *Apollo Belvedere*, whose similar role of *alexikakos* ("warder-off of evil") Rubens clearly appreciated, as his quotation of this statue in the Medici cycle (*The Council of the Gods*) demonstrates.

Since both the cartoon and the bozzetto are lost, we have only the modello to compare with the final tapestry. As in *The Sacrifice of the Old Covenant*, there are certain pentimenti in the columns: again Rubens was still working out aspects of the framing device at the modello stage. The left column base has been extended so as to be seen from the right (in the tapestry, from the left side). Similarly the column has been filled out to the right, the original spiraling line still showing through. Between the modello and the tapestry there are slight modifications in the three putti who hang the tapestry, the inscription on the altar, and the placement of the kneeling couple on the steps. One disappointing change is found in the expression of the old priest who in the modello looks fearfully out of the corners of his eyes at the apparition. (In the tapestry he merely gazes blankly toward the viewer.) The toppled figure in front, along with the falling objects and the spilling wine, adds particular drama in the tapestry by his rather ambiguous placement.

Elbern has claimed that Rubens "in true Baroque style" has transgressed the "limits of pictorial reality" and that "persons from one reality reach or step over into the other."[2] In these foreground figures, placed so far forward that they seem about to fall through the picture plane, the transition from real space (the architectural setting) to the fictive tapestry space is so subtle that only after considerable analysis can the viewer determine where that tapestry begins and ends. But the illusionistic device, though stretched to extremes, is never transgressed and remains consistent, as one might well expect from the care with which it is worked out during the preliminary stages.

A drawing (Boymans-van Beuningen Museum, Rotterdam), has been attributed to Rubens by N. Beets as a preparatory stage preceding the modello.[3] As in the previous case, however, it is clearly a drawing by a follower of Rubens, based on the modello. Several oil copies of the mo-

\day, one of which was attributed by Haverkamp Begemann
 ~~~~ himself (Coll. Mme. Henri Heugel, Paris), but is now cor-
~~~ly considered a studio copy.[4]

The composition was engraved by Schelte a Bolswert, whose print
included the inscription "*Cede Deo Mala*," thus placing the scene more
explicitly within the realm of allegory and underscoring its Counter-Reformational significance. Other engravings by François Ragot (after Bolswert) and by E. Picart le Romain were later executed.[5] The composition,
a masterpiece of Baroque drama, evidently enjoyed great popularity in
the seventeenth century.

In view of Rubens's lifelong interest in classical antiquity and its
harmonious coexistence with his devout Catholicism, the iconography of
this tapestry might come as some surprise. In his previous tapestry cycles
the scenes including Roman (pagan) sacrificial elements were treated with
solemnity and a certain sympathy on Rubens's part. The Constantine
cycle may be said to typify the artist's attitude towards classical paganism, which was seen as a prologue to Christian Rome; the transition was
officially initiated by the Emperor Constantine himself, the very subject
of that cycle. In the Decius tapestries, the pagan sacrifices are treated
almost as a prefiguration of their Christian successors: as a means by
which the hero Decius comes to know God's will for him and his people.
But here in the Eucharist cycle, Christian revelation is clearly presented
in violent conflict with the world of ancient Rome.

This explicit opposition raises the questions of Rubens's primary
source for the scene and its role within the cycle. What historical moment—if any—does the tapestry illustrate? How does Rubens's choice
of subject relate to the rest of the cycle and, more generally, to its Counter-
Reformational context?

It seems unlikely that this scene illustrates a specific historical inci-
dent, an actual disruption within a particular Roman temple. It is more
probable that Rubens intended a more generalized reference to the historical victory of Christianity over Roman paganism toward the end of
the fourth century A.D. In any event, the historical context of this allegory is not the reign of Constantine but the subsequent reign of the Emperor Theodosius. The story of Constantine, the subject of Rubens's
earlier cycle, represents the early peaceful transition from paganism to
Christianity. Constantine's conversion, however, by no means resulted in
a complete religious transformation of the Empire. In general, the Constantinian rule marked only a gradual displacement of paganism by Christianity. But this trend was shortlived, and under Julian ("the Apostate")
paganism experienced a new revival and an apparent triumph over Christianity. He organized a pagan priesthood, opened new temples, and ac-

tively took part in ritual sacrifices. He did all he could to encourage strife among the Christians; he abolished Constantine's famous Christian standard, the "labarum," and introduced a school reform that "forbade the Christian masters of rhetorical grammar to teach unless they came over to the worship of the gods."[6]

This pyrrhic triumph of paganism, however, was soon to be reversed once and for all under the reign of Theodosius the Great (379–95), who mercilessly combated both heretics and pagans. He issued several decrees prohibiting animal sacrifices, divinations, and temple worship. His last decree, issued in 392, referred to the old Roman religion as a "pagan superstition" and "prohibited completely the offering of sacrifices, burning of incense, hanging of garlands, libations, divinations, and so forth"[7]— in short, everything that Rubens illustrates in this tapestry. In Rome, Theodosius removed the Altar of Victory from the Senate, where it had been returned after Constantine's reign by Julian the Apostate. As the historian Alexander Vasiliev has noted, Theodosius's victory over paganism was coupled with a victory for orthodox Christianity. Rather than tolerate competing doctrines, he designated the Nicene Creed "as the only legal creed," thus laying "an absolute veto upon all other tendencies in the Christian fold, as well as upon paganism."[8]

Historically the defeat of paganism thus corresponded to the triumph of orthodoxy, and this fact is implicit in Rubens's selection and treatment of the subject in the Eucharist cycle. From the time of the Reformation the Protestants were fond of charging the Church with residual paganism in its liturgy of the Mass—specifically, in its doctrine of sacrifice. In choosing to depict the Theodosian victory of Christianity over paganism as part of the epic history of the sacrament, Rubens, in effect, took the traditional Protestant accusation, reversed it, and exploited it as a piece of rhetorical counterattack. The scene is to be read not only as the historical victory of the Eucharist over pagan sacrifices but, allegorically, as the supremacy of the traditional Catholic doctrine of the efficacy of the sacrament. Just as Theodosius triumphed over both pagans and heretics, so does this tapestry—like several parallel subjects in the Jesuit ceiling program—suggest a dual victory with decidedly Counter-Reformational implications: the incomparable power of the Eucharist. The futility of pagan exercises in the face of the Eucharistic apparition anticipates, by analogy, the inevitable defeat of Protestantism. In this way the tapestry is closely related to and complemented by its companion, *The Victory of Eucharistic Truth over Heresy*.

The Victory of Eucharistic Truth over Heresy

In *The Victory of Eucharistic Truth over Heresy* (Fig. 16) the sense of violence and confusion introduced by the previous tapestry is further

heightened, as is the degree of allegory. In the center of a turbulent battlefield, which is strewn with bodies, smoke-filled, and infested with fire-
breathing monsters, arise the allegorical figures of Time and Truth. Winged
Time, the ancient man with a long white beard, raises his traditional
scythe of destruction while his other arm embraces the beautiful and
partially naked Truth. She points upward to a scroll which, along with
garlands of fruit, hangs in front of the tapestry. On it are inscribed the
words of Christ's institution of the Eucharist, the words of consecration
at each mass: "*Hoc est [enim] Corpus Meum.*" On each side the winged
monsters of Heresy menacingly breathe flames and smoke at her, but she
remains secure and unperturbed.

At the right of the tapestry (*left* in the modello) two partially nude
and muscular men flee from the scene, reaching forward in fear. The
foremost, dressed in red, holds a dagger: he, Rooses has suggested, personifies Rebellion, while his companion, in white drapery and wearing a
turban, represents Falsehood.[9] The latter appears to be an Arab, in which
case he might be interpreted more specifically as symbolizing the infidel.
Balancing these two, in the foreground, are two entering bearded figures,
fully clothed, each carrying a loosely bound book or sheaf of papers.
Smith identified them as two Evangelists, St. Matthew and St. Mark,[10]
but a more recent suggestion is that they are allegorical personifications
of the Old and New Testaments: the rear and older of the two men is the
Old and the nearer, younger man is the New Testament (dressed in sandals
and stockings, he also wears more modern clothing.)[11] More likely they
are meant to represent two Catholic theologians.

One walks, apparently exhausted, over a prostrate body. Dressed in
antique ecclesiastical robes, the latter may represent the early Christian
heretic Arius. Before him is sprawled another defeated figure, nude and
grasping a monstrance: he is Tanchelm, the twelfth-century heretic of
Antwerp, who led a revolt profaning and destroying tabernacles and the
sacred elements. He was defeated by St. Norbert, who restored devotion
to the sacrament in the area and who was traditionally represented in art
as standing over Tanchelm's body, as we find in Rubens's contemporary
oil sketch (Private collection, Atlanta) for a sculpture of the pair to be
placed on the pediment of the high altar for the Norbertine Abbey of
St. Michael's (now destroyed) in Antwerp.[12] (In this cycle, however,
St. Norbert is to appear separately in the tapestry of Eucharistic saints.)
Beside the heretic lies the contorted dragon of Heresy, in addition to two
more contemporary heretics. Luther, dressed in his white Augustinian
habit, lies with his head against a toppling altar (a Roman altar, recalling
the previous tapestry). He has just let fall a page of one of his treatises.
The sacrificial altar here is used with emblematic significance and refers
to Luther's attack on the Eucharist: "The Mass is not a sacrifice."[13]

Calvin, beside him, remains sitting and continues to defend his doctrines, pointing to a page of a book, probably his *Institutes*. In the background a young man holding a hammer appears to clutch a woman and child. He represents Iconoclasm, for on close inspection we find that it is a *statue* of the Madonna and Child that he is pulling down to destroy.

No putti are shown setting the tapestry in place, but on the ledge lies a lion (the tapestry draped over its back), holding in its claws a dead fox. The lion here symbolizes the Catholic Faith; the fox, the wiles of Heresy. As in *The Sacrifice of the Old Covenant*, these emblematic additions serve as a commentary on the tapestry's meaning, recalling similar devices used by Rubens in his designs for title pages. So, too, do the allegorical snake-like monsters, the iconoclast's hammer, the statue, and the antique altar all refer to the destructive aspects of heresy and recall Rubens's earlier use of such details for the title page of F. Haraeus's *Annales ducum seu principum Brabantiae totiusque Belgii III* (1623), at the bottom of which a similar monster of war (outside the temple of Janus) overturns a sacrificial altar, and scattered on the ground are a crucifix, broken statue, hammer, trumpets, drum, and helmet. Such allegorical "footnotes"—especially the Roman altar, now given Christian significance—are essential clues to the tapestry's Counter-Reformational meaning.

Several of the more prominent figures similarly recall earlier works by the artist. The image of Time uplifting Truth had been recently used in the final panel of the Medici cycle (*K.d.K.* 263). In the tapestry the pair is given a greater sense of animation, and Truth—now Eucharistic Truth—is appropriately provided with more clothing. The monster Heresy recalls the Hydra of discord in *The Reconciliation of Maria de' Medici and her Son* (Louvre, Paris, *K.d.K.* 262), as well as the dragon in *The Fall of the Rebel Angels* (Alte Pinakothek, Munich, *K.d.K.* 240); the sprawled figure of Tanchelm recalls the defeated Satan in the modello of the latter subject for the Jesuit ceiling (Musées royaux des beaux-arts, Brussels, *K.d.K.* 214), as well as Rubens's sculptural version of St. Norbert mentioned earlier.

In this tapestry, as in the Medici cycle, Rubens fuses specific, identifiable portraits with purely emblematic devices and combines history with allegory in representing the ultimate defeat of Lutheranism and Calvinism, the two primary challenges faced by Catholicism. Moving across the "battlefield," destruction will soon overcome these more recent heretics just as it already has Arius and Tanchelm, and they too will be trampled (along with their writings) by the two theologians. Time alone, here brandishing his reaper, which is notably absent in the Medici cycle painting, presides over the victory as both destroyer and preserver. Juxtaposed with the chaos and ugliness of Heresy, which is typified by the contorted Tanchelm, is the image of idealism in the ascending figure of Catholic Truth. This effective contrast is common throughout the religious art of the Counter-Reformation, especially in such closely related subjects as *St. Michael Triumphing over Satan*.

The bozzetto (Fitzwilliam Museum, Cambridge, Fig. 16) provides an interesting comparison with the tapestry, for it reveals that Rubens originally conceived the scene as a view of a battlefield. Here Truth, recalling a Roman Victory, strides over the plain, pointing to the banner and inscription unfurled in the sky. There is here no indication of the figure of Time, who was subsequently introduced between the bozzetto and the modello; that is, probably after Rubens's consultation with the Infanta and her theological advisors. In other details, however, the bozzetto is close to the final composition and includes the two theologians, the two fleeing figures, monsters, and three heretics (along with their attributes). There is also a sketchy reference in the background to the iconoclast and the statue. The flying inscription, however, is shown as part of the tapestry design, rather than part of the surrounding architecture; and below the tapestry, instead of the lion and fox, is placed a cockle shell flanked by two griffins. The architecture and tapestry-device, both carefully defined, distinguish the bozzetto from the preceding ones. It is clear that by now the device was no longer added as an experimental afterthought, but was fully developed as part of the overall composition.

A pen-and-wash drawing of the bozzetto preserved in the British Museum was thought by Hind to be a preparatory sketch by the master.[14] As in the previous cases, however, it represents a copy (not by Rubens) after the bozzetto, as Haverkamp Begemann correctly described it in his 1953 catalogue of the Rotterdam exhibition.[15] A second drawing in black chalk (Louvre, Paris), was attributed by Fritz Lugt to Rubens as a preparatory study.[16] It includes a detailed study of the lion and fox together with a single Solomonic column. While recognizing the style as wholly typical of Rubens, Lugt had some reservations about the drawing of the animals in which he had expected *"une touche plus caractéristique."* Indeed the handling is rather weak and too linear in some passages. A comparison with the Prado modello reveals no differences at all between the animals in each or between the two columns (the drawing corresponds to the modello's right column). Such an exact repetition deprives the drawing of any logical place within the evolution of the composition and indicates that it surely represents a workshop study based on the finished modello.

The cartoon no longer exists, but a comparison between the modello (Prado, Madrid, Fig. 17) and the final tapestry reveals no substantial changes, only the usual elaboration of details in the architecture, tapestry border, and so forth. The predominant use of grays, browns, and blues in the draperies complements the thick, smoky atmosphere of the sky against which Truth, dressed in glistening white, radiates a golden light. Those elements that so enliven the modello—the loose flowing drapery, the smoke and flames, the juxtaposition of glowing light and thick clouds— suffered most in the transition from oil to tapestry. The modello, there- fore, is all the more to be enjoyed as an independent composition. (Of course, like the other Prado modelli it should be restored to its original dimensions.) Its great compositional strength is reflected in the many copies which were later painted.[17] The composition, like its companion *Victory*, evidently enjoyed widespread popularity and was engraved by A. Lommelin, who added the inscription *"Tempus Veritatem Producens."*

The inscription on the reproductive engraving recalls another, more famous, proverb that enjoyed a rich literary and iconographic history throughout the sixteenth and seventeenth centuries: *"Veritas filia Tem- poris"*—Truth is the daughter of Time. In an extremely illuminating study Fritz Saxl has traced the various—and largely propagandistic—uses of this theme throughout the Reformation and Counter-Reformation.[18] Both sides invoked and illustrated those words with equal conviction that they would vindicate their cause and that time would bear out the truth of their respective claims. In showing his figure Truth pointing upwards to the inscription *"Hoc est Corpus Meum,"* Rubens defines her role in one particular controversy. It is the Truth of the Catholic doctrine of transub- stantiation that Time will uplift and reveal over the tumult of heresy.

That among those overthrown by the glory of Truth is the Church's first major heretic, Arius, not only emphasizes the long history of dissen- sion in which the contemporary Protestant challenges appear as mere recurrences, but also recalls the words of Constantine's solemn procla- mation over the adoption of the Nicene Creed at the first Church Council, which had rejected Arianism: "The devil," the Emperor wrote, "will no longer have any power over us, since all that he had malignantly devised for our destruction has been entirely overthrown from the foundations. The Splendor of Truth has dissipated at the command of God those dis- sensions, schisms, tumults, and so to speak deadly poisons of discord."[19] The document is recorded in Socrates's *Historia ecclesiastica*, and in view of his evident interest in early Christian history one wonders whether Rubens might not have known of this text. He may well have come across it while studying the life of Constantine for his previous tapestry cycle, which, as David Dubon has shown, derives its scenes from the works of such early Christian historians as Eusebius.[20]

Rubens was surely aware of the "timeless" nature of heresy and strife within the Faith, and so in joining Father Time with his daughter

Truth the artist emphasized the dependence of the latter upon the former. Poussin was to use the pair in a ceiling painting commissioned in defense of the policies of Cardinal Richelieu.[21] Bernini was also to invoke this image in a private work in his own "defense," his famous, and unfinished, sculpture of Truth (Borghese Gallery, Rome) for which the figure of Time the Revealer was never executed.[22] But Rubens's adaptation of the familiar motif on behalf of one of the most fundamental Catholic doctrines remains unparalleled. Time here becomes far more than simply the revealer of Truth—or the destroyer of falsehood: he reveals himself as no less than Truth's savior and the metaphysical agent of her apotheosis, an aged counterpart to the youthful herald who similarly dispels the forces of paganism by raising the transcendent host and chalice.

In their mixture of historical figures or settings and the allegorical content, the two *Victory* tapestries provide an iconographic transition from the Old Testament typologies to the third major group, the *Triumphs*. As Elbern has noted, in the *Victories* the Eucharist is presented entirely "separated from the Christian sacrificial act and thus seemingly absolutized."[23] The drama of the heightened conflict between the allegorical personifications of the Eucharist and its historical enemies prepares the viewer for the triumphal processions. Iconographically as well as compositionally, the *Victories* establish the central role of allegories as fully living counterparts to the Biblical and historical characters within this religious epic.

5

The Triumphs

The *Triumphs*, though numbering only three out of the eleven narrative tapestries, provide the dramatic focal point for the entire cycle, which derives its title (*The Triumph of the Eucharist*) from them. The special attention paid to this group by past scholars and critics is readily understandable to even the most casual viewer. Rubens's treatment of this exciting subject, the allegorical triumphal procession *a lo divino,* to borrow a phrase from Spanish poetry, surpassed all his artistic prototypes and was never equaled by subsequent artists.

As in the group of prefigurations, in the three triumphs *all' antica* of the allegorical women *Fides*, *Caritas*, and *Ecclesia*, Rubens had a rich tradition from which to draw his iconography. Unlike the prefigurations, however, the *Triumphs* do not reflect a revival of medieval conventions but, rather, a relatively modern *typus* whose initial popularity in art and literature coincided with the Renaissance rediscovery of classical antiquity. During the Middle Ages one can find only remote references to the image of the allegorical chariot or procession. For example, in his commentary on *The Song of Songs*, Honorius of Autun pictured the Shulamite woman (symbolizing Synagogue eventually driven to Christian belief) as seated in a chariot representing the *Quadriga Christi*, whose wheels represented the four Gospels.[1] Such theological tracts had a direct influence on religious art; and in the late twelfth century illustration of Honorius's text ("My soul troubled me for the chariots of Aminadab," *Canticles*, VI, 12), the regal woman is found on a chariot the wheels of which are embossed with the four Gospel beasts.[2] In his *Purgatorio* (XXIX, 88–XXX, 21), Dante describes a similar vision of Beatrice (representing Faith) ascending a "triumphal chariot more glorious than those of Scipio and Augustus," this time mounted on two wheels representing the Old and New Testaments and drawn by a griffin—a combination of bird and quadruped—symbolizing the dual nature of Christ. And, significantly, she is invited to enter with words taken from *The Song of Songs*. Finally Walafrid Strabo had conceived of Christ's metaphysical victory as a triumphal march.[3]

But for the flood of triumphal imagery which began in the Renaissance, one must look to a secular source: the poetry of Petrarch. Although he did not invent the triumphal metaphor, it was Petrarch who infused it with an unprecedented evocative power. In the course of his archaeological studies he was responsible for the first true understanding of antique triumphs and triumphal arches, and he incorporated them in his Latin epic *Africa* in the description of the triumph of Scipio Africanus. In his later poem *I Trionfi*—the six successive triumphs of Love, Chastity, Death, Fame, Time, and Eternity—he created an entirely new *typus:* the allegorical triumph, an "apotheosis of abstractions," as Müller-Bochat describes it.[4] Both Petrarch's renewed interest in classical triumphs and the new allegorical conceit soon flourished in art as well as literature. On the relief sculpture *The Triumph of Alfonso of Aragon* (Castelnuovo, Naples), one discovers a mixture of sacred and profane allegory in conscious imitation of such antique prototypes as *The Triumph of Marcus Aurelius* (Capitoline Museum, Rome). In painting, the theme recurs in Piero della Francesca's portraits of Federico di Montefeltro and his wife Battista Sforza (Uffizi, Florence), complete with the Seven Virtues and a Victory crowning Federico, who like his wife is shown riding in a ceremonial chariot. The allegorical triumph *all' antica* was paralleled by purely historical or mythological subjects: triumphs of Caesar, of Titus and Vespasian, or of Bacchus. In addition to such literary and pictorial examples, the processional triumph became an increasingly popular form of public spectacle: in 1491 Lorenzo de' Medici staged a magnificent triumph of Aemilius Paullus in the streets of Florence. In this same year Mantegna painted his splendid cycle, *The Triumph of Caesar* (Hampton Court, London), which Rubens had studied during his stay at the court of the Duke of Mantua and of which he later painted a variation (National Gallery, London, *K.d.K.* 310).

It is both significant and ironic that a few years later, while busily exterminating all such vanities of his predecessor, Savonarola in turn appropriated the imagery of these pagan, worldly triumphs and recast it in a thoroughly Christian mold: the *Triumphus Crucis*. In this profoundly influential work he became the first writer to represent the history of the Faith allegorically as a triumphal procession. The idea of Christ as *triumphator*, as Mâle had noted, would have deeply shocked thirteenth-century Christians, especially Franciscans, as in fact it later did Pascal.[5] But Savonarola succeeded in infusing the image with a dignity and piety commensurate with his intense religious fervor. Christ, seated in a quadriga, displays his wounds; while in front of him march the patriarchs, prophets, and heroes of the Old Testament. Surrounding the carriage and propelling it are the Apostles and those who foretold of Christ. Behind Christ are the Christian martyrs, immediately followed by the Doctors of the Church, carrying their open books. This vivid description by the otherwise iconoclastic monk was to provide artists with a rich source of illustration. Botticelli, among others, made an engraving of the scene (now lost) which Vasari considered his best. In 1511 Titian designed a large woodcut (five separate blocks, more than twelve feet long) generally inspired by the *Triumphus Crucis* and perhaps specifically by Botticelli's engraving (although there is now no way of telling how much.)[6]

Whereas Savonarola's triumphator was the human Man of Sorrows, Titian substituted an Eternal Christ, who thus represents the entire Trinity. There are many interesting variations between the woodcut and the text, and most of Titian's innovations can be directly related to the history of illustrations of Petrarch's *Trionfi*.[7] In these illustrations *Divinità* (riding in the final chariot—not specifically mentioned in the text) replaced Petrarch's *Eternità*, although their equation is only implied by the poet. Several of the new iconographic details transferred to Titian's woodcut later became part of a standard vocabulary for all religious triumphs. In the woodcut the four beasts of the Evangelists pull the quadriga; Christ is seated on a globe encircled by the signs of the zodiac which signify his universal rule; and the four Church Fathers turn the wheels, propelling the Church eternally. Old Testament heroes and Christian martyrs alike hold up their symbolic attributes. Banners unfurl, and the long procession is heralded by angels carrying the cross. In the sky the instruments of Christ's Passion are transformed into emblems of his triumph.

Many copies of this woodcut were published, and they quickly spread north into France and the Netherlands where the theme of the religious triumph soon flourished in all the arts. For example, a stained glass window in the church at Brou can be recognized as having been based on the woodcut.[8] Another in St. Patrick, Rouen, represents a more original variation, a treatise on the Fall and Redemption: in the center the crucified Christ is shown on a chariot preceded by Old Testament figures. At the foot of the cross are placed several vases in front of which sits the Virgin, as a quotation from Savonarola explains.[9] The vases, in turn, refer to the sacraments of the Church. In the window above, Christ is shown standing on a quadriga, running over a figure of Death; and the image of a processional triumph is linked with allegorical military victories.

In other triumphs it was the Virgin who was chiefly honored, and the compositions were often complex. In Geoffroy Tory's *Triumph of the Virgin* (from *Heures de la Vierge*, 1542) one finds several references to antiquity, the *Trionfi*, and even contemporary poems.[10] In front of the chariot march the Seven Virtues, the Seven Liberal Arts, and the Nine Muses. Still other related subjects include the independent triumphs of the Seven Virtues and even the triumphs of the Seven Deadly Sins, of which an important and grandiose series of tapestries designed by Pieter Coeke van Aalst may have had some influence on Rubens's equally allegorical (but virtuous) counterparts.[11] In the Netherlands one of the earliest Christian triumphs is found on a choirstall, carved by Jan Terwen Aertsz (1511–89) in 1543, in the cathedral of Dordrecht; it represents a carriage in a triumph of the Eucharist.[12] In an engraving of a related Christian triumph the Flemish artist Jerome Cock depicted Christ standing on a similar carriage, armed with the standard of the Cross, while behind him march four defeated enemies: the Devil, the Flesh, Sin, and Death.[13]

In attempting to establish an immediate context for Rubens's tapestries, however, one must turn to the series of six paintings depicting allegorical triumphs of the Catholic Church by his former teacher, Otto van Veen.[14] Painted in 1616, just ten years before the Eucharist cycle, these dry, academic, and repetitive compositions foreshadow very little of Rubens's intensely dramatic scenes. Nevertheless, they do establish several iconographic motifs that reappear in Rubens's own processional triumphs. For example, in Van Veen's *Triumph of the Crucified Christ* (Bayerische Staatsgemäldesammlungen, Munich) both Caritas and Fides are shown sitting at the foot of the cross. Rubens was to take these two personifications and give each a separate chariot, indeed a separate composition. More striking is the fact that in Van Veen's *Triumph of the Catholic Church* (Bayerische Staatsgemäldesammlungen), Ecclesia rides in a chariot drawn by four white horses, just as in the corresponding tapestry by Rubens. The putti hovering over it and bearing instruments of the Passion were to become still another element adopted by Rubens. Therefore, while it has been said that Rubens owed as little to his early teacher as Manet did to Couture, it nevertheless appears that Van Veen at this relatively late date was useful in providing Rubens with an important and contemporary source for his allegorical triumphs.

In addition to the pictorial precedents which may have influenced Rubens's triumph group one can cite a striking example of the religious, specifically Counter-Reformational, triumph in literature: *Triumphos Divinos* by the Spanish poet and playwright Lope de Vega. Published in 1625, the epic treated a similar series of triumphs *a lo divino* and ended with a triumph of the Eucharist. The intriguing coincidence of the date of the poem with Rubens's commission has led to the speculation that Lope may have exerted a direct influence upon Rubens, comparable to Savonarola's upon Titian.[15] We shall return to this question shortly.

One important source for Rubens's group of triumphs was the actual ceremonial triumph in Antwerp, the *Blijde Intrede* of Albert and Isabella in 1599, just a year before the young Rubens departed for Italy. The importance of this civic display for Rubens's own commission later in his life, the *Pompa Introitus Ferdinandi* held in 1635 for Isabella's successor, the Archduke Ferdinand, has been noted by Martin in his monograph on the latter.[16] Not only did the earlier triumphal entry, with impressive (if temporary) monuments to mark the political significance of the occasion, make a lasting impression on the young Antwerp artist, but Rubens may well have taken part in the execution of those decorations which were supervised by his former teacher, Otto van Veen. Of course, Rubens's *Pompa Introitus* represents a major transformation of the traditional elements of the ceremonial triumph into his own personal formulation, as Martin has shown. But in an important sense this later translation had been prepared by his adaptation of the triumphal imagery in his triad of allegorical tapestries.

Perhaps still closer as background imagery for these tapestries are the triumphal cars and chariots which were filled with costumed personifications and paraded around the streets of Antwerp and Brussels during the annual *ommegang* celebrations. One significant example of this colorful religious festival is recorded in the painting by Denis van Asloot of the 1615 *ommegang* (Victoria and Albert Museum, London). That procession, held on May 31, was unusual as it was celebrated in honor of the Infanta Isabella, not the Virgin (who was traditionally "Queen of the Fête").[17] The ceremonial triumph became, in effect, a personal triumph of Isabella and a celebration of her enlightened policies and her reign of peace which the Southern Netherlands enjoyed as a result of the Twelve Years' truce, signed in 1609. No doubt this triumph played a special role in the genesis of the allegorical triumphs she commissioned a decade later to celebrate, proleptically, a renewed reign of peace for her land and her faith.

In the light of this living tradition, the Eucharist's triumphal carriages can be seen as falling both conceptually and chronologically between the floats mentioned above and Rubens's magnificent *Car of Calloo*, designed for the *ommegang* of 1638. The car as well as the placement thereon of the allegorical (living) figures is recorded in Rubens's oil sketch (Koninklijk Museum, Antwerp, *K.d.K.* 412) and reproduced in Van Thulden's etching.

The parallel between the Eucharist *Triumphs* and actual civic celebrations must not be pressed too far, just as one must resist drawing too many parallels between Baroque theater and the visual arts. But in the cases of Rubens and Bernini a certain degree of cross-influence is not only reasonable but inevitable. Just as Bernini was active in both the visual arts and theater (as set designer, playwright, and sometimes even actor), so Rubens bridged the gap between these media by his activity in staged triumphs. The influences run both ways: as the fictive processions in the Eucharist tapestries draw from "live" precedents, so do the acutal *Pompa Introitus* of 1635 and the *Car of Calloo* of 1638 look back to their allegorical and illusionistic predecessors in the Eucharist cycle. Thus Rubens maintained a lively dialogue between illusion and reality, art and nature.

As a final backdrop to this rich and complex group of tapestries it is worth noting that not only did the triumph develop as an artistic, literary, and ceremonial *typus* during the two centuries preceding Rubens, but that a parallel development can be traced in liturgy beginning in the late Middle Ages and culminating in the sixteenth and seventeenth centuries, a development which centered around a new mystical devotion to the Eucharist.

In the history of Eucharistic processions for the feast of Corpus Christi, one discovers a gradual yet thorough transformation.[18] The feast, originally established by Pope Urban IV in a bull of 1264 as an expiational devotion to the sacrament (resulting from a vision by St. Juliana of Lièges, who was told that Holy Thursday alone was not sufficient), soon became an occasion for processions. At first these resembled the *viaticum*, the transporting of the sacrament to the sick or from one church to another, and they were performed with great simplicity. Later, crystal reliquaries were substituted as greater emphasis was placed on spectacle. Finally a variety of elaborate monstrances were introduced. At first biers were used to carry them, indicating a deliberate association with the Ark. Later these became actual carriages as the processions became increasingly festive and triumphal with the inclusion of pennants, crosses, and processional candles or torches.

The clergy, like the secular court, were often girded with floral crowns, and all classes of people joined in. Martyrs were added to the procession by carrying their reliquaries; images of saints and holy kings joined the throng until finally the cortège became a triumph comparable to those ancient prototypes described by the Italian humanists. Thus the feast of Corpus Christi was transformed from its original function as a penitential and expiational solemnity into a triumphal event, a gradual development which was accelerated and intensified by the Counter-Reformation. The Council of Trent strongly defended and further encouraged such liturgical processions as both a suitable devotion to the sacrament and an appropriate weapon to be used against the Protestants, "to confound the heretics."[19] It is with a keen awareness of such militant overtones that one must view the following tapestries, remembering that these allegorical triumphal processions provided, above all else, a visionary backdrop for the actual liturgical processions of the Descalzas Reales on Corpus Christi and Good Friday. In this respect they truly become living allegory.

The Triumph of Faith

In the first of the *Triumphs*, that of *Fides Catholica* (as the cartouche in the center reads), Faith is shown standing upon her processional chariot, holding a chalice crowned by a Host as she turns to look back on her train of captive followers (Fig. 19). The first, a bearded man holding an astrolabe in one hand and a book in the other, personifies Astronomy. Behind him walks an old, partially crippled man leaning on a walking stick who, resembling traditional portrayals of Socrates, represents Philosophy. Rooses identified him as Stoic Philosophy, but this is inconsistent with his Socratic features.[20] Behind his stooped back, one catches a glimpse of a much younger face looking up yearningly at Fides, who returns the look. Rooses identified him as Epicurean Philosophy, but more probably he represents Poetry in view of his only visible attribute, the crown of laurel. At his side walks Nature, with five breasts. Holding her skirts, arms crossed, and looking humbly at the ground in front of her, this figure derives from a female captive in Giulio Romano's *Triumph of Titus and Vespasian* (Louvre, Paris).

In the darkness from which these figures have emerged, beside the column, appear the face and upraised hand of one final figure. He is black, bearded, and wears an exotic headdress with a gold earring; like Poetry he looks up in supplication to Faith. He has been alternately identified as an Indian, thus symbolizing the New World missions, and as the continent Africa. (Both Rooses and Tormo simply mention him as an otherwise unidentified Negro.)[21] He cannot, however, be an American Indian since his facial characteristics and dress are distinctly Near Eastern. More likely he typifies Moorish (Islamic) Philosophy, finally brought into line with the rest who follow obediently behind the true Faith: as such he would have particular significance in an allegory designed for a Spanish royal convent.

On the carriage, at the feet of Faith, rests a large globe symbolizing (along with the captives) the universality of her rule. In front kneels an angel of the Passion holding a large wooden cross, its diagonal placement paralleling Faith's stance and gesture. Together with the instruments of the Passion, carried by two putti (one holds the four nails, the other, the crown of thorns and loincloth), it refers to Christ's sacrifice and therefore immediately—and physically—precedes the sacrament (chalice and Host). The cross and chalice are traditional attributes of Faith, who recalls, especially in the raised gesture, Titian's *Faith Adored by Doge Grimani* (Ducal Palace, Venice) which Rubens may well have known from his early years in Italy. In the Titian painting Faith herself holds the cross. Rubens, however, had already used the motif of an additional figure—an attendant angel—holding the cross in front of Faith in his altarpiece for the Jesuit church in Antwerp, *The Miracles of St. Francis Xavier* (Kunsthistorisches Museum, Vienna, *K.d.K.* 205), in which a globe is also included at her side. Faith is thus associated exclusively with the sacrament, which she alone is entrusted to hold.

Directly above the captive train fly two additional angels, the foremost raising a torch and with the other hand pointing toward the chariot which is propelled by two angels in front and two putti behind. The illusionistic tapestry, hung between the Doric columns by three putti, is thus almost completely filled by the figures, but a small clump of vegetation, along with the brief glimpses of background landscape, indicates a natural setting for the allegorical group. An effective contrast is achieved between the three "real" putti (one casts a sharp shadow against the tapestry as he hangs the cartouche in place) and the putti depicted within the illusionistic tapestry: once again Rubens exploits the juxtaposition of visual reality and illusion.

In front of the tapestry stands a decorative pedestal with a shell-like encasement, upon which rests a crucible and over which hovers a heart surrounded by flames. The pedestal is similar in shape to the flat-topped chariot, while the heart and crucible recall the chalice and Host (enveloped in an even brighter light). The heart suggests the popular devotion to the Sacred Heart, which flourished during the Counter-Reformation. The objects are guarded by two strangely beautiful sphinxes. In Synesisus's *De Regno*, the sphinx symbolizes the virtues of fortitude and prudence, as Rubens was later to use it on his Arch at St. Michael's for the *Pompa Introitus* in 1635.[22] Perhaps then the two may here also refer to these virtues as necessary guardians of the faith. More likely, however, they symbolize the aspect of mystery in the faith, an interpretation of the motif which arose out of Renaissance efforts to understand the sphinxes of Greek and Roman antiquity.[23] In the post-Tridentine period that mystery was most perfectly identified with the sacrament itself and was accessible only to those who, like the allegorical figures here, obediently followed the one true faith.

In the figure of Fides Rubens has created an image of incomparable and unearthly beauty. Her stance—feet firmly placed together, one hand resting against her hip—emphasizes her strength and resolution. As a personification, she is wholly in keeping with the aspirations and joyous optimism of seventeenth-century Catholicism, as well as with the artist's own temperament and faith. One additional detail worth noting is that the emblematic pedestal (similar to those of preceding tapestries) is repeated above in the relief work on the entablature between the columns.

The bozzetto (Fitzwilliam Museum, Cambridge, Fig. 18) reveals several minor changes between the artist's first formulation and the finished tapestry. Faith is relatively larger; her chariot, smaller. The angel holding the cross stands rather than kneels while the angels preceding the cross blow trumpets instead of carrying the instruments of the Passion. Philosophy is shown without a walking stick, and his companion carries a *caduceus* instead of an astrolabe (thus he was later changed from Medicine to Astronomy). The Moor is not shown, nor are the angels flying above. Only the two putti who hang the cartouche are included, below which two sphinxes flank a second cartouche. But in comparison with previous bozzetti, this composition is in some respects remarkably detailed: the architectural setting indicates that the tapestry is to be seen from the right (as it is in the final version). The wide range of contrasts, especially in the use of light and shadow (the brightness of the Host juxtaposed with the cloudy darkness of the upper left), and the free and energetic brushwork already convey the sense of motion found in the tapestry.

Although still exhibited as one of Rubens's autograph modelli, the Prado panel of this subject is definitely not the modello on which the cartoon (Louvre, Paris: now on deposit in Valenciennes) was based, but a very inferior copy. Moreover, the fact that, unlike the six original sketches, the additional areas of architecture are not added strips of wood but are part of one single panel argues that this copy was painted after the Prado modelli had been altered to create a uniform set. Yet this panel was exhibited in the 1937 Brussels Exhibition as the original together with a "replica" of it (Coll. E. Tourney-Solvay, Brussels: now in the Musées royaux des beaux-arts, Fig. 19), but as Alfred Scharf pointed out at the time, the two attributions should be reversed, for the latter is the original.[24]

The cartoon, though executed by studio assistants, presents a stunning composition. The bright halo behind Faith's head has become entirely diffused. In general the dramatic use of light and shadow has been intensified from the modello, as have the expressions and gestures. Simply by raising the wrist slightly, Faith's delicate gesture of holding the chalice has become assertive: she lifts the radiant chalice higher so that it may be seen by all the followers. The angel holding the cross is leaning farther back and now looks up with a typically Baroque expression of intense adoration. Faith's swirling, tumultuous drapery assumes almost a life of its own. As insubstantial as the clouds, it heightens the contrast between pure spirit and the baser earthly figures of the captive train who march behind her. The composition was engraved from the modello by Nicholas

Lauwers. On the cartouche (the modello's is empty) he added the inscription "*Novae Legis Triumphus*."

The *Triumph of Faith* can be seen as growing out of the rich tradition of allegorical triumphs in art, specifically the Christian triumph which was first spelled out by Savonarola's *Triumphus Crucis* and was first given visual form in Titian's woodcut of 1511. Rubens's inclusion of the instruments of the Passion, the angelic heralds in the air, and the procession of followers behind the chariot all recall the Titian woodcut and, more immediately, Van Veen's allegorical triumphs of the Catholic Church. Even in his use of the flat-topped carriage as a kind of moving stage on which the allegorical figures stand or kneel recalls these two prototypes as well as the ceremonial floats of the annual *ommegangen*.

Rubens's version of the Christian triumph *all' antica* is essentially a product of his age, an allegory of his time. Particularly original—and revealing—in this respect is the train of captives following Faith. The personification of Astronomy reminds us that at this time the Church was struggling with the implications of the Copernican revolution and that the reigning Pope Urban VIII (who appears in one of the altar tapestries) finally forced his friend Galileo to renounce his claims to absolute truth. Science might proclaim new theories, but ultimate truth was still in the domain of the Faith. Similarly, the inclusion of Philosophy reminds us that the seventeenth century witnessed a flourishing of various schools of philosophy. It also recalls Rubens's own interest in neo-Stoicism and the circle of Justus Lipsius. But philosophy, like science, is also subject to faith. No less so is nature, the special concern of scientists and artists alike in the Baroque age.

Rubens's combination of allegorical figures elaborates on the theme of the universality of faith (also symbolized by the globe). It also reflects some primary religious questions of his day: namely, the relationship between faith and science, faith and philosophy, faith and nature. In this Counter-Reformational cycle those relationships are reduced to an unambiguous image of victor and captive, and the triumphal imagery is appropriately *Roman*.

The Triumph of Divine Love

In *The Triumph of Divine Love* (Fig. 21) Caritas stands on a small processional chariot drawn by two lions. She holds one of her children in a tender embrace while the two others stand at her side. Immediately in front of her stands a pelican, piercing its breast to feed its young, a traditional symbol of Christ's love and sacrifice. In the air around her head fly twelve putti (only eleven are visible; the twelfth is behind Caritas). Some have birds' wings; the others, butterfly wings, and one holds a flaming torch. Through the circle opens an expanse of sky and background landscape, of which far more is visible than in the preceding triumph. On the ground are three additional putti. One rides a lion, holding its mane in one hand while in his other he uses an arrow as a crop. He turns and looks back at his companions. One stoops over in order to burn two intertwined snakes (symbols of sin and evil) with his torch; the other raises a flaming heart in his left hand and holds a bow in the other.

These motifs of love (sacred and profane)—Cupid's bow and arrow, the flaming torch, the flaming heart, and putti—are repeated in various decorative elements. In the center of the chariot's wheel is a carved seraph from which radiate alternating arrows and shafts of flame as spokes. This unusual detail may refer to the ecstasy of St. Theresa in which all three—the angel, arrow, and burning flame—are combined in her description of divine love; but in any case, as symbols of love the motifs are commonplace. Above the tapestry, which hangs between two Doric columns (no additional putti are shown hanging it), is strung a garland of fruit and flowers. In the center, between two crossed torches, hangs a cartouche inscribed "*Amor Divinus*." Below the bottom ledge, in the center, is placed a flaming heart pierced by two crossed arrows encased in an ornamental shell adorned with flowers. On each side is a cornucopia from which emerge flames and smoke and on which sits a dove, another emblem of love.

Rubens's combination of Caritas with these evocative symbols recalls another *Triumph of Caritas* in the Brussels tapestry cycle, *The Triumph of the Seven Virtues* in Vienna.[25] In the latter, Caritas stands, surrounded by three children, on her chariot and holds a flaming heart in her left hand. Also included is a pelican, similarly shown opening its breast. The personification of Caritas also appears in Van Veen's *Triumph of the Crucified Christ*, where she is seated at the foot of the cross with Fides.

Rubens, however, adds to the traditional Caritas another level of meaning. The two lions who pull her triumphal chariot link the image with the classical goddess Cybele, the Mother of the Gods, who on Roman coins was similarly represented.[26] In a title page illustration, Rubens was to show the goddess—here in reference to Maria de' Medici, the Queen Mother—seated between her two lions.[27] The implied reference to Cybele in this tapestry reveals the artist's characteristic appropriation of a classical motif for a Christian subject. As Mother of the Gods, she refers to Mary, Mother of God (*Theotokos*); and in this context it is especially revealing that her features, in addition to her blue and red drapery (traditionally used in representations of the Madonna), recall several of Rubens's paintings of the Virgin and Child (for example, the wing of the *Christ à la Paille* altarpiece, Musées royaux des beaux-arts, Antwerp, *K.d.K.* 161) and even *The Apocalyptic Woman* (Alte Pinakothek, Munich, *K.d.K.* 240), who was traditionally identified with the Virgin. In the latter, painted only a few years earlier, one notes the same long flowing hair, facial features, and loose cascades of drapery. She treads on a serpent surrounding the globe, while in the tapestry that task is delegated to one of her assistants who purges evil from the world with the torch of divine love.

More generally, the tapestry recalls *The Exchange of Princesses* from the Medici cycle (*K.d.K.* 256) in its similar arrangement of putti linking hands in the air, putti with torches, and garlands. In the Medici painting, the curtain hanging between two columns and pulled back by putti bears a remarkable similarity to the manner in which the tapestry is arranged between its two columns. The resemblance is even more apparent in the bozzetto (Fitzwilliam Museum, Cambridge, Fig. 20), in which Rubens originally intended a putto to drape the tapestry over the right column. (He later chose to show the tapestry tied around the column from behind.) In other respects the bozzetto reveals few differences from the final conception. The putto burning the snakes was originally painted looking downward, as a pentimento indicates, but was later turned backward toward his companion. (In the modello Rubens was to revert to the original position.) The cartouche is absent from the bozzetto, as are the garlands and the decorative objects below the tapestry where one finds only an empty stand flanked by two torches. It is noteworthy that in the bozzetto the architecture was to be seen from directly in front, whereas in the final tapestry the viewer faces it from the right side.

In the modello (Prado, Madrid, Fig. 21) there are several pentimenti, especially on the base of the left column, indicating that Rubens changed the angle of perspective during this second preparatory stage. The modello—again, minus the later additional strips of wood—captures an unusual aura of peacefulness, warmth, and tenderness, in contrast with its highly dramatic and heroic predecessors. The chromatic progressions of reds (drapery, hearts, ribbons), golds (architecture, chariot, flames), and blues (drapery, sky, water) further evoke an overall sense of harmony and peace which is most poignantly reflected in the image of Caritas who, despite all the triumphal trappings, appears strangely serene and even withdrawn.

If this composition is the least triumphal of the tapestries described so far it is also the least explicit in Eucharistic imagery, especially in comparison with the two other triumphs. The only specific reference to the Eucharist is the pelican. Feeding its young with its own body and blood, it symbolizes both the sacrificial nature of the Mass and the doctrine of transubstantiation, in which God nourishes his children with his actual body and blood—the two Eucharistic dogmas which Counter-Reformation art asserted in the face of Protestant denials. More generally, the subject of Caritas (along with the various emblems of love) represents a theme common to all the typological and allegorical tapestries of the cycle. Underlying the more formal doctrines of sacrifice and real presence is the theme of divine love, and significantly it was St. Thomas Aquinas, author of the Corpus Christi sequence, who described the Eucharist as the "Sacrament of Love."[28] Central as it is to the iconographic program, this tapestry therefore hardly requires further justification for its prominent position within the cycle.

The cartoon (Fig. 22), discovered in an English private collection, now hangs with its four companions in the Ringling Museum (Sarasota).[29] In general, it represents a faithful studio translation of the modello (it has subsequently been cut down at top and bottom). The magnificent head of the putto riding the lion, however, reveals Rubens's own hand. The landscape, by a studio collaborator, is especially compelling, as are the lions which may likewise include some finishing touches by the master. The putto entering at the right, carrying a flaming heart suggests in facial type and coloring the influence of Jacob Jordaens. Whether Jordaens himself collaborated with Rubens on the preparation of the Eucharist cartoons must remain a matter of speculation. The fact that he participated in Rubens's next cycle, *The Achilles Series*, and probably also in *The Constantine Series*, makes the possibility an attractive one.

In Leningrad (Hermitage, print room), is preserved a sheet of various pen-and-ink sketches, including a full-length figure of woman holding one child while two others stand beside her. Above her head "caritas" is written in red chalk. M. Dobroklonsky has related the drawing to this tapestry.[30] Certain similarities are evident, but whether it actually represents a study for this particular composition is by no means clear. In view of the other figures on the sheet, which have no connection with the cycle, it would be dangerous to assume any direct relationship between the drawing and the tapestry. More likely, it provides yet another example of Rubens's characteristic use of the same vocabulary of images. The modello was engraved by A. Lommelin, who added the inscription "*Amoris Divini Triumphus*" at the top.

The Triumph of the Church

In contrast with its predecessors, the third and final triumph, *The Triumph of the Church* (Fig. 24), reveals the artist at his most hyperbolic, animated, and fully Baroque. Not only is it the largest tapestry of the cycle (7.5 meters long), but it is also the most crowded with allegorical figures and symbols. Compositionally it is the most vibrant and dramatic of the series and can be understood iconographically as the climax of the entire procession. Representing the triumph of the Catholic Church, it is also the most explicitly Counter-Reformational.

Ecclesia, seated in an elaborate, golden quadriga, holds in front of her a large, jeweled monstrance which radiates spiritual light. A beautiful, typically Rubensian personification with long, flowing blonde hair and sumptuous ecclesiastical robes (an angel behind her carries the train of her cape), she recalls her earlier appearances in title pages designed by Rubens.[31] Directly above, a winged Victory is about to crown her with the papal tiara. The quadriga is pulled by four white horses which in turn are led by three women. The first, wearing a lion's skin over her head and carrying a staff, represents Fortitude, and the others (preceded by a fourth who carries the *labarum*) may thus represent the remaining three cardinal virtues, but only Fortitude is given any distinct attributes.[32]

In the air the procession is heralded by three celestial figures. The first two blow the trumpets of Fame, and the third, a Victory, holds out a laurel crown in one hand and a palm branch in the other. Riding the foremost horse is a winged Genius, crowned with laurel and carrying a processional baldachin with the two crossed keys of the Papacy, which he personifies. Behind him appear the heads of two additional women, also crowned with laurel. One holds up an olive branch, behind which flies a white dove. Recalling the dove of Noah's Ark (a typological reference to the Church as the new "vessel of salvation"), it symbolizes Peace. Directly below it, an angel seated on the front edge of the chariot gathers the reins in one hand and in his other holds a short whip.

Beneath the quadriga lie the bodies of three defeated figures. The blackened face and torch identify the first as Fury. Caught between the wheel is Discord with her serpentine hair. Finally, crushed under the rear wheel, lying on his back, and exhaling smoke is Hate with his animal-like face. The tapestry is hung in place between the Solomonic columns by two putti. The architectural setting is decked with a long garland, and in the center a cartouche (adorned with cherubs' heads) bears the inscription "*Ecclesiae Triumphus.*" Directly below, in front of the tapestry, rests a globe encircled by a snake biting its tail, a symbol for Eternity. On one side is a palm branch; on top of the globe, a laurel crown; and on the other side, the rudder of Providence. These common symbols—the globe, serpent, laurel crown, and rudder—later appear on a title page designed by Rubens for H. Goltzuis's *Icones Imperatorum Romanorum.*[33] As an emblematic gloss on the tapestry scene they signify the triumph of Ecclesia as an eternal, universal victory, guided by Providence. The figures crushed beneath the wheels refer to the more violent and destructive elements of Protestant heresy and recall the figures in *The Victory of Truth over Heresy*.[34]

In the foreground march two additional defeated figures. One with asses' ears and Silenus-like features represents Ignorance; the other, blindfolded, is Blindness.[35] Directing him forward and holding a lamp is the beautiful female personification of Light or Wisdom in the service of Ecclesia. Once again the triumph of good over evil is conveyed by the juxtaposition of beauty (the radiant Ecclesia) with ugliness, baseness, and deformity, as in the previous *Victory* tapestries or *The Triumph of Faith*. Here also the Eucharist is given the central role in the victory. Ecclesia is shown holding no other attribute but the monstrance, upon which all attention is directed; and her personal triumph becomes, by extension, the supreme triumph of the sacrament itself.

In depicting the moment just before the victor is crowned in a triumphal procession, this tapestry takes its place in a long tradition of classical triumphs—both antique and Renaissance. Among Rubens's own works it recalls a similar moment in the Constantine tapestries, *The Entry into Rome*, in which we find a similar prancing horse, its hooves raised high off the ground, and the flying personifications of Fame and Victory. These elements also recur in the Medici cycle's *Triumph at Juliers* (*K.d.K.* 225). And when Rubens later designed *The Entry into Paris* (Uffizi, Florence, *K.d.K.* 317) for the ill-fated Henry IV cycle, it was—like its religious counterpart—conceived as a triumph *all' antica*. Finally, ten years after the Eucharist cycle Rubens again used the motifs of the woman with billowing drapery (in this case, Providence) leading the victor's horse, a similar winged Victory with laurel crown and the trampled bodies of the defeated in *The Advent of the Prince* for the *Pompa Introitus*. This final variation was conceived as a tapestry hanging within a stage setting, being arranged by putti similar to those hanging *The Victory over Paganism*.[36]

In its unique combination of rich allegory and compositional clarity *The Triumph of the Church* surpasses all its secular counterparts. Jacob Burckhardt, who knew it only from an engraving, described the scene as "incredibly rich, yet not overloaded, and full of room to breathe"—a remarkable contrast with its companion, *The Triumph of Faith*, which he found "a crude and unpleasant composition."[37] One especially impressive passage is the group of four horses and women in front with its subtle variation of repeated forms, the wavelike motion of the raised hooves, the effective modulation of colors (pinks, blues, golds), and the varied angles of view in the figures. The procession is, to borrow Müller-Bochat's phrase, a true "*triumphus triumphi*"[38] and makes its ancestors, dating all the way back to Petrarch, appear pale and artificial by comparison.

The bozzetto (Fitzwilliam Museum, Cambridge, Fig. 23) is the liveliest and surest in execution of its group, with very few pentimenti and only minor alterations at later stages. The cartouche, garlands, and putti were, as in previous examples, added in the modello. Here one finds flanking the globe two lions which were later to be replaced by the palm and rudder, more specific references to the Church's triumph. (The lion, as we have seen, was later added to the modello of *The Victory over Heresy*.) But the tapestry-device and its architectural setting had already been carefully worked out in terms of perspective—it is the only tapestry to be seen straight on—and lighting (from right to left), and this bozzetto therefore probably represents one of the last to have been executed.

The modello (Prado, Madrid, Fig. 24) is unquestionably the most lively of its group, as well as one of the most finished. No major pentimenti occur, even around the columns. In fact, comparing this panel with the tapestry—the cartoon, unfortunately, no longer exists—we find that the composition was later simplified rather than elaborated: the two faces peering from behind the horse of the Papacy were dropped from Ecclesia's retinue. In the modello only two figures seem to lie beneath the quadriga. Furor's torch is included, but not his face. But the fact that he appears in the bozzetto (although Gerson failed to notice him)[39] as well as in the Bolswert engraving based on this modello, indicates that his absence is probably due to some damage in this area rather than to a deliberate omission. As this portion of the panel is unusually dark, careful cleaning might restore the image.

The composition was engraved by no fewer than five different artists. Bolswert's print includes in the empty cartouche of the modello the inscription "*Ecclesia per S. Eucharistiam Triumphans*." In addition, several copies of the modello were painted (one is in the Cleveland Museum of Art), and a copy of the cartoon by Van Thulden remains in St. Peter's Church, Ghent.[40]

At this point it is worth considering the question of a possible relationship between Lope de Vega's *Triumphos Divinos* and Rubens's three triumphs. In support of the hypothesis that "the origin of the commission [the Eucharist tapestries] and the works of Peter Paul Rubens that resulted from it are to be seen in the *Triumphos Divinos* by Lope,"[41] Müller-Bochat has attempted to demonstrate not only that Rubens owed the prominent allegorical *typus* of the military and clearly Counter-Reformational triumph *a lo divino* to Lope but also that he relied on the poet for many of his iconographical details. His argument rests primarily on an iconographic correlation between the last tapestry, *The Triumph of the Church*, and the fourth chariot of Lope's procession. This correlation, however, is at best superficial. For example, he equates Lope's ship, in which Ecclesia rides, with Rubens's golden quadriga which, he argues, is also in "the form of a ship."[42] But the equation is visually unsatisfactory. Although Rubens's chariot may imply a ship, Lope's six white sea-horses can hardly be identified with the four horses of the tapestry.

To argue that Rubens's compositions are *derived* from Lope's verses is to mistake a thematically related work of art (having the same purpose and arising from the same wellspring of imagery) for a definite prototype. Furthermore, for each similarity that Müller-Bochat cites between Rubens and Lope, one can point to a visual, and hence far more immediate, prototype in representations of the allegorical triumph, most notably in the recent cycle by Otto van Veen.[43]

In view of the fact that no unique correlations can be drawn between Rubens's compositions and Lope's descriptions, one can assume only a very general influence on the artist by the poet, if any at all. Whether the *Triumphos Divinos* was read by the Infanta or Rubens and was subsequently influential in the inclusion of equally heroic triumphs within this cycle is, of course, another question altogether. The coincidence of dates, as well as the similarity of themes, makes the possibility of even an indirect connection between the leading Spanish playwright and the foremost Flemish painter an appealing matter for conjecture. It is possible that a study of Lope's popularity and influence in the Spanish Netherlands might yield some additional insight. But in seeking Rubens's primary sources for this unique series of Eucharistic triumphs we return to the rich pictorial tradition which Rubens inherited and to his own imagination, his extraordinary ability to reshape and revivify that tradition.

6

The Entourage

Closely related to the *Triumphs* are the two tapestries of the four Evangelists and Eucharistic saints. Whether they ought to be considered iconographically as an entourage following the processional chariots, as Müller-Bochat has suggested,[1] or as the "announcers and defenders of the Eucharist" and therefore preceding the chariots, as Elbern maintains, is a matter of conjecture. While admitting that Müller-Bochat's grouping of the entourage behind the carriage of the triumphant Ecclesia is a "thoroughly tenable disposition," Elbern defends his own placement before the triumphal carriage on the analogy of other pictorial parallels in which such groups (Evangelists and Church Fathers) conventionally appear before the carriage, as in Van Veen's cycle.[2] He furthermore cites certain iconographic "interweavings" to justify this location between the two *Victory* tapestries and the *Triumphs*. Elbern interprets *The Four Evangelists* as being responsible for *The Victory of the Eucharist over Paganism* and *The Church Fathers and Saints* as responsible for *The Victory of Eucharistic Truth over Heresy*, noting the inclusion of St. Norbert and Tanchelm respectively.

The latter observation raises a third possible placement, considered neither by Elbern nor by Müller-Bochat, but recently suggested by Müller Hofstede: namely, *before* the *Victory* tapestries, where as historical figure groups they might be understood to bridge the Old Testament typologies and the Christian allegories.[3] However, the question of placement inevitably depends upon the intended arrangement of the entire cycle, which will be taken up in Part III. For the moment, it is more useful to consider the pair separately as a fourth group.

The Four Evangelists

The four Evangelists (Fig. 27) are shown walking in an open landscape, accompanied by their four Apocalyptic beasts. In front is St. Luke with the ox (of which only the head is visible), an allusion to sacrifice and his traditional attribute since his Gospel begins with the sacrifice of Zachariah. Next is St. Mark, his back turned to the viewer, holding his Gospel under his left arm; beside him walks the lion, the symbol of the Resurrection, also turning away. In the center stands St. Matthew, holding his large Gospel open while the angel above him (his attribute, since he begins his Gospel with the human genealogy of Christ) points up to the sky with one hand and to a passage in the text with the other. The gesture recalls that of Truth in *The Victory of Eucharistic Truth over Heresy*. Somewhat apart from the others stands St. John, the youngest of the four—he alone is without a beard—who looks up yearningly at the eagle, one hand resting against his chest. According to the Bestiaries the eagle alone is able to look directly into the sun and thus refers to John's Apocalyptic vision. The inclusion of these beasts, which derive from the vision of Ezekiel, represents, as in the typologies, the survival of medieval iconography in the religious art of the Counter-Reformation and recalls, for instance, the iconography of Domenichino's *Four Evangelists* in the frescoed spandrels of Sant' Andrea della Valle in Rome,[4] as well as Rubens's earlier painting of *The Four Evangelists* (Bildergalerie, Potsdam-Sanssouci, ca. 1614, *K.d.K.* 68), to which we shall return presently.

St. John is shown holding a golden chalice containing a serpent. This traditional attribute, which appears in several other paintings of the saint by Rubens, refers to an apocryphal story from *The Golden Legend*, in which John, presented with a cup of poison (usually depicted as a snake) as a test of his faith, made a cross over it, drank it, and then proceeded to revive the two unfortunate men who had just died from drinking the same potion.[5] In this tapestry, the cup is clearly a chalice and thus conveys an appropriate allusion to the Eucharist.

Smith understood the group walking as "performing the command of their Lord—'Go, preach the gospel to every creature.' "[6] More probably their directional movement is intended to convey the sense of a triumphal procession. Rubens's prominent inclusion of the Evangelists in this cycle underscores their significance as witnesses and recorders of Eucharistic doctrine. The first three all recount the institution of the Eucharist, and St. John's Gospel, which alone omits the actual consecration at the Last Supper, is especially charged with Eucharistic imagery and doctrine (e.g., "*Hic est panis qui de coelo descendit. . . .*"), which was to be quoted in the engraving of the companion tapestry of *Eucharistic Saints*.

The feigned tapestry is hung from three gold rings and is draped by two putti over a garland suspended between two Solomonic columns. In front, at the bottom, is a cockleshell, a traditional symbol of the Resurrection. On its left is placed a cornucopia of fruit, symbolizing the rich abundance issuing forth from the Gospels and, sacramentally, from the Eucharist; on the right is a dolphin, another Christian symbol of Resurrection.

In the bozzetto (Fitzwilliam Museum, Fig. 25) the figures originally filled less of the tapestry: there is more open space, and the figures stand farther back in the landscape and are viewed from a high vantage point. St. John's eagle is fully shown, and the saint enters from the left, in profile, with greater movement and more animated gesture. His chalice was originally to be held in the left hand. The bozzetto omits the two putti of the final tapestry and reveals, at the bottom, a cartouche instead of the cockleshell and two dolphins instead of one. But the architectural frame anticipates the final tapestry (to be seen from the left and lit from the upper left). For this reason the panel can be assumed to be one of the later bozzetti executed.

The modello (Coll. Mrs. Dent-Brocklehurst, Sudeley Castle, Glos., Fig. 26) can be identified as the sketch seen by Waagen in the London house of James Morrison[7] (and earlier, by Smith, in the collection of E. Gray).[8] With no significant pentimenti it, too, should be considered among the later works executed for the cycle. Recently rediscovered by Jaffé,[9] the sketch appears relatively finished in details—the garlands, folds, cockleshell, cornucopia, and dolphin—yet also characterized by rapid, lively brushwork. A comparison between this panel and the version in the Prado which was included in the 1972 catalogue as one of Rubens's original modelli and had been accepted as autograph by Tormo and Van Puyvelde,[10] reveals that the latter is a copy, though not a particularly faithful or skillful one. The architectural orders of the Prado sketch have been changed from Solomonic to Doric, and its composition has been considerably widened in order to create a set of uniform size. As in the Prado copy of *The Triumph of Faith*, the enlargement was not achieved by added strips of wood. Rather, a single panel was cut to the uniform dimensions, thus indicating a late copy probably dated after the modelli had been sent to Spain in 1648. The Prado also possesses another enlarged copy, again on a single panel of wood. Here, however, the columns are Solomonic, though increased to four. This weak copy has never been seriously attributed to the master.[11]

The cartoon (Ringling Museum, Sarasota, Fig. 27), aside from the usual refinements and elaborations of detail, is essentially a faithful repetition of the modello with only minor modifications. The gaze of the right cherub is now directed more toward the viewer, and at the lower right corner there is added a glimpse of background landscape. St. John's expression has also been modified from one of surprise to a typically Baroque expression of intense devotion in the upturned eyes of a saint in ecstasy. Waagen, who saw the canvas in the collection of the Duke of Westminster, in this instance rightly observed that "it is doubtful whether [Rubens] himself ever touched these great pictures."[12] In general, the figures are rather dry and formal. No additional copies of either the modello or cartoon are known. The composition was engraved from the modello by Schelte a Bolswert and again by Nicholas Lauwers.

Rubens had treated the subject of the four Evangelists at least once before in *The Four Evangelists* in Potsdam (*K.d.K.* 68). Rooses dated this painting around 1630, but Oldenbourg, followed by Vlieghe, considered ca. 1614 more likely.[13] Stylistically it resembles the other large and finished works of Rubens's early Antwerp period and thus may, like the Caen *Abraham and Melchizedek* of 1616, be considered a prototype for the Eucharist tapestry. In the Potsdam painting, St. Matthew's angel already plays a central role, but unlike his tapestry counterpart he points only *downward* to Matthew's Gospel on the table, rather than heavenward. And unlike the tapestry, this scene illustrates the authors of the three synoptic Gospels (Matthew, Mark, and Luke) grouped together at the table. Just as Matthew is the only one shown writing, since his Gospel was traditionally considered to be the first written, so John, standing apart at the right, is shown just arriving on the scene. He turns his head upward toward the eagle, his private source of inspiration, and remains oblivious to the three synoptic authors who receive their inspiration from Matthew's angel. Thus Rubens conveyed in the arrangement and varied activity of the Evangelists the contemporary, and official Tridentine, view of the relationship between the four Gospels: Mark and Luke closely followed St. Matthew whereas John (much younger) wrote his later and independently.[14]

Irving Lavin has recently explored the strong Counter-Reformational implications of Caravaggio's two *St. Matthew* altarpieces for the Contarelli Chapel in San Luigi dei Francesi—in particular, the Catholic belief that Matthew's was the first recorded Gospel and that St. Jerome's Vulgate was the most (indeed the only) reliable translation from the original Hebrew. Both these concerns are, as Lavin shows, incorporated in Caravaggio's first (and ultimately rejected) altarpiece for that chapel.[15] In the contemporary Potsdam picture of the four Evangelists, Rubens appears to have drawn from Caravaggio's second and final Evangelist portrait of St. Matthew. Particularly significant is the emphasis in both cases upon the angel's rhetorical gesture, which was later to be retained in his Eucharist tapestry. In this respect, the tapestry reveals Rubens's enduring debt to Caravaggio.

The idea of grouping all four Evangelists as a single picture can be traced back, according to Vlieghe, to Correggio's painting of 1521 (Museul de Arte, Bucharest). The subject was apparently first treated in the Netherlands by Frans Floris; and his painting, now lost, is recorded in a print dated 1566.[16] The theme gained popularity and can be found among the works of Pieter Aertsen (Kunsthistorisches Museum, Vienna) and Joachim Beuckelaer (Staatliche Gemäldegalerie, Dresden), to name two Netherlandish forerunners of Rubens. Rubens, however, was the first northern artist to introduce the subject into a monumental cycle of decoration. He was surely the only artist to represent it as a large tapestry.

Eucharistic Saints

In the companion tapestry of *Eucharistic Saints* (Fig. 30), a similar group is presented standing in a landscape, glimpses of which appear between the figures. There is again an implied processional movement. To one side St. Jerome, dressed in cardinal's robes, is shown reading from a book, probably his Vulgate translation of the Bible. Beside him, St. Norbert in his white Praemonstratensian habit with four-cornered hat is seen in profile, walking and carrying the sacrament beneath his robes.[17] This figure has also been identified as St. Albert, the patron saint of Isabella's deceased husband, the Archduke Albert.[18] But both the saint's habit and the act of carrying the sacrament clearly suggest St. Norbert as the correct identification and recall the defeated heretic Tanchelm in the preceding *Victory of Eucharistic Truth*. St. Norbert is usually shown carrying a monstrance, as in the statue of the saint designed by Rubens for the Abbey of St. Michael's in Antwerp, now preserved in the parish church of Zundert.[19] In this tapestry, however, the sacrament is concealed under his robes, and the honor of carrying the monstrance is reserved for St. Clare, who, as we shall see, holds a special and appropriate place of importance within this cycle.

In the center foreground stands St. Thomas Aquinas in his Dominican robes. In one hand he holds a book of his writings; his other points directly upwards, recalling the gestures of Eucharistic Truth and St. Matthew's angel, which reaffirms the primary role of these figures as proclaimers of the Eucharistic doctrine. On his chest is represented a large sun. This attribute refers to the vision of a Dominican monk who saw St. Thomas with such a sun glowing on his chest and alludes to his role as illuminator of Church doctrine. St. Thomas was, furthermore, frequently represented in art with the Dove of the Holy Spirit speaking in his ear. In this instance, however, the Dove hovers in the air, wings outstretched, directly above him and St. Clare of Assisi, signifying in its radiating light the source of doctrinal inspiration.

St. Clare, dressed in the Franciscan habit of the Poor Clares, of which she was the founder (and hence the patron saint of the Descalzas Reales), stands holding an elaborate monstrance in both hands. The monstrance, her traditional attribute, refers to the miracle which saved her order when the convent was attacked by Saracens employed by the Emperor Frederick II against the Pope. Already an old woman, she arose from her sick bed, took the sacrament to a window, and raised it before the soldiers scaling the walls, at which they fell back, took flight, and the convent was saved. The miracle is represented in Rubens's ceiling painting for the Jesuit church, in which the aged Clare is shown seated on a hilltop facing the Saracen camp, holding the sacrament.[20]

Rubens's description of an elaborate monstrance in the Eucharist cycle, as in the Jesuit ceiling painting, was clearly intended to emphasize the role of the sacrament in the miracle. It also serves as both an allegorical and a liturgical reference, recalling simultaneously the monstrance held by Ecclesia in the preceding tapestry and those used in contemporary Eucharistic processions or in the service of benediction. The saint's features are clearly those of the Infanta, whose second name was Clara, since St. Clare was one of her patron saints. Thus Rubens's patron is given the highest place of honor within the cycle which she commissioned. Here identified with the convent's patron saint, she stands beneath the Dove of the Holy Spirit surrounded by the four Latin Doctors of the Church and two of the leading defenders of the Eucharist. Most important, she alone of the earthly figures is entrusted with the monstrance containing the sacrament so that, in effect, she is given an active (albeit illusionistic) part in the Eucharistic celebration of her convent.

At the left of St. Clare stands St. Gregory the Great. The author of the *Liber Moralium* and the *Dialogues*, Gregory was responsible for most of the Canon and prayers of the Mass. Dressed in his pontifical robes and tiara, he holds the triple-cross staff of the Papacy and turns to face St. Thomas. Also turning, with his back to the viewer, is St. Ambrose, Archbishop of Milan, dressed accordingly in bishop's robes and miter. As author of the *De Mysteriis*, he asserted the dogma of Divine Presence in the Eucharist. Finally at the far right is St. Augustine, Archbishop of Hippo, recognizable by his black beard and his crosier and miter. His treatise *De Trinitate* illuminated various sacramental facets of the Eucharist. Only his face is visible, as he stares out at the viewer. Of the entire group St. Jerome alone is not immediately associated with the Eucharist. However, the legend of his last communion had by Rubens's time become a favorite subject in art, and it is probably for this reason that he is given a place among the throng of Eucharistic defenders. In addition, as author of the Vulgate, he was especially venerated during the Counter-Reformation.

Like *The Four Evangelists*, the tapestry is shown hung by two putti between columns (in this case, Doric). A garland of fruit is strung across the top, and in the center a cherub's bust is flanked by crossed trumpets over which is draped a long scroll. Below, in the center, rests an ornamental pedestal (like those of preceding tapestries) and on it are placed a book and an antique double-mouth lamp. The latter, an emblem of knowledge, refers directly to the Church Doctors above; but it also recalls the tabernacle lamp in *The Sacrifice of the Old Covenant* and thus is given Eucharistic significance. On either side one finds open books, inkwells, and quills, referring to the long written tradition of Catholic doctrine, dating back to the Patristic period. These objects serve as a vivid contrast to the heretical literature strewn about Luther and Calvin in *The Victory of Eucharistic Truth*. As a composition, the tapestry is the least dramatic and the most formal and static of the entire cycle so far, recalling the long tradition of the *sacra conversazione* in art, from which it derives: in this adaptation, the enthroned Virgin is replaced by the sacrament (the Body of Christ) as the object of veneration.

The bozzetto (Fitzwilliam Museum, Cambridge, Fig. 28) reveals the same grouping of figures with only minor differences from the final composition. St. Norbert looks upward and carries, instead of the sacrament, a staff over his shoulder. The dove is not yet introduced into the scene. St. Clare is here shown in profile, and there are as yet no indications that her features were meant to be those of the Infanta. Tormo has suggested that Rubens left them out of this sketch so as not to embarrass his patron (*"alarmarle la modestia"*) when the preliminary sketches were presented for her approval.[21] But it may simply be that the thought of using her portrait for St. Clare had not yet occurred to him. On the far right St. Augustine is barely visible, but perhaps this area has suffered some damage. What is surprising is that although the tapestry-device has already been clearly developed—even the two putti and garlands are included—there seems to be no indication of columns. It is difficult to determine whether the tapestry was meant to cover them, or whether in this study Rubens intended to eliminate them altogether. Other details, of course, were to be added later: the books, writing materials, lamp, scroll, angel's head, and trumpets.

In the modello (Prado, Madrid, Fig. 29) the feigned tapestry is now placed within the familiar architectural setting. The figure of St. Clare has turned toward the viewer, and St. Norbert, looking straight ahead, holds the sacrament beneath his garment. St. Thomas's gesture has been modified from an upraised, open hand to one pointing directly above. Glimpses of landscape appear between the figures, and the literary emblems have been introduced in front of the tapestry. Although considerably altered since the bozzetto, the architectural elements reveal no important pentimenti. The final tapestry, here represented in mirror image, was clearly to be seen from the left, the light also falling from the upper left.

In the cartoon (Ringling Museum, Sarasota, Fig. 30) one finds only minor reworkings of the modello. St. Clare's face is now clearly the Infanta's; no doubt Rubens's assistants merely copied it from a version of Rubens's recent portrait of her or its engraving. The Dove of the Holy Spirit is here enlarged, more clearly presented against the sun which shines through the clouds directly behind it—an effective juxtaposition of natural and spiritual light. A Eucharistic vine has been added above the head of St. Gregory. Its shadow, along with that of the right putti, which is cast upon the tapestry emphasizes still a third source of light outside the illusionistic tapestry and further stresses Rubens's deliberate contrast between "real" and pictorial space. As in the other cartoons, the figures are dryly painted, the faces are somewhat frozen, and there is little indication of the master's own hand in this final stage, although the figure of St. Clare appears somewhat stronger than the others. Perhaps here, if anywhere, Rubens might have applied a few correcting touches to the Infanta's portrait.

The composition was engraved from the modello by Schelte a Bolswert and Coenrad Lauwers (after Bolswert). On the scroll is inscribed "*Hic est Panis qui de Coelo Descendit*" (John, VI, 50).[22] The inscription recalls the Old Testament prefiguration of the manna: just as the Israelites were nourished by manna sent from God, so are the Church Fathers and Saints nourished by the Eucharist. And as the manna was later stored in the Ark, so is Eucharistic doctrine preserved in their writings. Once again a Counter-Reformational thrust is introduced into what might otherwise appear to be a conventional gathering of familiar saints.

In this final tapestry of the processional series all the personages are united by their common devotion to, and historical defense of, the Eucharist. They are thereby related not only to one another but, as a group of Eucharistic defenders, to the rest of the cycle. Their inclusion in the program, as a complement to the four Evangelists (the heralds of the Eucharist), recalls the comparable role of saints in the traditional Italian *sacra conversazione* and in such early Netherlandish antecedents as the Van Eyck's *Adoration of the Lamb* in the Ghent altarpiece. As part of a conceptual (if not actual) procession, the personages recall their graphic counterparts in Titian's woodcut. But their individual and collective identification with the Eucharist suggests, as a primary source, Raphael's famous Vatican fresco, the *Disputa*, which includes not only a gathering of early Church Fathers but also the monstrance as their central object of adoration and, directly above, the Dove of the Holy Spirit.

We know that Raphael's fresco was closely studied by Rubens while he was in Rome, for upon his return to Antwerp in 1608 he soon executed, as one of his earliest church commissions, a large altarpiece which was clearly based on it. In fact, it is not too much to claim that *The Real Presence in the Holy Sacrament* (ca. 1609), painted for the Chapel of the Holy Sacrament in the Dominican church in Antwerp, represents a conscious translation of Raphael's fresco into a Counter-Reformational idiom as well as Rubens's own Baroque style. In Vlieghe's apt words, "the scene is no doubt to be regarded as depicting the development, in the course of church history, of the recognition by theologians and exegetes of the doctrine of transubstantiation, emphasized as an article of faith by the Council of Trent."[23] Vlieghe goes on to point out that this interpretation "is borne out by the earliest known description of the picture, dating from 24 July 1616, in an inventory of the chapel of the Sodality of the Sweet Name of Jesus in the former Dominican church at Antwerp: *'Een constich stuck schilderije van de Realiteyt van den Heyligen Sacramente geschildert bij mijnheer Peeter Paulo Rubbens* (An artful painting of the Reality of the Holy Sacrament, by Peter Paul Rubens).' "

The message of the painting is spelled out by the four gospels which, opened to appropriate passages, are held above the altar by angels. Just as these texts anticipate the inclusion of their respective authors in the Eucharist cycle, so do we find below the four Latin Doctors of the Church (Sts. Gregory, Augustine, Ambrose, and Jerome) standing in the foreground in front of the altar upon which rests the sacrament in its monstrance. To the left of the altar is seated St. Thomas Aquinas (again, with the sun on his chest) and, next to him, Pope Urban IV, who instituted the feast of Corpus Christi. The altarpiece provides, then, a source for the tapestry of *Eucharistic Saints*, as well as its companion piece, *The Four Evangelists*. We shall soon discover that this important altarpiece anticipates not only such iconographic details but also a more fundamental relationship between the "entourage" panels. Furthermore, it plays an important role in the genesis of the next group of tapestries, *The Adoration of the Sacrament*.

7

The Altar Group

Completing the Eucharist cycle is a separate but related group of five tapestries (Fig. 31) which were hung around the high altar on the two occasions of solemn processions: the feast of Corpus Christi and Good Friday. Together these tapestries form a monumental altarpiece combining an apotheosis with a Eucharistic adoration. In four equal-sized tapestries, celestial beings and, below them, earthly representatives of Church and State are assembled in adoration of the Blessed Sacrament. The fifth and smaller piece is devoted to the sacrament itself, which is exposed in a monstrance held aloft by two small angels. In their correct arrangement, which will be described presently, the panels reveal a composition divided into two tiers or levels. On the bottom kneel the rulers of the Church and State in an open landscape. In each case, a narrow tapestry is framed by two Doric columns, creating the illusion of an open loggia. No longer does Rubens depict the scene on an illusionistic tapestry.

On the left kneel the ecclesiastical rulers (in the oil sketch: on the right). Two angels in the upper right corner direct their attention upwards to the miraculous appearance of the sacrament. The foremost figure, kneeling in profile with arms folded against his chest and wearing a papal *camauro* and *mozzetta*, has been identified by Held as Pope Urban VIII, who was reigning at the time of the commission.[1] Beside him rests his papal tiara on a small cushion. To his left kneels a cardinal who, though possessing distinctive features (he is old, tired, and perhaps even ill), has yet to be identified. Behind the Pope and partially concealed by the column kneels a bishop with his back to the viewer, arrayed in gold robes and holding a crozier. He, too, remains unidentified, as do the four additional clerics. One, standing in the rear, holds the triple-cross staff of the papacy; another who kneels facing the viewer is dressed in Dominican robes.

The accompanying tapestry of temporal rulers presents a similar and complementary configuration. In the foreground, somewhat removed from the rest of the group, kneels the Emperor Philip II, dressed in imperial robes. On a cushion beside him rest his crown and, next to it, the orb and scepter. His right hand rests on the sword hilt—a gesture signifying his role as defender of the Faith and, in this context, the sacrament itself—while his left hand extends in a gesture of adoration. The back of his cape is adorned with the Hapsburg eagle, the symbol of the House of Austria. Behind the Emperor and to his right kneel King Philip IV of Spain in a similar pose and, at his side, Queen Isabella, whose right hand is placed at her breast in a gesture of penitence. In the background kneels the Infanta Isabella, dressed in her habit of the Poor Clares, her hands folded in prayer. Behind the kneeling rulers stand two military figures in armor holding flags. According to Tormo they probably represent Sts. Rudolf and Leopold, patron saints of the House of Austria.[2] Their flags balance the triple-cross in the preceding tapestry. In the upper left corner a small angel points upward, directing our attention to the Eucharistic vision.

Corresponding to the two lower tapestries is a pair of equal size, each framed with Solomonic columns. Through this upper loggia one views a choir of angels, some singing, others playing musical instruments. In the foreground of the left tapestry an angel crowned with a floral wreath plays a lute, accompanied by an angelic trio playing wind instruments. Several other angels are grouped behind them, and these gradually dissolve into the clouds, brightly illuminated by the burning light of the sacrament at the upper right. In front of the columns rests an ornamental pedestal flanked by two small cornucopia.

The right tapestry reveals a similar group, in mirror image, completing the antiphonal choir. In the foreground an angel plays a cello, while behind him another with his back to the viewer is shown playing a lute, and a third plays a violin. In the background small putti sing from a book while above them angels reach upward, soaring toward the source of heavenly light. Again, in front of the columns is a pedestal with two flanking cornucopia.

The fifth tapestry is smaller than the others and represents an arch and parapet through which we see two small angels (putti) holding the elaborate monstrance. The architectural framing includes two small pilasters with composite capitals. The entablature is meant to be continuous with that of the flanking Solomonic pair. Finally, the extremely ornate, lanternlike monstrance resembles those held by Ecclesia and St. Clare in the processional series.

The adoration of the sacrament was an especially popular subject in art during the Counter-Reformation, and it took several forms of representation. Often the Four Fathers of the Church are gathered around the sacrament, as in Rubens's altarpiece of *The Real Presence in the Holy*

Sacrament, described above. Other variations on this theme include the sacrament adored by the seven virtues, the five senses, the four continents, or similar allegorical groupings.

Rubens's deliberate choice of historical and even contemporary figures in place of allegorical personifications reflects the immediate Counter-Reformational, and political, context of this otherwise devotional subject. Their inclusion also underscores the fact that the commission was designed for a *royal* convent, founded by a dynasty (the Hapsburgs) which considered itself the special guardian of the Catholic Faith. The prominence given to the angelic choir in turn reflects the traditionally close association between angels and the sacrament. Rubens's composition may refer specifically to the "Bread of Angels" in Aquinas's hymn "*Lauda Sion*," which was chanted at every celebration of the feast of Corpus Christi: "*Ecce panis angelorum. . . .*"[3] In view of the many references to Aquinas and Corpus Christi throughout the cycle, such an allusion seems wholly appropriate.

In the mystical and devotional literature of the Middle Ages the "bread of angels"—originally a reference to manna—and the Eucharist were considered synonymous, but the iconographic (as opposed to purely decorative) inclusion of angels in Eucharistic subjects in art did not fully develop until the late Renaissance. However, it soon became a standard motif in post-Tridentine art and appears in such works as Tintoretto's late *Last Supper* (San Giorgio Maggiore, Venice, 1593), in which the mystical light emanating from the sacrament miraculously calls forth the ghostly images of angels.[4] In his altar tapestries, then, Rubens sought to combine two hierarchies (natural and supernatural) into a single composition: a heavenly chorus in praise of the sacrament and, below, a gathering of witnesses representing the highest earthly authorities of Church and State.

Exactly how these tapestries were to be arranged has been a subject of disagreement among scholars. Rooses was the first to recognize that they were designed to hang as a single composition. He did so on the basis of a small copy on copper, then in the collection of Abbé Le Monnier in Paris.[5] This panel depicts the same groups of earthly rulers assembled outdoors, looking up to the host of musical angels surrounding the sacrament in the clouds. It combines the compositions of the five altar tapestries minus the architectural setting, and thus for Rooses it offered a key to their proper arrangement.

Tormo, however, interpreted the Le Monnier copy as a record of Rubens's original—but unexecuted—design for a large single hanging (either canvas or tapestry) to cover the altar of the convent chapel throughout Good Friday in keeping with the prevailing custom among Spanish churches. Discovering that a single tapestry would be too heavy,

Tormo reasoned, Rubens apparently decided to divide it into several smaller pieces, each with its own architectural frame, as in the large preceding tapestries.[6] In his reconstruction of the tapestries around the empty tabernacle over the high altar (Fig. 32), Tormo added two additional pieces (*The Allegory of Eternity* and *King David with Musical Angels*) and hypothesized a third "lost" tapestry whose place in the reconstruction he filled by reproducing the *David* in reverse. Adding the latter and its "lost" counterpart to each side of *The Angels with Monstrance*, Tormo visualized the complete set as a three-tiered structure which, he points out, would have corresponded to the altar's actual reredos by Gaspar Becerra.[7] The reredos was destroyed in a fire, but is known from the artist's drawing, which describes a three-storied structure divided into sections by columns of varying orders.[8] But Tormo's reconstruction—admittedly hypothetical—is compositionally unsatisfactory. The King David pair appears out of place and of the wrong dimensions. *The Allegory of Eternity*, placed between the two bottom tapestries, also fails to correspond to the dimensions of the others, and its framing device omits completely the otherwise consistent use of illusionistic architecture. Iconographically it also has no place between the two groups of historical figures.

Fortunately, Held subsequently identified Rubens's original construction of the tapestries *in situ*: his preliminary oil sketch (The Art Institute, Chicago, Fig. 31) for the entire altar group.[9] The sketch is clearly related to the bozzetti for the preceding tapestries: it is exactly twice as high, since it comprises *two* tiers of tapestries. Four equal tapestries are described, two at each side. Between the upper pair is located the smaller *Angels with Monstrance*. At the bottom of the sketch, between the lower pair, Held has identified the *mensa* of an altar covered with a white cloth, above which hangs a sixth small (and apparently either never woven or lost) tapestry: framed with a simple gold border, it depicts a hanging garland and at each side the Eucharistic elements, loaves of bread and chalice of wine.[10] Directly above it, in the center of the bozzetto, is represented a grill with eight horizontal and seven vertical bars (approximately 3 × 3.5 meters).[11] Behind this grill there appears a faint image of a seated or kneeling woman. Only the roughly sketched head is illuminated, and it is difficult to tell whether the figure sits beneath a baldachin or, more likely, between two curtains drawn back at each side. Such grills were common in cloistered convents to separate the nuns *in clausura* from the rest of the congregation, but its appearance behind and above the main altar—where Becerra's reredos was presumably standing—presents a problem. Perhaps at the time of painting the sketch Rubens mistakenly assumed that the actual grill in the chapel (at the west end, overlooking the choir) was located behind the altar. We should not, however, rule out the possibility that like the surrounding portico Rubens's grill represents a fictive architectural element, a temporary or perhaps even a painted grill set in place above the high altar when the tapestries were hung. Whether real or illusionistic, the grill provides both a striking architectural contrast to the surrounding columns and an effective compositional and iconographic contrast to the spacious realm described in the tapestries, its darkness juxtaposed with the incomparable light of the Eucharist.

In all other respects, the Chicago bozzetto is remarkably explicit about the arrangement of the tapestries, and Tormo's hypothetical additions (which will be discussed individually later) may now be ruled out completely. Comparing the panel with the other bozzetti, one notes that while the architectural façade of these tapestries was worked out in full there is nowhere any suggestion of the usual tapestry-device within it. One peculiarity that makes it unique among the series of bozzetti (to which it surely belongs) is that the composition is already shown in the reverse sense. Why Rubens altered his usual procedure in this case may only be surmised. As a symmetrical composition, with none of the directional movement found in the processional series, there was far less need to paint the sketch in its final sense in order to convey to his patron the effect of the tapestries. It is also possible that since this was one of the last bozzetti executed—as the sureness of architectural detail would imply—the Infanta had become accustomed to the process of reversal in the modelli and could imagine the final altar tapestries without requiring Rubens to make the adjustment in his sketch.

The bozzetto's reversal facilitates a comparison between that sketch and its corresponding modelli, of which three out of the total five have been located and identified by Held.[12] The modello for *The Adoration of the Sacrament by the Ecclesiastical Hierarchy* (Speed Museum, Louisville, Fig. 33) reveals a simplification and condensation of the group depicted in the Chicago bozzetto. For example, Rubens abandoned the idea of showing the Pope (originally bareheaded) swinging a censer, and eliminated the acolyte who in the bozzetto stood between him and the cardinal. The three figures—Pope, cardinal, and Dominican monk—have been moved forward, closer to the picture plane, and are thus given more prominence. Many of the additional lightly sketched background figures (and crosiers) have also been eliminated in favor of a more sharply focused composition. The Louisville modello reveals a substitution of the two putti for the one angel (in the bozzetto) who communicates the Eucharistic vision to the Church leaders. No cartoons for any of the altar tapestries appear to have survived,[13] but a comparison between this modello and the final tapestry indicates that little was changed beyond this point except that the columns were described as more clearly free-standing; that is, as part of an open loggia—the figures being visible on both sides of them—and not simply as a framing device. The facial expressions, as in previous tapestries, unfortunately lost much of their expressiveness in the successive translations from modello to cartoon to tapestry.

No modello has so far been discovered for *The Rulers of the House of Austria*, but a comparison between the bozzetto and the final tapestry reveals a similar evolution. The rulers have become more formally grouped than in the Chicago sketch, and the Emperor is given a more prominent position (originally he was shown with his back to the viewer). The bozzetto included only one military saint, and the crowns and imperial attributes were scattered on the ground. A second saint was later introduced, probably in the modello, the objects were more carefully arranged, and the crowd of background figures was completely eliminated.

The modelli for the two tapestries of angelic musicians were first identified by Held in the panel entitled *Musician Angels* in Sanssouci (Grosse Bildergalerie, Fig. 34).[14] As one can see from even a photograph, the two modelli have been joined to form a single composition, and the architectural framework has been painted over. Traces of the two outer columns can still be observed beneath the overpainting, and cleaning would undoubtedly restore the panels to much of their original state. That their alteration dates back to the seventeenth century is proved by an early reproductive etching (by Cornelis Schut?) which was published by Evers and later identified by Held.[15]

Comparing these modelli with the bozzetto, one notes that the right group of instrumentalists (that is, the left tapestry) has been brought together into a tighter configuration closer to the picture plane and that the lute player has been turned to face the viewer. The left panel (for the right tapestry) reflects a similar concentration and increased monumentality, but the basic composition of the bozzetto has been retained. No modello has been located for the central tapestry with the monstrance, but Rubens surely painted one.[16]

In the light of existing pieces (bozzetti and modelli), Held was able to establish that the Le Monnier copy—so central to Rooses's and Tormo's discussion of the altar group—was based on the Chicago sketch, as a comparison of the compositional details reveals. As a free copy (or variant) of the bozzetto, it is remarkably sophisticated. The unknown artist evidently realized that the Chicago sketch was painted in reverse, perhaps noting that the angels all played their instruments with their left hands or, if he was more discerning, that the ecclesiastical and secular authorities were placed on the "wrong" sides of the sacrament.[17] (The ecclesiastical rulers should be given the place of chief prominence: on the right side of the sacrament, the Gospel side of the altar, or the left side of the sketch, as one faces it.) Reversing the bozzetto, the artist set the figures in a spacious landscape, completely ignoring Rubens's architectural elements.

In subject as well as function and compositional structure, this final group of tapestries recalls several of the artist's earlier commissions for major altarpieces. This derivation is logical, for the tapestries were essentially conceived as an altarpiece, one of unprecedented scale and medium. A detailed analysis of its architectural components will be taken up in Part III; for the moment we may simply observe that the use of two architectural orders in this illusionistic loggia reinforces the compositional and iconographic division of the Eucharistic adoration into two levels and realms: heaven and earth. The meeting of the two in one composition— specifically, in an adoration of the Eucharist—derives from the 1609 altarpiece of *The Real Presence in the Holy Sacrament*, which, as we have seen, provided an important source for other tapestries in this cycle as well. There too, the sacrament, exposed in a monstrance, is surrounded and worshipped by both heavenly and earthly congregations. But the thematic similarity underscores an important distinction between the two Eucharistic altarpieces. In the earlier case, the sacrament is found in its natural setting, on the altar. In the tapestry group, it has been raised to a celestial plane and is suspended by angels well above the heads of the human gathering. Rubens has described not only the *adoration* of the Eucharist but also its *apotheosis*, and for a prototype within his own oeuvre we must look to his project to decorate the apse of the Chiesa Nuova in Rome (1606–1608), his most important Italian commission.[18]

Originally Rubens had painted there a single altarpiece representing a famous icon of the Virgin being set into place by putti over a triumphal arch below which stood a group of early Christian saints. The original altarpiece (now in Grenoble) was no sooner installed than Rubens decided to replace it. The second version was expanded into three large panels (of slate) which still remain *in situ*. The saints were moved to the two side panels and the altarpiece proper was devoted entirely to the miraculous icon which now was set into the painting along with its sculptured frame. The subject of this altarpiece had been transformed into an explicit apotheosis of the Virgin, via her icon; and the relatively lower placement of the two side paintings enabled Rubens to describe the saints as looking *up* to this supernatural appearance. Thus the tapestries of *The Adoration of the Sacrament* may be seen as a variation upon the formula established by Rubens in his final version of the Chiesa Nuova cycle. The pictorial celebration of the Virgin's iconic presence was translated into a comparable apotheosis and adoration of the Real Presence of her son.

Finally, the altar tapestries find their closest parallel and ultimate source in Rubens's early altarpiece for his first Italian patron, Duke Vincenzo Gonzaga: *The Adoration of the Trinity by the House of Mantua* (1604–1605), originally painted for the Jesuit church in Mantua (today in the Ducal Palace, *K.d.K* 13). The altarpiece, now fragmented, originally represented Vincenzo Gonzaga and his family kneeling in prayer, looking up to a miraculous apparition of the Trinity surrounded by angels and putti.[19] Like the tapestries, this altarpiece is devoted to the theme of adoration and is divided into two levels. In each case the kneeling figures on either side of the altar represent actual persons (notably, members of a ruling family). The Mantuan altarpiece incorporates a two-storied loggia—or colonnade—as both an internal framing device and a means of suggesting the two-tiered nature of the sacred event, the meeting of heaven and earth. Finally, the miraculous apparition of the Trinity is represented as a tapestry carried by the angels. It is clear that the early Mantuan altarpiece served as an important source not only for the composition of Rubens's grand "altarpiece in tapestries" but also for his use of architecture and even the notion of illusionistic tapestries. The painting contained, as will be shown in Part III, an early and tentative introduction of motifs and devices which would later be fully exploited in the Eucharist tapestries.

8

Additional Tapestries

In addition to the preceding tapestries which make up the Eucharist cycle there are four small pieces whose relationship to the program is far from certain. Nevertheless, inasmuch as they hang in the Descalzas Reales and were designed by Rubens, they too should be considered within the context of the cycle. The first, *King David Playing the Harp, Accompanied by Singing Angels* (Fig. 35), was thought by Tormo to be part of the altar group. Although the Chicago bozzetto refutes Tormo's hypothesis, the piece should not necessarily be denied a place within the cycle. In several respects—both compositional and iconographic—it appears to be related to other tapestries within the series. King David, crowned with laurel, his gold crown at his feet, sits in the clouds playing a golden harp to the accompaniment of angels singing from a long scroll of music. David and two of the three angels behind him gaze upward as they sing. The figures are bathed in bright sunlight from the upper left (this fact alone rules out Tormo's placement of the tapestry to the *left* of the monstrance). The composition is framed by a trapezoidal window flanked by two composite pilasters and adorned with decorative relief work. Its architectural frame is identical to that of the central altar tapestry, *The Angels Carrying the Monstrance*. The two pilasters are to be viewed from the right, as indicated by their foreshortening, and they are illuminated from the left (right, in sketch).

This unusual subject represents a heavenly—and timeless—vision of the Psalmist (with whom King David was traditionally identified) playing and singing amid an angelic host, perhaps as an allusion to Psalm 148: "Praise the Lord from the heavens, praise him in the heights; Praise him all you his angels, praise him all you his hosts. . . ." The image may also recall the popular Baroque subject of David (the then youthful king) playing his harp before the Ark of the Covenant after it had been successfully transported to Jerusalem. This subject, found in II Samuel (VI, 17), is closely related to Rubens's fourth Old Testament prefiguration which illustrates a triumphal and musical procession of Hebrews carrying the

Ark. In that prefiguration, as we have seen, Rubens chose not to depict the familiar image of David dancing before the Ark; King David appears nowhere in that tapestry. All the more significant, then, is the fact that Rubens designed a separate tapestry in which David is raised to a new level and plays not before the Ark of the Old Covenant but before the New Ark: God's sacramental presence in the monstrance, the central panel of the altar group, with which this tapestry seems to be most closely related both architecturally and iconographically.

A similar figure of David appears in an early pen-and-ink drawing by the artist dated about 1611, perhaps a study for an illustration for a psalter or breviary.[1] David is shown kneeling on the ground, surrounded by musical instruments, playing his harp as he looks up to heaven where a chorus of angels playing musical instruments surrounds a bright sun (symbolizing God) inscribed with the phrase *"Soli deo gloria."* The drawing, in turn, recalls a contemporary etching by Peter de Witt, called Candido (ca. 1548–1628), illustrating Psalm 148: *David Playing His Harp Amid a Heavenly Host*, which similarly includes an angelic choir surrounding the sun as a symbol (inscribed with Hebrew letters) for God.[2]

Rubens's drawing, along with the print, is of particular interest not only for its close similarities to the later tapestry of David but also for its inclusion of musical angels, which anticipate the upper tapestries in the altar group. It seems that when designing these tapestries Rubens once again turned to an earlier (and perhaps unused) composition for the basic arrangement of the angelic choir. The drawing's combination of the heavenly chorus with the singing David may even offer an iconographic as well as compositional justification for associating the David tapestry with the rest of the Eucharist cycle—or at least with the altar group. The modello (Barnes Foundation, Merion, Fig. 35) tends to support such a relationship: Rubens himself designed the piece with an architectural framing conceived as an integral part of the composition, as it is in all the preceding tapestries. For the moment, the connection between this tapestry and the Eucharist cycle should remain an open question. Arguing against its having been designed as part of the larger cycle is the fact that it does not resemble (either in size or conception) the processional series and has no apparent place within the altar group. It may therefore represent a later donation by the Infanta to the convent—literally, an "additional" tapestry designed to harmonize with (but not to form part of) the Eucharist cycle. In favor of its inclusion with the rest of the tapestries is the fact that its architectural frame is identical to the centerpiece of the altar group, to which its iconography conforms. The question of its original or subsequent possible location within the cycle will be considered in the next section (Part III).

The second additional tapestry, the so-called *Allegory of Eternity* (Fig. 36)[3] which is also incorrectly included by Tormo among the altar group, is less clearly related to the cycle. An old woman, dressed in a Franciscan habit, sits on a rock in an open landscape. Through her hands she passes a cord on which are strung medallions of Popes as she looks up at an angel, who with one hand grasps the cord and with his other holds a snake biting its tail (the symbol of Eternity). In front of her stand three putti, each holding a section of the cord. A similar personification (of *Successio*) also wearing a veil and shown with a long string of medals, is included in Otto van Veen's *Triumph of the Catholic Church*, where she is shown riding in front of Ecclesia, her cord draped over the outside of the chariot and dragging along the ground as the procession moves onward.[4] Once again it seems that Rubens looked to this important source of triumphal and allegorical imagery. The three putti, in turn, recall Rubens's three Fates who string out the life cord (or Destiny) of Maria de' Medici (*K.d.K.* 243) in the Medici cycle.

The modello for the tapestry (Fine Arts Gallery, San Diego, Fig. 36) reveals that instead of medals Rubens originally painted roses on the cord, and that the snake biting its tail was first conceived as a ring. This sketch was interpreted by Panofsky as representing an elaborate allegory of eternity, based on Cesare Ripa's *Iconologia*: Old Age ("*habito di Matrona*") is shown with a veil covering both her shoulders. Rubens has substituted a thread (of human life) for her traditional attribute, a globe which is a more cosmic symbol for Time. The three putti may be interpreted as Past, Present, and Future. Panofsky notes that Past holds an empty cord, and Present appropriately is shown with fewer roses than Future. The thread "after having passed through these stages of 'temporary' life is then passed on to Eternity and her genius, the putto, symbolizing the future, longingly looking up to the genius of Eternity while the putto of the past 'looks forward' to that of the present, and the putto of the present to that of the future."[5]

While recognizing the symbols of time and eternity, Tormo offered a more specifically Franciscan interpretation in reading the medals (he did not know the modello) as references to Franciscan popes and other leaders from that order. Thus he entitled it *An Allegory of Franciscan Asceticism and its Recompense*.[6] Rooses, who first discussed the composition, assumed that it was an integral part of the Eucharist cycle; he entitled it *The Dogma of the Eucharist Confirmed by the Popes*.[7] His assumption was based on his knowing the tapestry only from a later reweaving in which the composition was set between two Solomonic columns with two garlands of flowers and fruits, in the middle of which was placed an angel's head with wings between two crossed trumpets. Hence its apparent connection with the preceding tapestries. The original, however, includes only a simple gold frame.

Recently Held has suggested that in the light of a similar personification in Rubens's title page for Dionysius Mudzaert's *De kerkelijke Historie . . .* (1622), this tapestry should be interpreted as an allegory of ecclesiastic history.[8] At the right of the title page, for which Rubens's original drawing is preserved in the Teylers Foundation in Haarlem, there stands an elderly veiled woman holding a cord with medallions of popes; and at her feet a child reaches up to grasp the cord with both hands. Held, following Rooses, identifies her as a personification of Ecclesiastic History.[9]

The formal and iconographic similarities between this figure and the chief personification in the subsequent tapestry argue strongly in favor of a similar meaning in each case. (Both allegories also include the emblem of Eternity, a snake biting its tail.) The iconography of the title page reflects, as Held observes, "the strongly polemical character of the book,"[10] and it is within such a Counter-Reformational context that the personification should be interpreted. Her close association with Ecclesia (seated above her), together with her chief attribute, the cord of papal medallions, recalls Otto van Veen's *Triumph of the Catholic Church* in which a similar figure, identified by an inscription as *Successio* (Succession), is accompanied by *Vetustas* (Age) and *Universitas* (Universality).[11] The three personifications, who ride in front of the enthroned Ecclesia, represent three chief claims invoked by the Church during the Counter-Reformation. In his tapestry, as in the title page, it appears that Rubens combined Vetustas and Successio into one personification, an old woman who holds the line of papal succession. The scene may therefore be interpreted as an allegory of Apostolic Succession, the doctrine upon which rests all Catholic claims to supreme authority. The unbroken cord passes from Youth to Age to Eternity; Apostolic Succession is described as a continuous line connecting the past, present, and future of the Church and as our one link to eternity. The natural setting reinforces this doctrinal interpretation of Rubens's allegory, for his ecclesiastic personification is shown seated on a rock, the traditional symbol (introduced by Christ himself) for St. Peter, upon whom the Catholic Church was founded: "*Tu es Petrus et super hanc Petram aedificabo Ecclesiam meam . . .*"

Whether this piece (which will be referred to as hereafter as *The Allegory of Apostolic Succession*) deserves a place within the Eucharist series remains, as Held notes, "a matter of conjecture."[12] The absence of Eucharistic references as well as architectural framing raises considerable doubt. Furthermore, the modello is usually dated, on purely stylistic grounds, between 1630–35; that is, several years later than our cycle. We shall return to this question presently, after considering the following two companion pieces.

Closely related to *The Allegory of Apostolic Succession* are two smaller tapestries similarly depicting female personifications with putti. These, too, are bordered by a simple gold frame. In one, Caritas is shown with her three children seated before a cliff and holding a torch which rests on top of a globe (Fig. 37). Entitling the piece *An Allegory of Charity Illumined by Dogma*, Tormo believed that it was designed not by Rubens but by a pupil.[13] The original modello, however, has recently been identified by Held (Mead Art Building, Amherst College, Amherst, Fig. 37) and firmly establishes the design as Rubens's own.[14] Again the lack of any Eucharistic iconography, together with the fact that Caritas is already given her own tapestry in the Eucharistic procession, raises strong doubts that the tapestry was designed as part of the original cycle.

Its companion piece, *An Allegory of Divine Wisdom*, was also thought by Tormo to be designed by a pupil.[15] A woman is shown seated, legs crossed, and writing in a book as she pauses to receive inspiration from the Dove of the Holy Spirit whispering in her ear. Müller Hofstede has observed that this image derives from Michelangelo's sibyls—in particular, the Erythraean sibyl—of the Sistine ceiling frescoes.[16] On a step beside her stands a small angel holding the writing instruments. Once again, the original modello (Fig. 38), now lost but reproduced in a 1931 sales catalogue and identified by Held,[17] establishes beyond question that this tapestry was the master's own design. A small bozzetto for the piece, also identified by Held (Musée des beaux-arts, Tournai) reveals essentially the same composition as the final tapestry, but reversed.[18]

Although the above three tapestries have no obvious place within the Eucharist cycle and may have been commissioned by the Infanta at a later date as subsequent gifts to her convent, there is some evidence that such additional (more modest and smaller) tapestries were already considered by Rubens at an early point in designing the cycle. In the Chicago bozzetto one such tapestry is depicted over the altar, between the two main panels. Strictly speaking, this piece (which may or may not have been executed) is not designed as an integral part of the altar group inasmuch as it does not share the unified illusion of the surrounding five panels. Rather, it serves a more modest and decorative function as a covering for a relatively small space between the altar and grill. In no way does it incorporate any architectural illusion, but is conceived simply as a picture with an illusionistic gold frame. The fact that the three additional tapestries described above are identically framed suggests that, like the "filler" tapestry in the Chicago sketch they, too, may have been designed for spaces not covered by the larger cycle. Perhaps they were meant to hang above side altars during Corpus Christi and Good Friday as temporary altarpieces, recalling Rubens's two large paintings (*K.d.K* 204, 205) for the Jesuit church in Antwerp which were designed to be installed interchangeably at the high altar depending upon the feast day being celebrated. Even if the tapestries represent later donations by the Infanta, they may be said to be related to the Eucharist cycle insofar as their conception and design derive from the Chicago bozzetto. In either case, we have a fairly certain *terminus ante quem* for their design: 1633, the year of the Infanta's death.[19]

9

A Related Sketch

In general, the iconographic program for the Eucharist cycle was already established at the bozzetto stage. Most of the changes and modifications between the bozzetti and modelli involve details and not a radical recasting of the subjects. There is, however, one exception. One sketch indicates a fundamental change in the program after the bozzetto stage: the small panel entitled *The Triumph of Hope*, which appeared on the art market in 1967 and which was correctly identified as a bozzetto for an unexecuted tapestry within this series.[1] This magnificent sketch (now in a private collection, U.S.A., Fig. 39), like its companion bozzetti, reveals a fictive tapestry draped within an architectural setting—in this case, of Doric columns. Only one (at the left) is shown freestanding; the two at the right have been covered by the tapestry so that only their capitals and bases are still visible, although a pentimento reveals that Rubens originally painted them in full.

On the illusionistic tapestry is depicted a sailing vessel being rowed by four angels and steered by a winged and haloed female figure. One hand rests on the tiller while the other holds a flower, an attribute which identifies her as the personification of Hope (*Spes*). Several putti busily unfurl the two sails, and at the bow of the ship is mounted a lantern, vaguely resembling a monstrance, within which burns a candle. No other details which might provide clues to this scene's iconographic significance are to be found; the four large shields beside the rowing angels are blank. The ship has apparently just set off from port, its pilot looking back over her shoulder as she steers its course.

On Roman coins *Spes* was usually represented as a woman walking rapidly, her drapery flowing behind her; she holds up a flowering stem, her chief attribute.[2] In early Christian iconography she was most commonly associated with an anchor. The ship did not appear as a symbol for Hope until toward the end of the fifteenth century when as Mâle has observed, a new iconography for the virtues was established in France.[3] In manuscript illuminations Hope is sometimes shown wearing a ship on her head as an emblematic hat, as she is depicted in a woodcut (1545) by H. Vogtherr the elder.[4] In Andrea Alciati's *Emblemata* (first edition Augsburg, 1531), *Spes Proxima* was illustrated by a ship in a storm. Rubens's representation of Hope as winged perhaps derives from an engraving by Hans Sebald Beham, in which the winged virtue is shown walking along the deck of a ship. In Joachim Camerarius's emblem book of 1590, her flowering stem was given a religious meaning.[5] Recalling the flowering rod of Aaron, it became an emblem for hope in God, a nuance that was possibly also intended by Rubens.

The identification of this sketch as an allegory of hope suggests its place in Rubens's original program for the tapestry cycle. As a triumph of Hope, it falls between the two triumphs of Faith and Charity. Evidently Rubens originally planned, as a group, the triumphs of the three theological virtues, all similarly framed by Doric columns. Yet this triumph stands apart from its companions, as its heroine rides not in a chariot but on a ship. In fact, it is the only marine composition in the entire cycle.

In placing Hope at the tiller of her ship Rubens was following a tradition established in sixteenth century Flemish tapestries devoted to this subject. One such tapestry (Museum of Fine Arts, Moscow) shows Hope at the helm of a ship caught in a storm. In the foreground are several Old Testament figures who, saved by God from death, illustrate the efficacy of hope. The inscription above spells out the theme of the allegory:

Irruat horribilis quamquam presentia mortis
Tuta tamen spes est in bonitate Dei.

The emphasis of this early tapestry, which was probably once part of a set of the seven virtues, is essentially Protestant: man's salvation lies in the firm hope of God's beneficence.[6]

For Rubens's triumphal and Catholic variation on this subject we must look to a later tapestry, *The Triumph of Spes* in the Viennese set of *The Seven Virtues*, from which *The Triumph of Caritas* may have similarly provided a source for Rubens's treatment of that subject. In this series, as in Rubens's, Faith and Charity ride in triumphal wagons while Hope is shown seated in a ship, the description of which anticipates Rubens's vessel: each appears more ceremonial than seaworthy. The style of the Vienna tapestry (also of Flemish origin) reflects strong Italian influences. Its interpretation of the subject is decidedly Catholic, which reflects its patronage. The series (1572) belonged to Queen Catherine of Poland, the sister of the Holy Roman Emperor, Maximilian II. The inscription, unlike that of the Moscow panels, is in Roman letters (instead of Gothic) and expresses the Catholic belief that grace alone is not sufficient for salvation;

it must be combined with *merit* (good works): "*Spes est certa expectatio futurae beatitudinis ex meritis et gratia proveniens.*"[7]

If the Vienna tapestry—or a replica thereof—provided Rubens with an iconological prototype for his own tapestry design, his composition was equally an adaptation of one of the panels in the recently completed Medici cycle which also represented an allegorical launching: *The Majority of King Louis XIII* (*K.d.K.* 258). Here the young monarch, like Hope, is shown at the tiller of a similar vessel which is rowed by four virtues (each identified by a shield beside her). Most probably Rubens intended the rowers on Hope's ship to be the cardinal virtues, also identifiable by the shields. Thus would all seven virtues be found in his three triumphs.

One perplexing aspect of the Eucharist bozzetto is that, unlike the Medici canvas, it shows the rowers facing the wrong direction: one usually rows facing the stern. Yet recent X-rays of the bozzetto for the Medici canvas reveal that Rubens originally painted two of the virtues similarly rowing in the wrong direction.[8] It is hard to imagine that Rubens would have made the same mistake twice. Perhaps he felt that the virtues ought to be shown facing the lantern (monstrance) even if it resulted in a certain awkwardness in rowing.

In adapting the Medici composition to his allegory of Hope, Rubens may have wanted to convey the notion of "new" Hope at the helm of the *navis ecclesiae* (or the Spanish state, to which the vessel may equally refer, just as its counterpart in the Medici cycle symbolizes France). Indirectly, the boat may also allude to Spain's overseas territories and the Church's far missions, both of which offered primary causes for their hope of future triumph.

In Juan de Boria's *Empresas Morales* (1581) the lantern is explained as a symbol for the light of faith.[9] The lantern which is prominently placed on the bow of Hope's vessel is no doubt also intended to connote a metaphysical illumination. Held has proposed that Rubens's lantern may also be meant to imply a monstrance.[10] Although Müller Hofstede rejected this suggestion on the grounds that it is a typical ship's lantern,[11] the allusion does seem probable, as monstrances were often represented as mystical lanterns radiating heavenly light—as are the three other monstrances in this cycle—thereby equating the two objects iconographically.

We do not know why Rubens ultimately decided to drop this subject from the cycle, thus breaking up the traditional triad of Faith, Hope, and Charity. Perhaps he felt that its imagery was too far removed from the accompanying triumphs: the allegory is the least "triumphal" of the three. But in this case we would expect him to redesign the triumph, not drop it from the cycle altogether. Müller Hofstede is correct in claiming that Rubens must have had very weighty reasons (*"schwerwiegende Gründe"*) for abandoning the subject and leaving the triumphs of the three theological virtues incomplete.[12] It is virtually inconceivable that Rubens would have tolerated such an obvious gap in the iconographic program. Far from abandoning the triumph of Hope, Rubens probably chose to replace it with a new allegory, one that was both more triumphal and more expressive of the Eucharistic theme of the cycle, *The Triumph of the Church*. It should be noted that the bozzetto for this subject appears, as previously observed, to have been painted later than the other bozzetti. More telling is the fact that Rubens here incorporated much of the imagery from the abandoned triumph: the monstrance which functions as a lantern, the virtues leading the four horses, and even the unusual chariot which resembles Hope's ship. That Rubens intended Ecclesia's chariot to suggest a ship is confirmed by his reuse of the triumphal vehicle for the *Car of Calloo* (1638), where it is clearly identified as a ship (with masts and a tiller) although it, too, rides on dry land and is pulled by horses. Finally, in the modello of the new triumph we find, placed prominently in the foreground, the rudder of her ship.

That no modello is known to have been painted for *The Triumph of Hope* is confirmed by the fact that there exist no engravings or copies of the subject. This observation further strengthens the hypothesis that, once it was rejected, Rubens replaced the subject with the late bozzetto for *The Triumph of the Church*. In that substitution Rubens retained enough of the emblematic imagery of the shortlived allegory to preserve the integrity of the original group of three triumphs and, by implication, of the theological virtues. Finally, the decision to substitute *Ecclesia* for *Spes* can be understood as a reaffirmation—indeed a proclamation—of the central theme of the entire cycle. Hope is to be found in the Church; *Ecclesia* fully embodies *Spes*.

As we shall discover in the next section, however, the decision to drop the original plan for *The Triumph of Hope* involved more than simply designing a new triumph. It profoundly altered the outcome of another tapestry as well.

Part III

Sacred Architecture

10

The Reconstruction

Rubens's use of illusionistic architecture has been described repeatedly throughout the survey of individual tapestries in this study. As a recurring device—and the most striking aspect of the tapestry series—the unusual framing invites further analysis. Not only is it unique to this cycle, but it appears to be central to the overall conception and organization of the tapestries. Whereas in his two preceding tapestry cycles, the Decius Mus and Constantine series, Rubens evidently left the matter of designing the borders to the weavers, in the Eucharist cycle he not only chose to design the borders himself, but invented a framing device so original and so carefully integrated with each composition that it far surpasses all conventional tapestry borders. In the first eleven tapestries, each piece represents an illusionistic tapestry hung within such a setting of either Solomonic or Doric columns. In the altar group the same architecture is combined in a two-storied loggia, as the Chicago sketch illustrates.

Rubens's choices for the two alternating architectural orders recall several earlier examples within his oeuvre. The Solomonic column was a favorite motif, dating back to the artist's early years in Italy where it was first introduced in his altarpiece of *St. Helena and the True Cross* (Hospital, Grasse, *K.d.K.* 1). While in Rome, Rubens sketched such a column on the verso of his drawing of a figure from Raphael's Vatican fresco, *The Battle of the Milvan Bridge*.[1] This drawing may represent the artist's first recording of what was to become a common architectural element in later compositions. (Whether Rubens made the drawing from one of the original columns in St. Peter's or from Raphael's Vatican tapestry *The Healing of the Lame Man* is an open question, for both sources were known by him.)

In addition to the frequent appearance of the column in paintings (both religious and secular), several of which will be cited in the discussion of its iconographic meaning, it was also used by Rubens at least twice in designs for actual architecture. This may be seen in his preliminary drawing (Albertina, Vienna) for the high altar of the Jesuit Church in Antwerp and in his oil sketch (Metropolitan Museum, New York) for the altarpiece painted for the Carmelites in Antwerp. The subject of the latter, which is contemporary with the Eucharist cycle, is significantly *The Eucharist Triumphant over Sin and Death*. We shall return to these projects when considering the iconography of Rubens's architecture.

The rusticated and banded Doric (or Tuscan) columns likewise can be found in several of Rubens's paintings—for example in *St. Ambrose and the Emperor Theodosius* (Kunsthistorisches Museum, Vienna, *K.d.K* 191) and in *Henry IV Departs for Germany* (Louvre, Paris, *K.d.K.* 251) from the Medici cycle. Both reflect the portico in the courtyard of the artist's house in Antwerp, in which the banded column is a prominent feature. As an architectural motif, it was especially popular among the Italian mannerists and can be found among the palace façades illustrated in Rubens's book of engravings, *Palazzi di Genova*.[2]

It is clear that Rubens's selection of the two architectural motifs represents nothing unusual. By the time he set his brush to the Eucharist cycle both column types had acquired a respectable pedigree within his oeuvre. Their particular *combination*, however, as illusionistic settings for these tapestries is not so easily explained. It raises several questions, the most important of which concerns the intended location and arrangement of the tapestries themselves. Before we can pursue the meaning of Rubens's architecture we must first answer the basic question: Where and how were the tapestries designed to be hung?

In his monograph on the tapestry cycle, Tormo refered to the first eleven pieces as "processional" tapestries on the assumption that the Infanta had commissioned them to hang on the four walls of the open cloister in the Convent of the Descalzas Reales during the two Eucharistic processions of Good Friday and Corpus Christi.[3] He noted that the convent had traditionally borrowed tapestries from the royal collection for this purpose and that the Infanta's gift was intended to provide the nuns with a permanent set of processional hangings. The altar tapestries, however, although of equal height and sharing the same architectural framings (but not including feigned tapestries), were treated as an independent set that was designed for the high altar inside the church. For Tormo the commission was consequently understood as a double one: two separate series that Rubens partially unified by adopting the same two architectural settings of the processional tapestries for the altar group. In the altar group, Tormo explained, Rubens combined the columns in a rational, tiered structure which is characterized by a unified lighting and perspective and which thus creates the effect of a grand reredos comparable to the existing one by Gaspar Becerra.

In contrast with the altar tapestries, however, Tormo found no rational, unifying principle controlling the alternating columns of the processional series. Instead of following a *"rigio regla"* in dividing these eleven tapestries between the two orders, Rubens presumably followed his *"capricho"* (caprice).[4] It was only later when designing the altar tapestries that the artist seemingly chose to apply a rule to the architectural organization. In attempting to explain why Rubens failed to compose the first eleven with a consistent set of framings Tormo could only suggest that their placement in the narrow halls of the cloister made such an organizing principle unnecessary. The procession would pass from one tapestry to the next in much the same way that a person leafs through a book of engravings of different sizes and decorative frames.[5]

Assuming the cloister setting for the tapestries was therefore essential to Tormo's explanation for what might well appear a serious defect in Rubens's overall conception of the cycle. Having measured the halls of the cloister, he argued that when all the tapestries are hung, only ten meters of wall space (of a total of 87 meters) are left uncovered, thereby allowing for an entrance door, a sacristy door, and a small votive altar. In his calculation, however, Tormo included not only the eleven processional tapestries but also the four major panels of the altar group (the pair of angels and the two hierarchies). He justified this inclusion as being required by the dimensions of the halls: without the additional altar tapestries too much wall space would remain uncovered! Having previously described the last four panels as part of the bi-level altar group, Tormo finally concluded—with no attempt to explain the contradiction—that they, too, must have hung *on one level* as part of the linear procession of hangings.[6]

In his discussion of the eleven processional tapestries Elbern raised the question of the varying architectural orders and, in particular, the relationship between the eleven large tapestries and the altar group. Noting that the three *Triumphs* include two Doric and one Solomonic tapestry, while the *Victories* are each framed with Solomonic columns, he concluded that the processional series did not appear to be designed with the architectural coherence of the altar group. He added, however, that "it seems not impossible to come to some conclusions as to the sequence of the tapestries at their original location by studying the order of the columns."[7] More important, Elbern believed that in view of the iconographic program the eleven tapestries' intended location could not have been the open cloister but must have been the chapel itself. But he pursued the question of location no further, and scholars subsequently accepted the premise that the eleven tapestries form a linear processional arrangement. Such a view was central to Müller-Bochat's hypothesis that Rubens's cycle, as a visual triumphal procession, owed its origins to Lope's *Trium-*

phos Divinos. In short, the question of the tapestries' proper arrangement has consistently been treated as a question of their *order* within what was assumed to be a linear sequence.[8]

Ordinarily such an assumption might appear reasonable. But as regards these tapestries any attempt to establish a linear progression that is visually coherent is frustrated by Rubens's unique framing devices. In a linear sequence we should expect to find a uniform series of columns, entablatures, and bases. It is revealing that in a later reweaving of the tapestries (the eight panels in the Cathedral of Cologne) the weavers chose in several cases to disregard Rubens's architecture so that all the panels are uniformly framed with Solomonic columns. This set *was* meant to hang on one level, as illustrated in a nineteenth century print.[9] However, owing to Rubens's use of two architectural orders, all the proposed linear arrangements have left the impression of an arbitrariness on Rubens's part, the creation of architectural nonsense: an inconsistent colonade of interchanging orders. One can hardly imagine Rubens approving of such a structure. By the time he undertook the Eucharist cycle Rubens not only had published a book on architecture, the *Palazzi di Genova* (1622), but also had practiced architecture himself in designing much of his house (the new studio, portico, and garden pavilion) in Antwerp. He had also designed several architectural (and sculptural) structures, including the high altars of the Jesuit church and the Antwerp cathedral. On such projects he paid as much attention to the marble framing as to his own painting, as he confessed in a letter of 1614 to the Archduke Albert in which he stated that he had put "considerable effort into drawing up the plan for the entire work [the proposed high altar for the Ghent cathedral], as much for the marble ornamentation as for the picture. . . ."[10]

Rubens must have had a good reason for his apparent inconsistency of framings in the eleven large tapestries. To suggest, as Tormo did, that the lack of uniformity can be dismissed as the artist's "capricho" is to ignore the fact that throughout the various preliminary stages of design Rubens was scrupulous in describing these architectural settings. Each was to be seen from a slightly different perspective and, except for *Abraham and Melchizedek*, the architectural order for each tapestry had already been determined at the bozzetto stage. If in a hypothetical reconstruction the tapestries do not appear to fit together in a logical and unified scheme of decoration one may assume that the fault does not lie with Rubens. Another solution must be sought.[11]

If, for the moment, we abandon the notion of a linear progression and view the tapestries not as so many individual wall hangings but as parts of a conceptual whole, certain constants throughout the cycle come into focus. Just as all the tapestries reflect an iconographic unity, so do the eleven processional tapestries incorporate the same architectural elements as the altar group. Not only are they divided between the same architectural orders, but their heights also are identical.[12] These architectural consistencies suggest a key to the cycle's overall plan; and since a specific structure has already been established for the altar group by the Chicago sketch, an obvious hypothesis to test is that the artist intended the same structure, comprising Solomonic over Doric columns, to apply to the larger group as well.

An inspection of these eleven panels confirms this hypothesis. Here, as in the altar group, Rubens employed a consistent principle of alternating perspectives that *require* their being hung on two different levels. Every tapestry framed with Solomonic columns is meant to be seen from below: note that we can see the underside of the coffered ceiling but not the tops of the columns' bases. Every piece framed with Doric columns is composed to be viewed at eye level: now we look down on the bases, and the ceiling is less visible. This principle was applied not only to the illusionistic architecture but also to the compositions within the fictive tapestries. Compare, for instance, the triumphal processions of Ecclesia and of Caritas (Figs. 21, 24). The former we view *di sotto in su*, whereas the latter seems to pass by us at eye-level. This all-governing perspective reinforces the classically correct progression upwards from the simpler to the more elaborate order, from Doric to Composite. The tapestries must be hung accordingly.

A comparison of these same architectural elements reveals not only a vertical shift of viewpoint according to whether the order is Doric or Composite, but also several horizontal angles of view. Just as the perspective of the altar tapestries takes into account their placement to the left or right of the altar (and the viewer) so are the eleven larger tapestries also to be seen from varying degrees to the left and right. Similar distinctions arise, too, in their apparent sources of illumination.[13] Add to these factors the many variations in horizontal dimensions, and the evidence can suggest only that each tapestry was designed for a specific place within the convent chapel which was undoubtedly the intended location for the cycle as a whole. It is the only room in the convent large enough to hold the entire series on two levels, and in view of the iconography—including the depiction of an altar in the Chicago sketch—it is the logical setting for such a sumptuous program of religious decoration.

These factors in each tapestry's design now provide certain criteria—relative dimensions, angle of view, and lighting—for identifying tapestry pairings: that is, pieces that were designed to hang directly above or below another. Again, the result is consistent with the example offered by the Chicago sketch. Thus *The Four Evangelists* takes its place above *The*

Eucharistic Saints (Fig. 40); *The Victory of the Eucharist over Pagan Sacrifices* was to be hung over *The Sacrifice of the Old Covenant* (Fig. 41); and *The Victory of Eucharistic Truth over Heresy* was to be paralleled below by *The Triumph of Faith* (Fig. 42).

Each of the above pairs is unified with respect to lighting, angle of view, and dimensions, but also compositionally and iconographically. If we consider the positioning of *The Four Evangelists* over *The Eucharistic Saints* (Fig. 40), we find that the tapestries conform in their perspective and dimensions and that they share the same angle of view (slightly to the left) and a common source of lighting (from upper left). Compositionally, the two are related in the grouping of the figures and also in the contrapuntal gestures of St. Matthew's angel and, directly below, St. Thomas Aquinas. Iconographically, they create a logical pairing of the heralds and defenders of the Eucharist that has long been recognized by Elbern and others discussing the program of the cycle.[14] But the fact that the Evangelists are placed *over* the Church Fathers and Saints is significant, for it recalls the same hieratic placement in Rubens's altarpiece of *The Real Presence in the Holy Sacrament* which, as previously noted, provided an important source for both tapestries. As the saints stand under the Four Gospels in that early altarpiece so do their counterparts (in all but two cases, the same saints) now stand under the four authors of those texts.

The second verifiable tapestry pair comprises *The Victory of the Eucharist over Paganism* and, directly below it, *The Sacrifice of the Old Covenant* (Fig. 41). Once again, the perspective is consistent—each is to be seen from the left—and the two also share a common source of light (at the upper left). Like the previous pair the two tapestries also reveal several compositional as well as iconographic correspondences. For example, the columns of the two temple porticoes (Roman and Jewish) fall into line,[15] as do the two altars of sacrifice. Outside each structure at the upper left appears the chief embodiment of God's Eucharistic Presence: the sacrament carried by the divine herald and the Ark carried by the Chosen People. These two tapestries of similar dimensions were thus conceived as a pair presenting contrasting views of pre-Christian sacrifices. In one, the sacrifices are overthrown by the Eucharist; in the other, they are to be fulfilled by what they prefigure.

Another pair that also reveals both architectural and compositional parallels comprises *The Victory of Eucharistic Truth over Heresy* placed over *The Triumph of Faith* (Fig. 42). Again one finds a consistent light source (upper right) and perspective (viewed from the right) and similar overall dimensions: the difference of 20 cm. in length is trivial and may be due to stretching. Several compositional parallels include the contrast between the flying monsters of Heresy and the angels carrying instruments of the Passion, the weary figures which enter each tapestry at the left, the billowing drapery of the female personifications, and finally their repeated gestures which recall those of Matthew's angel and Aquinas. As Faith raises her chalice and host, Truth points upward to the flying inscription that applies equally to both allegories: *Hoc est Corpus Meum.* The fact that this pair has the same dimensions as the preceding one and is designed in mirror image with respect to light source and viewpoint suggests that the two were intended to be seen as a double pair (perhaps facing each other across the chapel). Each pair appears to parallel and to complement the other iconographically as well. Just as on the upper level *The Victory of the Eucharist over Paganism* anticipates *The Victory of Eucharistic Truth over Heresy*, so does its counterpart below, *The Sacrifice of the Old Covenant*, anticipate *The Triumph of Faith.* The Ark prefigures the chalice and host held by Faith, and the sacrifices of the former are complemented by the references to Christ's Passion in the latter.

Not all the tapestries, however, lend themselves so conveniently to such pairing. The two smaller Old Testament typologies—*Moses and the Discovery of Manna* and *Elijah and the Angel* (Figs. 6, 10)—appear to form a horizontal pair of upper-level tapestries in view of their relative perspectives and common lighting from right to left, but there are no corresponding tapestries to be placed directly below them. Similarly *The Triumph of the Church*, the largest tapestry and the only one to be viewed straight on (Fig. 24), is also part of the upper level and has no apparent corresponding lower piece. On the other hand, *The Triumph of Divine Love* (Fig. 21) presents a lower-level tapestry for which no obvious upper complement exists unless *David Playing the Harp Amidst Singing Angels* (Fig. 35), which is similar in width and is also to be seen from the far right and lit from the upper left, was intended to be located above it. If so, its unusual size and framing may have been due to some specific architectural feature in the church, as in the altar group where the Chicago sketch indicates that a large central area (represented by the grill) required a fifth, smaller, tapestry to complete the group. Finally, *Abraham and Melchizedek* viewed and lit from the right (Fig. 45), with only one column visible, is to be placed on the ground level but with no identical counterpart above it.

The fact that several of the tapestries were not paired should come as no great surprise when we consider that they were intended to be hung within the chapel. The varying dimensions and groupings depended in large part upon the existing architectural aspects of the room. Doorways had to be taken into account, perhaps side altars were to remain accessible, and, of course, windows had to be left uncovered.[16]

In view of the evident care with which Rubens designed the tapestries to "fit together," it would be gratifying to be able to offer a reconstruction showing exactly where each tapestry was intended to hang. Unfortunately, owing to the chapel's subsequent remodeling and the present limited accessibility of the convent, such a reconstruction has yet to be established.[17] Paradoxically, it seems that the renovation of the chapel eventually resulted in the tapestries' no longer being displayed there but rather in the adjoining cloister. The continuous series of hooks around its four walls indicates that several tapestries were probably hung there, which, in turn, evidently misled Tormo to assume that Rubens's cycle was originally intended for that location.

The visitor to the Descalzas Reales today would have some difficulty imagining Rubens's sumptuous tapestries hanging within the decorative, paneled interior of the convent chapel (Fig. 43). The bare walls of the cloister appear to offer a far more receptive setting for the heavy Baroque columns, elaborate relief work, and gold highlighting of Rubens's illusionistic architecture. However, if one imagines the Rococo paneling stripped away and pictures the stark, probably brick interior of the chapel in Rubens's day—the convent was, after all, built in the time of Philip II[18]—one can appreciate the tapestries in a new light. Not only did Rubens design a series of festive hangings for the austere church interior, but he effectively created an entirely new classical architecture for the room by means of his elaborate framing device of Doric and Solomonic columns. And while the precise location of each tapestry will have to await further study of the building's architectural history, certain principles underlying the program of decoration may be reasonably assumed.

The tapestries were almost certainly designed to cover all the free wall space of the church, transforming it into a unified interior of two continuous bands of columns. The altar group was architecturally, as well as iconographically, an integral part of the larger tapestry group. Furthermore, the tapestries were organized according to a coherent principle of lighting and perspective which accounts for the distinct variations among them. The importance of varying viewpoints (or perspective) has been demonstrated by Held's definitive reconstruction of Rubens's Whitehall ceiling paintings.[19] Raphael's tapestries for the Sistine Chapel likewise reflect a similar attention to relative viewpoint. John White and John Shearman, in attempting to reconstruct these tapestries at their original locations, adopted four main assumptions: 1) that the chronology of the subject matter must remain consistent; 2) that the series is unified with respect to the chapel's lighting; 3) that the existing tapestries represent the entire series; and 4) that each sequence originates at the altar, as in all the other decorative programs in the chapel. On this basis, the authors established a convincing reconstruction.[20] Essential to their efforts was a detailed knowledge of the room's architectural features, and fortunately the Sistine Chapel has remained relatively unaltered to the present day. The chapel of the Descalzas Reales, on the other hand, presents severe problems in this respect. But given sufficient access to its architectural history, there is no doubt that one might eventually determine the original setting for each of the Eucharist tapestries.

A full reconstruction of the Eucharist cycle should be based on a set of assumptions similar to those adopted by White and Shearman: 1) the tapestries' illusionistic architecture was designed to conform to a rational principle of perspective; 2) there is a logical and consistent scheme of lighting for their settings, whether the source is an actual window or the spiritual light from the monstrance in the altar group; 3) the series must maintain an iconographic continuity (as we have seen, for example, in the pairings); and 4) all the main tapestries must be accounted for. The usual arrangement for such cycles of church decoration begins at the altar and continues around the building, ending at the altar. Since Raphael's tapestries were conceived as a double cycle—one half devoted to St. Paul and the other half to St. Peter—they present an exception in that each half began at the altar and proceeded down the nave of the chapel. Nevertheless, the point of origin was the main altar. In determining the placement of Rubens's cycle one should give special attention to this convention of church decoration, especially since the subject—the Eucharist—both originates and is preserved at the altar, where we find its apotheosis and adoration. Presenting both a compositional and thematic variation on traditional representations of the Ascension, the altar group provides the most vivid statement of the doctrine of Transubstantiation—the transformation of natural substances into pure divinity—and thus represents an appropriate focal point for the entire cycle.

The Redesigned Modello

A survey of the preparatory sketches for this cycle indicates that as early as the first stage in design—the series of bozzetti—Rubens took into account each tapestry's intended location within the convent chapel. For example, if we place the bozzetto of *The Victory of Eucharistic Truth over Heresy* above the corresponding sketch for *The Triumph of Faith* (Fig. 44) we find not only that the architectural and visual coherence is comparable to the Chicago bozzetto but also that the viewpoint and lighting (both from the right) as well as the relative dimensions are the same as in the finished tapestries. This observation, together with the architectural structure of the entire cycle, provides an explanation for the one glaring exception to Rubens's normal procedure in designing each tapestry for the cycle: the unique case of *Abraham and Melchizedek*, for which Rubens changed his original conception and ended by painting two finished modelli. As noted earlier, they differ noticeably in their dimensions and architectural orders, as well as in compositional details. Such changes alone, however, would hardly have necessitated an entirely new modello; they could easily have been made at the cartoon stage or through an intermediate drawing (and Rubens was an economical painter). Consequently, Elbern concluded that the Prado version does not represent a preparatory sketch after all but an independent reworking of the subject after the tapestry had been executed.[21]

But the change in columns and dimensions signifies something far more fundamental than a change in details. It indicates an entirely new location for the subject within the cycle (and the convent chapel). This relocation required a complete change in the perspective governing both the architecture and the composition which, in turn, caused Rubens to paint a new modello. The flight of steps offers the most striking evidence of that essential shift in viewpoint. Whereas in the Prado sketch the steps (and figures) are seen from far below (Fig. 3), in the Washington revision they are now viewed at eye-level (Fig. 5).

At some point between these two modelli, then, Rubens decided to move the tapestry to a new location which required a complete reworking of its perspective and architectural design. That decision may be linked directly to the bozzetto for *The Triumph of Hope*, discussed earlier. In all respects save subject matter, this bozzetto (Fig. 39) corresponds more closely to the Washington modello than does the Fitzwilliam bozzetto of *Abraham and Melchizedek*. If we reverse the modello (Fig. 45) so that both sketches may now be compared in the same sense—that of the final tapestry—we discover how precise those correspondences are. The two sketches share not only the same relative dimensions, direction of lighting (from the upper right), and angle of view (from the right, at eye-level), but also the unique architectural feature of only one exposed column (on the left) balanced by a pair (on the right) which is covered by the feigned tapestry. Even the manner of draping that tapestry remains constant.

These unique correspondences between the bozzetto for *The Triumph of Hope* and the final modello for *Abraham and Melchizedek* suggest a simple explanation for the problem of the two modelli: after Rubens decided to drop *The Triumph of Hope* from the cycle, he quite literally dropped *Abraham and Melchizedek* from the upper level to take its place. When we recall that Rubens appears to have replaced *The Triumph of Hope* with *The Triumph of the Church*—an upper-level tapestry—the decision to move *Abraham and Melchizedek* can be related to both *Triumphs*.

That Rubens removed the tapestry of *Abraham and Melchizedek* from the upper level may be interpreted as further confirmation of our hypothesis that he added, at a relatively late stage, *The Triumph of the Church* to that level. The bozzetto for *The Triumph of Hope* was thereby reincorporated in *two* tapestries. While much of its imagery was transferred to the newly conceived *Triumph of the Church*, its physical characteristics were applied to the redesigned *Abraham and Melchizedek*. The fact that in the Washington modello the bozzetto's relative dimensions, architectural features, perspective, and light source were all retained in full indicates how carefully every tapestry was planned to cover a designated space.

This proposed relocation and principle of reconstruction for the Eucharist tapestries not only throw new light on such individual oil sketches but also illuminate the cycle as a whole. Instead of seeing it as a divided commission—an altar group plus a separate processional series—we may now appreciate it fully as a unified, carefully orchestrated program of church decoration in which the allegorical history of the sacrament is both architecturally and conceptually integrated with its final apotheosis over the high altar. The series has truly become a *cycle*.

11

The Concetto

Rubens's novel combination of fictive tapestries and illusionistic architecture was conceived as more than a means of providing sumptuous and festive decoration for the convent chapel during its two annual triumphal processions of the Eucharist. Its purpose was to create within that chapel an entirely new edifice with a specific meaning of its own. Both the fictive tapestries and the architecture were essential to the concetto of the cycle. It was through these two unusual devices that Rubens visually expressed the meaning of the Eucharist tapestries.

The Fictive Tapestries

The notion of fictive (or illusionistic) tapestries became a popular motif in monumental wall painting during the sixteenth century in Italy. Italian mannerist painters, with their love of spatial ambiguities, often applied this device to programs of fresco decoration, both secular and ecclesiastical. As Ursula Reinhardt has shown in her survey of the fictive tapestry in sixteenth century art, the motif can be traced to two important sources, both late works designed by Raphael and executed by his pupils after his death: the frescoes in the Sala di Costantino in the Vatican (1520–24) and the loggia of the Villa Farnesina.[1]

The fresco cycle for the Sala di Costantino illustrates the life of Constantine in a series of four illusionistic tapestries with narrow borders that are shown tightly stretched and nailed to the walls of the room. These frescoes were executed by Raphael's leading pupil, Giulio Romano, who was soon to become instrumental in carrying Roman mannerism north to Mantua after the sack of Rome in 1527. In the mythological cycle of the Farnesina loggia the central fresco, *The Marriage of Amor and Psyche*, also executed by Giulio, was similarly represented as a tapestry, in this case one that is stretched above the room.

Both of these two late commissions of Raphael were well known by Rubens, who, as a young artist in Rome, had ample opportunity to study them. There is evidence that they had a significant influence on several of Rubens's works painted after his return to Antwerp. The Farnesina frescoes have been identifed as sources for some of his large mythological paintings: for example, *Cupid Supplicating Jupiter* (Forbes Collection, New York) which J. R. Martin and Claudia Bruno have shown to derive in part from two of Raphael's frescoes in the Farnesina.[2] The Sala di Costantino, in turn, provided an essential source and possibly even the original idea for the tapestry cycle devoted to the life of Constantine. Indeed Rubens's choice of this subject for an actual tapestry series may have been suggested by the fact that the most famous precedent for a monumental representation of Constantine's life was conceived as an illusionistic tapestry cycle. One concrete—if modest—record of Rubens's interest in the frescoes is his drawing of a figure from *The Battle of the Milvian Bridge*,[3] on the back of which is found a Solomonic column reflecting the second Vatican source for Rubens's Eucharist tapestries, the architectural motif which will be considered presently.

In the light of Rubens's general debt to Raphael's Sistine tapestries as the High Renaissance ancestor of his cycle of religious tapestries, his incorporation of fictive tapestries in the Eucharist cycle assumes a new significance. Both Rubens and Raphael were painters with large studios who took a special interest in tapestry design, and both substantially affected its development by translating their mode of monumental painting into that medium. It has long been recognized that Raphael's Sistine tapestries had a profound influence on the subsequent course of tapestry design in the sixteenth century. His *Apostles* series raised the medium of tapestry to an unprecedented level of appreciation among artists and patrons; and the motif of the illusionistic tapestry, as Reinhardt notes, offers an additional reflection of the high esteem in which tapestries were held.[4] Finally, a direct link between the motif and Raphael's tapestries can be found in Giulio Romano, for prior to painting the illusionistic tapestries in the Sala di Costantino he had assisted Raphael in painting the cartoons for the *Lives of the Apostles* series.

Like Giulio, Rubens bridged the gap between the fiction and the reality by painting both actual and illusionistic tapestries. Yet while following the lead of Raphael and Giulio, Rubens took an unprecedented step: he *combined* fictive with real tapestries. He seized upon a popular device in fresco decoration and returned it to its source, so to speak, by representing feigned tapestries within actual tapestries. In the Eucharist tapestries Rubens fused the two High Renaissance prototypes, the Sistine tapestries and the Constantine frescoes. This fusion of media and spatial illusion is both typical of the High Baroque and characteristic of Rubens. But before attempting to place it in its proper context within the artist's oeuvre, we should consider two additional and more contemporary Italian sources for Rubens's fictive tapestries. Like the Constantine frescoes, both are found in Rome. More important, they represent major programs of church decoration that were undertaken on the eve of Rubens's arrival in that city.

In 1598 Baldassare Croce began to fresco the nave of the newly restored basilica of Santa Susanna in Rome, the new façade of which had been designed by Carlo Maderno. The subject of these frescoes was the story of Susanna and the Elders, and the Old Testament heroine Susanna was here portrayed as an obvious prototype for the early Christian saint and martyr of the same name. The large, colorful frescoes were conceived as tapestries with elaborate wide borders, hanging within illusionistic Solomonic columns which were painted by the quadraturist Matteo Zoccolino.[5] Over the tapestries are draped festive garlands, and in the center of each hangs a cartouche. These close correspondences with Rubens's Eucharist tapestries, their date, their location within an important early Christian basilica, and their function as Old Testament prefigurations all suggest that the frescoes provide a likely prototype for Rubens's fictive tapestries. Most striking is the originality of their conception. While the convention of fictive tapestries still reflects its primary debt to the Sala di Costantino it has been exploited and combined with monumental illusionistic architecture in a truly proto-Baroque manner that evidently left a lasting impression upon the young Flemish painter.

The second and more significant precedent for Rubens's application of the mannerist device is found in the transept of the Lateran, where Pope Clement VIII commissioned Giuseppe Cesari, the Cavaliere d'Arpino, to decorate with huge frescoes the area surrounding his magnificent Sacrament Altar (1600–1601).[6] That altar, as we have seen, offered a venerated, monumental, and thoroughly Counter-Reformational precedent for the iconography of Rubens's Old Testament prefigurations. No less influential were Cesari's accompanying frescoes illustrating the life of Constantine, including the foundation and dedication of the Lateran, the Cathedral of Rome, a donation to the Papacy by the first Christian emperor.

The Lateran frescoes were conceived as illusionistic tapestries. The device was not simply applied as a means of creating a luxurious and festive tapestry cycle in permanent form but, in view of its location and subject matter, was no doubt employed as a deliberate allusion to its counterpart (and origins) in the Sala di Costantino. Pope Clement intended his frescoes to rival as well as to revive Raphael's and Giulio's cycle across the river in the Vatican Palace.

The fictive tapestry survived well into the seventeenth century. Francesco Albani introduced it into his frescoes (1609) for the gallery of Palazzo Giustiniani Odescalchi at Bassano di Sutri. And Domenichino, perhaps following Albani's lead, adopted the device for his frescoes of the life of Apollo, painted in 1615–16 for the Villa Aldobrandini at Frascati (now in the National Gallery in London). Nevertheless, as Reinhardt observes, there is virtually nothing original in either treatment of the mannerist convention. Rather, she considers the Lateran frescoes to be "*le point culminant*" of the fictive tapestry which originates with Raphael.[7] Therefore it seems appropriate that just as Rubens's Eucharist tapestries look back to the frescoes in Santa Susanna in their combination of fictive tapestries and architectural enframements, so do they recall in their association with the Eucharist and a Counter-Reformational program the "permanent" display of tapestries in the Lateran transept. If the latter cycle represents the culmination of a device in fresco decoration, it also represents a crucial point of departure for Rubens's High Baroque transformation of the motif. We shall now consider the nature of that transformation and its special meaning for the iconography of the Eucharist cycle.

Compared with the virtual catalogue of Italian precedents, the fictive tapestries in the Eucharist cycle reflect a striking degree of naturalism which is characteristic both of Rubens and of the Baroque age in general. A mannerist *trompe-l'oeil* device is here exploited with unprecedented persuasiveness; for the first time it becomes a truly convincing illusion.

Previously, the fictive tapestry was identified by a traditional tapestry border and by some indication of its attachment to the frescoed walls. Occasionally, the fact that the scenes were to be understood as hangings was further indicated by showing a corner or side partially curled, as in the Lateran and Santa Susanna frescoes. Of the latter examples it is fair to say that their identification as fictive tapestries depends almost entirely upon such a detail. One might well mistake the Santa Susanna frescoes for wall paintings framed by architecture, were it not for the fact that they are shown partially rolled at the bottom. A more dramatic way of conveying the illusion is found in the Sala di Costantino, where in *The Donation of Constantine* two putti (one at each side) pull back the tapestry and reveal part of the cloth's reverse side. Just as Rubens adopted the combination of tapestry and architecture from the Santa Susanna frescoes, so did he incorporate this device from the Sala di Costantino in several of the Eucharist tapestries. Rubens, however, exploited the device in a far more expressive and convincing way: his putti do not simply fly inwards symmetrically to call attention to the tapestries; they are shown actually hanging them.

If we compare the tapestry of *Abraham and Melchizedek* with both the Constantine frescoes and the scenes in Santa Susanna we recognize not only Rubens's dependence upon each but, more important, we observe that he has combined and exaggerated their illusionistic devices in a typically Baroque manner. The putti are shown busily hanging and draping the tapestry across its architectural setting. The borders are not neatly curled but are turned inside out, crumpled, and casting shadows. Rubens's fictive tapestry looks like a heavy and unwieldy fabric that is draped rather casually over the architecture rather than being neatly framed by it.

Rubens, then, unlike his predecessors, placed special emphasis on the physical properties of his fictive tapestries as large, bulky hangings. Evidently he wished to stress that the eleven large panels represent *actual* tapestries, some even in the process of being arranged by a heavenly crew, and are not simply a conventional device. In this respect they are distinguishable from the altar group, which contains no such tapestries but substitutes natural space and living figures for their woven counterparts. For all the emphasis on the physical characteristics of the fictive tapestries, however, the narrative scenes in no way appear to be limited by the fact that they are ostensibly two-dimensional representations. The figures and settings of the tapestries-within-tapestries appear no less real than the architecture, objects, and putti before them in the viewer's own space.

So convincing is the illusion of space and activity *within* the fictive tapestries that their two-dimensional nature seems to have been suspended. Figures, objects, and settings within the fictive tapestries are no less naturalistic than those in front of the hangings; the space described within those tapestries is a continuation of our own. The sense of continuous space that penetrates the plane of the fictive tapestries is achieved chiefly through the application of a single, unified perspective to each panel. As noted earlier, a single viewpoint governs both the illusionistic architecture and the composition of the fictive tapestry. All the figures depicted on upper-level (fictive) tapestries are seen *di sotto in su* as if they were freestanding figures and not mere representations, while their counterparts below are viewed at eye-level. In each case the compositions conform not to some ideal perspective (as in the traditional *quadro riportato*) but to the same viewpoint as their physical setting. The figures all look as if they could easily pass from the realm of illusion into reality, as if they could step out of their tapestries and stand within the illusionistic architecture, in the viewer's own space. This deliberate continuity of spaces has resulted in at least one significant misinterpretation of the fictive tapestries.

In his survey of *tableaux vivants* throughout the Renaissance—particularly those designed for street shows—George Kernodle has observed that painted cloths and tapestries were frequently used as backgrounds for the boxlike stages. Noting that "Renaissance painters in both Italy and Flanders were very fond of landscapes as backgrounds, putting them behind almost any kind of scene or a single or group portrait," he cites the Eucharist tapestries as a specific example of "how cloths painted as landscapes could be hung back of tableaux vivants set in a shallow stage framed by a proscenium."[8] Rubens's fictive tapestries are interpreted as "a loose cloth spread under and over a cord or part of the proscenium above," and therefore Kernodle "suspect[s] that Rubens was borrowing directly from the street-show that he saw and helped design."

While the Eucharist tapestries may, as we have seen, recall in part such "street-shows" as the *Blijde Intrede* of 1599 and the annual *ommegang* displays, Kernodle's interpretation of the fictive tapestries and their architectural settings as backdrops and stages for live actors in a series of *tableaux vivants* derives from a basic misreading of the visual evidence. As real as they may appear, the figures cannot be understood to stand in front of the fictive tapestries: they are clearly described as part of those tapestries. We have only to cite the *Abraham and Melchizedek* panel, which reveals a putto draping the tapestry around a pair of columns (seen above and below the cloth). Real actors here would have no place to stand; the horse and boy and soldiers move freely in space only because they belong to the space of the fictive tapestry (Fig. 5).

What we confront in these tapestries, therefore, is not the simple and logical illusion of a *tableau vivant*. Rubens was, in fact, to represent the *tableau vivant* in his designs for the *Pompa Introitus Ferdinandi*, where the illusion of actors within the temporary stages intentionally recalled their live predecessors which had been replaced by paintings. In the Eucharist cycle, however, Rubens created a more complex illusion: he suggested two distinct spatial entities defined by two traditionally separate media (tapestry and architecture) and then proceeded to unify the spaces and dissolve the boundaries separating one realm of art from another.

Rubens's fascination with the integration of space and media can be traced back to his early altarpiece of *The Trinity Adored by the House of Mantua* (K.d.K. 13), where the Trinity is represented on a tapestry. Here the tapestry is not attached to an architectural setting but is temporarily suspended between two colonnades by angels, which anticipates the Eucharist tapestries.[9] More important is the fact that although the subject is presented as an image on a tapestry which is clearly defined by a decorative border (as in the Eucharist cycle), the figures appear to inhabit a space continuous with the rest of the altarpiece, as if, miraculously, the tapestry reveals not a two-dimensional image but a view into another realm. Here, too, the effect is achieved by describing the figures from a natural viewpoint, *di sotto in su*, as if they were physically present above the kneeling members of the Gonzaga family.

Rubens's exploitation of this device can be seen as far more than a play of spatial, illusionistic effects. Its purpose was to illustrate the efficacy of religious art in a manner consistent with the prescriptions of the Council of Trent. During its twenty-fifth session on 3 and 4 December 1563, the Council defended "the legitimate use of images," proclaiming that:

> the images of Christ, of the Virgin Mother of God, and of the other saints are to be placed and retained especially in the churches, and that due honor and veneration is to be given them; not, however, that any divinity or virtue is believed to be in them by reason of which they are to be venerated, or that something is to be asked of them, or that trust is to be placed in images, as was done of old by the Gentiles who placed their trust in idols; but because the honor which is shown them is referred to the prototypes which they represent, so that by means of the images which we kiss and before which we uncover the head and prostrate ourselves, we adore Christ and venerate the saints whose likeness they bear. That is what was defined by the decrees of the councils, especially of the Second Council of Nicaea, against the opponents of images.[10]

In the Gonzaga altarpiece, Rubens depicts a sacred image and, through his use of naturalism and perspective, transforms the image into the reality and refers the viewer and worshipper beyond the picture plane to the prototype itself. Rubens was later to exploit the fusion of media for the same purpose in his definitive altarpiece for the Chiesa Nuova. There an actual icon with its own sculptural frame—truly existing in our own space—was inserted into Rubens's painting and was represented as carried by angels so as to exist within the picture's space as well, and thereby provide the link between the two. The saints in the two side pictures look diagonally across the sanctuary toward the altar where they adore the image of the Virgin. Thus the intervening space becomes spiritually charged.

The concept of charged space across which one work of art relates to another was not invented by Rubens. We find a similar device employed in Caravaggio's paintings (1601) for the Cerasi Chapel in Sta. Maria del Popolo, which receive their apparent illumination—across actual space—from a frescoed Dove of the Holy Spirit in the vault.[11] More suggestive of Rubens's program is the contemporary altarpiece by Annibale Carracci (1601–1603) painted for the Salviati Chapel in San Gregorio al Celio. Here the kneeling St. Gregory was similarly shown gazing (praying) across the chapel at an icon of the Virgin located above the altar.[12] In view of the recent date, the saint's identity, the object of veneration, and the relative placement of the large canvas and the icon (at a ninety-degree angle), there can be little doubt that Rubens derived his final solution for the Chiesa Nuova project from Annibale, to whom he looked for inspiration on several other occasions (the Farnese Gallery held a special place of importance for Rubens's later mythologies). But although Rubens cannot be credited with inventing the typically Baroque unification of real and fictive space, he was to develop it well beyond the range of his predecessors and just short of its full exploitation in the works of Gian Lorenzo Bernini. That development may be traced briefly in a series of three major altarpieces designed by Rubens following his return to Antwerp.[13]

In his altarpiece of *The Raising of the Cross* for the Church of St. Walburgis in Antwerp, Rubens included above the main triptych a niche in which was inserted a small painting of God the Father on either side of which stood a cut-out angel. Rooses was evidently the first to observe that the representation of God the Father "filled an effective part in the drama" since He was shown as the object of Christ's upturned gaze.[14] Thus two separate compartments of the altar were psychologically and spiritually (as well as physically) integrated.

Rubens took an important step in the subsequent high altar for the Kapellekerk in Brussels (1616–1617), combining not only two compartments of this more modern (portico) altar, but also two different media. The large painting of *The Assumption of the Virgin* similarly presents its subject looking heavenward to God the Father, who is located directly above (again in a decorative niche). But He no longer belongs to the realm of painting. Instead He protrudes slightly into the viewer's own space as a sculptured relief, probably executed by Hans van Mildert.[15] Likewise the two flanking angels, now reclining on curved pediments, have been translated from painted cut-outs into freestanding sculptures. Consequently the figures behind the picture plane (the Virgin and accompanying angels) are now related to figures who inhabit the actual space of the chapel.

The integration of the two spaces and media was fully realized in the high altar for the Antwerp Cathedral. Its design evolved over several years, and the altar was not completed until 1626—that is, just at the time when Rubens was beginning work on the Eucharist cycle. Unfortunately, while the original painting (again, *The Assumption of the Virgin*) remains *in situ*, the marble altar has not survived to this day: it was dismantled in the early nineteenth century. However, on the basis of an engraving by Lommelin (Fig. 46), it is possible to visualize the effect of the now complete fusion of the painted realm behind the picture plane and the viewer's own space. Katharine Fremantle has given the following, highly evocative description:

> Sculptured angels, resting on a broken pediment above the frame of the picture, leant down with palm branches and with wreaths in their hands, as another angel does within the painting, proffering them to the ascending Virgin depicted below, while Christ was represented in sculpture in a niche in the centre of the pediment, looking down towards her and offering her a crown which, as she ascended, she held steadily in view. The crown was evidently the most firmly established point in the painting's turbulent composition, though it was outside the picture of itself. Above the figure of Christ—which seems to have been slightly larger in scale than the figures in the painting but would have been in keeping with them when seen from below—the Holy Spirit appeared in the form of a dove, and higher still, in the tympanum of the pediment which surmounted the center of the altarpiece, God the Father was represented, holding his hands open and outstretched as though in a gesture of welcome. Here it is clear that architecture and sculpture were used not as frame for a painting but as an integral part of a unified composition; the meaning of the painting was emphasized and completed by the sculpture and by the architectonic arrangement of the altarpiece as a whole, and the assumption of the Virgin was shown not simply as a take-off for heaven (as, looking at the painting only, one might assume) but in its entirety, and as though it were taking place not in fictive space beyond a picture-frame, but in the very presence of the worshippers in the church.[16]

The fact that Christ holds the Virgin's crown toward the viewer implies that her ascent, far from being strictly vertical, is soon to break into the sanctuary, into our own space. In this respect, the altar anticipates by more than thirty years the concetto of Bernini's church in Ariccia, in which *The Assumption of the Virgin*, painted above the high altar, finds its imminent conclusion in the dome of the church itself.[17]

Compared with such an altarpiece, the subsequent Eucharist commission offered Rubens a greater challenge: to achieve a similar psychospatial effect, but now restricted to a single medium. No longer did the artist have the benefit of real sculpture and architecture with which to combine his painting. But through his ingenious use of tapestries within tapestries Rubens once again created images that transcend their natural boundaries. The device served another function as well, for unlike his predecessors Rubens gave it an iconographic meaning, one that expresses the concetto governing the entire cycle. That meaning, in turn, offers an additional explanation for Rubens's unusual emphasis on the motif of the fictive tapestry.

In his discussion of the large processional tapestries Elbern offered the intriguing suggestion that Rubens designed eleven such hangings as a deliberate reference to the eleven "curtains" of the Jewish Tabernacle as prescribed in the Book of Exodus: "Thou shalt make also eleven curtains of goats' hair, to cover the top of the Tabernacle'' (Exodus, XXVI, 7).[18] That is to say, Rubens's tapestries were conceived as a specific allusion to the hangings that surrounded the Jewish Holy of Holies, the sacred dwelling place of God in the Temple. Such a typological concetto is consistent with the cycle's iconographic program. Not only does it extend the concept of Old Testament prefigurations which, as we have seen, are so important to this cycle, but it also throws new light on the unusual and perhaps unprecedented fourth subject of that group: *The Sacrifice of the Old Covenant* (Fig. 13). This tapestry combines several prototypes for the Eucharist, and establishes a specific correlation between the Hebrew Tabernacle and its Christian successor. In the upper left corner, we catch a glimpse of the Tabernacle, the destination toward which the triumphal procession of the Ark proceeds. One of the Tabernacle's curtains is pulled back in a way that parallels the fictive tapestry, the corner of which is drawn up by a putto who is about to attach it to the cornice of Rubens's illusionistic architecture.

Elbern's hypothesis was further developed by Müller Hofstede, who introduced an essential modification. He suggested that the allusion to the Tabernacle curtains was made not by the physical tapestries of the processional series but by Rubens's eleven fictive tapestries therein.[19] Müller Hofstede did not consider the question of where or how the tapestries were to be hung. The fact that all the Eucharist tapestries were intended to hang together in the convent chapel, however, confirms his hypothesis. In this case, there are at least sixteen separate pieces in all, not eleven, and the symbolic importance that Elbern attached to the processional tapestries would appear to be denied by the inclusion of the altar group as part of the same cycle. But if, as Müller Hofstede suggests, we are meant to count only what the artist *describes* as tapestries, we find exactly eleven fictive hangings which can now be understood as signifying more than an illusionistic *tour de force*.

The iconographic meaning of the fictive tapestries explains why Rubens did not extend this device to the altar group. The fact that it appears only eleven times was essential to its iconographic function—and to the concetto of the entire cycle. That the altar group does not include such tapestries underscores their significance. But the allusion to the Tabernacle, the Holy of Holies, was not restricted to the fictive tapestry. So central was it to the meaning of this cycle that it was incorporated into the illusionistic architecture as well. The key to that meaning is provided by the Solomonic columns.

The Solomonic Columns

The twisted Solomonic columns are so called because of their antique prototypes in St. Peter's Basilica in Rome. According to legend, these marble columns—there were originally twelve—were brought from the Temple of Solomon in Jerusalem to Rome by the Emperor Constantine. Their history and incorporation in the presbytery of the Constantinian basilica has been traced by J. B. Ward Perkins.[20] But their strong dual association with the Constantinian high altar and tomb of the First Apostle and with the Temple of Solomon had been firmly established by artistic and literary tradition long before modern archaeological research into their origins.

We may consider two prominent examples with which Rubens surely was familiar. The first is Raphael's Sistine tapestry depicting *The Healing of the Lame Man* from *The Lives of the Apostles* series. The miracle, according to the Book of Acts (III, 1–11), took place within Solomon's Portico outside the Temple of Jerusalem. In Raphael's tapestry the scene is therefore described within a colonnade of Solomonic columns, as a reference to its Biblical setting. In his subsequent (school) fresco depicting *The Donation of Constantine* which we considered earlier apropos of the fictive tapestry, four identical columns are found at the entrance of the Constantinian shrine in Old St. Peter's. The deliberate association of the twisted columns in Old St. Peter's with the Temple of Jerusalem was expressed in Tiberio Alfarano's description of the basilica (*De basilicae vaticanae antiquissima et nova structura*) toward the end of the sixteenth century:

> The emperor Constantine and Pope Sylvester did no differently about the body and altar of the apostle Peter than Moses and Aaron had done about the Ark of the Covenant containing the tablets of the Law and the urn, which at God's command they constructed in the center of the Tabernacle inside the Holy of Holies under the wings of cherubim. And Solomon did the same in the Temple of the Lord.[21]

Among the various arrangements of the columns in depictions of Solomon's Temple there was a tradition that they actually surrounded the Holy of Holies (or Tabernacle), as illustrated in Jean Fouquet's miniature for his *Antiquités judaïques* (Fig. 47).[22] In his study of Bernini's reuse of eight of the original columns on the four piers at the crossing of St. Peter's, Irving Lavin suggests that Bernini intended an allusion to the Holy of Holies.[23] If so, we are faced with two contemporary (although independent) applications of the motif—with the same meaning—by the two giants of Baroque art: Rubens and Bernini. Both artists employed the

Solomonic columns as an allusion to the Temple of Jerusalem, now transformed into its Christian successor. Bernini's concetto for the crossing of St. Peter's involved what Lavin has described as a "topographical transfusion from Jerusalem to Rome."[24] Although it is unlikely that there was any direct connection between Bernini's use of the columns in his program for St. Peter's and Rubens's comparable application of the motif in the Eucharist cycle, they both shared one important precedent: Rubens's first major commission in Rome, his altarpiece of *St. Helen with the True Cross* (*K.d.K.* 1) for the Chapel of St. Helen in the Basilica of Sta. Croce in Gerusalemme (1601). This altarpiece provides a source not only for Bernini's statue of St. Helen for one of the pier niches but also for his use of Solomonic columns in the *baldacchino* over the high altar and tomb of St. Peter, as Lavin has shown.[25] As Rubens's first use of the Solomonic column, which was soon to become an important motif in his vocabulary of images, it also anticipates the concetto of the Eucharist cycle.

St. Helen is shown standing in the foreground with the True Cross. Through an arch behind her are two familiar Solomonic columns "employed in such a way—under the arches of a larger building, with no sign of a superstructure and with a drape hanging from the architrave—that might easily suggest a kind of Tabernacle."[26] Lavin explains their presence in this picture as a reference to a current tradition "according to which it was precisely the Empress Helen who obtained them in Jerusalem," and adds that "Helen is represented as if she were actually in Jerusalem." But the significance of Rubens's columns is not only as a means of locating the scene in Jerusalem (recalling Raphael's use of the columns in his Sistine tapestry) but also as an allusion to the idea of "topographical transfusion," the notion that Jerusalem has been brought to Rome. The architectural allusion within Rubens's altarpiece expresses visually a concetto that had already been spelled out by a lengthy inscription along the passageway to the chapel:

> This holy chapel is called Jerusalem because St. Helen, mother of Constantine the Great, returning from Jerusalem in the year of our Lord 321, having rediscovered the insignia of the Lord's victory, constructed it in her own chamber; and having brought back in her ship holy earth of Mount Calvary upon which the blood of Christ was poured out for the price of human redemption, and by the power of which entrance to the Heavenly Jerusalem was opened to mortals, she filled it to the lowest vault. For this reason the chapel itself and the whole basilica and all Rome deserved to be called the second Jerusalem, where the Lord for the strength of its faith wished to be crucified a second time in Peter, and where it is believed that the veneration of one God and the indeficient faith, by the prayers of the Lord and the favor of Peter, will remain until the last coming of the judging Lord in Rome, the sublime and mighty and therefore the true Jerusalem.[27]

This typological significance of the Solomonic columns for Rubens, first established in the St. Helen altarpiece, was retained (though often with variations) in subsequent works. For example, the colonnade of Solomonic columns in his next major altarpiece, *The Trinity Adored by the House of Mantua* (1603), represents a variation on the same concetto. Vincenzo Gonzaga and his family are to be understood as kneeling in the New Temple, in which they are permitted to behold the image of God (the Trinity). The combination of the columns and the cloth (or tapestry) suspended therein by the angels not only recalls the St. Helen altarpiece but suggests that the architecture here refers to the Tabernacle (the cloth referring to its veil): that is to say, to the new Holy of Holies, wherein God is no longer concealed in the Ark but now reveals himself to Duke Vincenzo's family and to the faithful who approach the altar to adore His sacramental presence.[28]

In his tapestry illustrating *The Baptism of Constantine* (ca. 1621) Rubens replaced the actual (straight) columns within the Lateran Baptistry, built by Constantine, with Solomonic columns. A deliberate inaccuracy, they are introduced as a personal reference to Constantine himself, as a reminder that he was responsible for transferring them from Jerusalem to Rome and for incorporating them in the New Temple, St. Peter's. As a reference to Jerusalem the columns may also allude to the major architectural undertakings by Constantine in the Holy Land, the most famous of which was his Church of the Holy Sepulchre. Finally, they signify the transformation of Rome into the New Jerusalem that was achieved by Constantine. Rubens's scene thus refers to the symbolic "baptism" of Rome and her empire, here represented by the Emperor's own baptism.

As a personal reference to Solomon, the motif appears in such allegorical representations as *The Proclamation of the Regency* (*K.d.K* 253) in the Medici cycle. Here the columns, together with the Solomonic "Throne of Wisdom," identify the Queen as the new Solomon. The columns also appear in *The Peaceful Reign of James I* for the Whitehall ceiling (*K.d.K.* 335) and with an identical meaning: the enthroned King is likewise celebrated as the new Solomon. (In each of the two cases, Rubens's allusion was regrettably far more flattering than accurate.)

The first record of Rubens's intending to use the Solomonic column as part of an actual structure, as Bernini was later to do in St. Peter's, is a preparatory drawing of the architecture and sculpture for the high altar of the Jesuit church in Antwerp (Albertina, Vienna). There the motif was intended to associate the new and lavish church with St. Peter's in Rome and thereby to emphasize the strong ties between the Jesuits and the Papacy. As such, the architecture of the marble altar parallels the architectural background in one of the two altarpieces: *The Miracles of St. Ignatius*, which Rubens describes as an allusion to the interior of St. Peter's.[29] As a reference to the Temple of Jerusalem these framing columns recall the iconographic concetto of the ceiling paintings, the typological pairing of the Old and New Testament subjects. The Jesuit church itself—commonly referred to as the "Marble Temple"—was to be viewed as a typological successor to Solomon's Temple in Jerusalem.

As it turned out, the altar for the Jesuit church did not incorporate these columns.[30] It is interesting that in the only subsequent example of their appearance in an architectural design by Rubens, the oil sketch (Metropolitan Museum, New York) for the high altar of the Carmelite church in Antwerp, he offered his patrons a choice of flanking columns: one Solomonic (on the right) and one Corinthian (on the left). The final altarpiece incorporated the latter and simpler type.[31] Yet this sketch sheds important light on the meaning of the Solomonic column in the Eucharist cycle, not only because of its proximity in date (ca. 1630) but because of its clearly related subject, *The Triumph of the Eucharist over Sin and Death.* Its Eucharistic imagery includes two familiar prefigurations: Melchizedek holding bread and wine and Elijah being handed the sacred elements by an angel. As in the Jesuit altar, the Solomonic column may here also represent an architectural parallel to the Biblical prefigurations.

The inclusion of the column in a work devoted to the Eucharist recalls that the Solomonic column itself includes an age-old symbol of the Eucharist: the putti and vine-scroll relief. That the Solomonic columns were thereby closely associated with the sacrament is indicated by their prominent place (supporting the pediment) in the altar of the Holy Sacrament in Old St. Peter's, which Rubens may well have known through a drawing or description. He surely would have been aware of their similar inclusion in the magnificent altar of the Precious Blood, in Sant'Andrea, Mantua. The chapel contains a relic of Christ's own blood, which the centurion Longinus was said to have collected from the wound he inflicted immediately preceding his conversion (the subject of Rubens's *Coup de Lance* altarpiece of 1620). According to one legend, Longinus was a native of Mantua and returned home with the blood, where he was eventually martyred.[32] The young Flemish artist in the household of the Duke of Mantua could hardly have failed to notice this important chapel.

The sacramental association of the Solomonic columns finds later expression in the illusionistic architecture which frames the cycle of frescoes in the Oratorio del Gonfalone in Rome (Fig. 48). Particularly significant is their presence in the background of Livio Agresti's *Last Supper.*[33] This late mannerist cycle illustrating Christ's Passion was surely known to Rubens, for it is only a short distance from the Chiesa Nuova, where he spent so much time during the second stay in Rome (1606–1608). Furthermore, his own altarpiece of *The Last Supper*, painted in 1632 (Brera, Milan, *K.d.K.* 203) similarly includes Solomonic columns in the background, where they are shown flanking a portal, thus indicating that Rubens was aware of such precedents and their sacramental significance. His particular description of the columns supporting a triangular pediment suggests a possible allusion to the Sacrament Altar in Old St. Peter's. That the painting was commissioned for an important altar of the Holy Sacrament (in the Cathedral of St. Rombaut in Mechlin) makes such an allusion all the more probable and meaningful.[34] Finally, when we recall that during this same decade (1630s) Bernini moved the remaining two Solomonic columns—the so-called sacramental pair—to a side altar within the new Sacrament Chapel in St. Peter's, the circle of associations is closed.[35]

Rubens's selection of the Solomonic columns for the higher level (both physically and hieratically) of his two architectural orders can be seen as a culmination of legend, symbolic associations, and iconographic traditions. Its meaning was topographical, typological, and sacramental. For all three aspects Rubens had several precedents on which to base his architectural concetto. Nevertheless, his adaptation of the sources was unprecedented. Not only was he the first artist to apply the motif to tapestry design, but he was also the first to combine it with fictive tapestries so that each illusionistic component reinforced the meaning of the other. Together they provided an iconographic as well as a formal framework for the cycle as a whole. The Eucharist cycle did more than decorate the convent chapel with a suitable series of Eucharistic subjects; it subordinated its setting to a single concetto. Upon entering the chapel, surrounded by the eleven sumptuous hangings and the Solomonic architecture, one set foot within another realm. By covering the walls of the chapel, Rubens's tapestries conceptually and illusionistically recreated the ancient, long since destroyed Holy of Holies, the Tabernacle of the Most High, now transformed into its Christian successor wherein the Ark is superseded by God's Eucharistic Presence.

Epilogue

Rubens was to employ illusionistic architecture once again as a framing device in his fourth and final tapestry cycle: *The Life of Achilles*. This set of eight episodes, designed in the early 1630s, probably for his father-in-law, the tapestry merchant Daniel Fourment, derives its internal frames directly from the Eucharist tapestries, as Haverkamp Begemann has observed.[1] The scenes are bordered above by a cornice, which is supported at each side by a sculptured term set in front of a plinth (Fig. 49). As in the Eucharist cycle, the cornices are decorated with garlands and cartouches. In several instances, these are shown being set into place by putti. Below, in front of the plinth, are placed emblematic objects, again recalling their prototypes in the Eucharist tapestries. None of the scenes are represented as fictive tapestries nor even, as Haverkamp Begemann has noted, as wall hangings (since the architecture casts no shadows on them).

The terms are described as freestanding, placed in front of "fictitious window frames" so that "the pictorial space and sometimes figures and objects placed in it continue beyond the terms."[2] In this respect the illusion is closest to that of the altar group in the Eucharist cycle. The chief difference between the two is that the columns have been replaced by the sculptured terms, painted white to emphasize their inanimate status. Haverkamp Begemann maintains that this distinction is more than formal:

> The terms are not merely decorative elements of fictitious frames, as the columns were in the Eucharist cycle. They represent deities and allegorical concepts that either emphasize certain aspects of the scenes they border, or stress the impact of the gods on the protagonists of the scenes, or simply clarify the subject. They vary from episode to episode, but in each case they are an integral part of the scene.[3]

Their iconographic significance is understood to derive from Rubens's early title page for François Aguilon's *Opticorum libri sex* (1613). In each case the terms "refer allegorically to and illuminate the central motif, which in the print is the title and by implication the subject of the publication, in the Achilles series an episode of the hero's life."[4]

Because Haverkamp Begemann considered the architecture of the Eucharist cycle "merely decorative," he saw the Achilles cycle as a major transformation of the tapestry border in which Rubens "went much further" and "intensified the relationship between scene and frame by introducing a mutual dependence between them in subject matter and 'message.'"[5] However, as we have seen, both the fictive tapestries and the illusionistic architecture represent far more than "merely decorative elements." Their iconological relationship to the subjects of that cycle was just as profound as that of their sculptural (and anecdotal) counterparts in the Achilles cycle. In this respect the Achilles series represents a translation more than a transformation of the Eucharist cycle: from architectural into sculptural iconography.

The framing terms are admittedly richer in allegorical detail than the columns and fictive tapestries of the preceding cycle. To this extent, one may speak of a further development of the framing device after the Eucharist tapestries. Nevertheless, their function is actually less ambitious: the terms provide individual allegorical commentaries on the scenes they frame but (unlike the Eucharist architecture) without any apparent suggestion of a larger, conceptual framework which both reinforces the significance of each scene and expresses the concetto of the overall cycle. If the frames of the Achilles tapestries look back to an early title page, the architectural concetto of the Eucharist cycle looks forward to Rubens's largest program of monumental and allegorical decoration: the stages and arches designed for the *Pompa Introitus Ferdinandi*, a secular counterpart to the sacred triumphal procession.

Just as Rubens recreated the triumph *all' antica* for his subsequent Henry IV cycle and the allegorical apotheosis for the Whitehall ceiling, in the *Pompa Introitus* he revived the two major components of an architectural concetto first expressed in the Eucharist style almost a decade earlier. A fictive tapestry was applied to the first stage of the long procession through the streets of Antwerp: *The Stage of Welcome*. The illusionistic tapestry, representing *The Advent of the Prince*, is shown in the process of being hung in place by three putti, who, as Martin has observed, derive from Rubens's modello for *The Victory of the Sacrament over Pagan Sacrifices*.[6] There are, of course, differences. The fictive tapestry is here depicted on canvas, not on an actual tapestry; and the framing architecture is no longer illusionistic, but real (if equally temporary).

The very nature of this late commission—combining painting, sculpture, and architecture—allowed Rubens to translate his earlier pictorial inventions into a characteristically 'Baroque *Gesamtkunstwerk*. It also offered him an appropriate occasion for recreating his architectural concetto of a two-storied structure alluding to the Temple of Jerusalem. This unique revival of that construction is found in *The Stage of the Infanta*, a funereal monument devoted to Isabella, who had died in 1633 (Fig. 50). Here Rubens painted the apotheosis of his recently deceased patron and framed it with the familiar Solomonic columns, which in turn were supported by banded Tuscan columns below. The stage resembles an exotic temple façade. In this instance, the meaning of the architectural invention is signified not by illusionistic hangings referring to curtains of the Holy of Holies (there would hardly have been room for the necessary eleven on such a stage). Instead, Rubens introduced another and more familiar reference to the Temple: the huge seven-branched candelabrum which crowns the top of the pediment. This element, as Gevartius explains in his text, refers to the candelabrum that was taken from the Temple of Jerusalem when it was sacked by the Emperor Titus in 70 A.D.[7]—a scene depicted in one of the reliefs on the Arch of Titus in Rome.

As a memorial to Isabella and as part of a monumental program designed for a triumphal procession, *The Stage of the Infanta* no doubt suggested to Rubens obvious parallels to the great cycle of tapestries she had commissioned him to design. Just as the two commissions reflected triumphant responses to recent military victories—Breda and Nördlingen, respectively—and renewed hope for peace, so did the Infanta's memorial deliberately share with the Eucharist cycle both its architectural allusion to the Temple and its central subject: an apotheosis. It appropriately recalled Isabella's grandest commission to Rubens and, in turn, his own most comprehensive, triumphal, and Baroque expression of the Catholic Faith.

Fig. 1.   Rubens, *The Infanta Isabella Clara Eugenia*.
The Norton Simon Museum of Art, Pasadena.

Fig. 2. Rubens, *Abraham and Melchizedek*, bozzetto.
Fitzwilliam Museum, Cambridge.

Fig. 3. Rubens, *Abraham and Melchizedek*, first modello.
Prado, Madrid.

Fig. 4. Rubens and assistants, *Abraham and Melchizedek*, cartoon. Ringling Museum, Sarasota.

Fig. 5.   Rubens, *Abraham and Melchizedek*, final modello. National Gallery, Washington.

Fig. 6. After Rubens, *Moses and the Discovery of Manna*, tapestry.
Descalzas Reales, Madrid.

Fig. 7. Rubens, *Moses and the Discovery of Manna*, bozzetto.
Musée Bonnat, Bayonne.

Fig. 8. Rubens, *Moses and the Discovery of Manna*, modello.
Los Angeles County Museum, Los Angeles.

Fig. 9. Rubens and assistants, *Moses and the Discovery of Manna*, cartoon.
Ringling Museum, Sarasota.

Fig. 10. After Rubens, *Elijah and the Angel*, tapestry.
Descalzas Reales, Madrid.

Fig. 11.   Rubens, *Elijah and the Angel*, bozzetto.
Musée Bonnat, Bayonne.

Fig. 12. Rubens, *Elijah and the Angel*, modello.
Musée Bonnat, Bayonne.

Fig. 13. Rubens, *The Sacrifice of the Old Covenant*, modello.
Coll. William A. Coolidge, Topsfield, Mass.

Fig. 14. After Rubens, *The Victory of the Sacrament over Pagan Sacrifices*, tapestry. Descalzas Reales, Madrid.

Sacrifices, modello.
Prado, Madrid.

Fig. 16.   Rubens, *The Victory of Eucharistic Truth over Heresy*,
bozzetto.
Fitzwilliam Museum, Cambridge.

Fig. 17. Rubens, *The Victory of Eucharistic Truth over Heresy*, modello. Prado, Madrid.

Fig. 18. Rubens, *The Triumph of Faith*, bozzetto.
Fitzwilliam Museum, Cambridge.

Fig. 19. Rubens, *The Triumph of Faith*, modello.
Musées royaux des beaux-arts, Brussels.

Fig. 20. Rubens, *The Triumph of Divine Love*, bozzetto.
Fitzwilliam Museum, Cambridge.

Fig. 21. Rubens, *The Triumph of Divine Love*, modello.
Prado, Madrid.

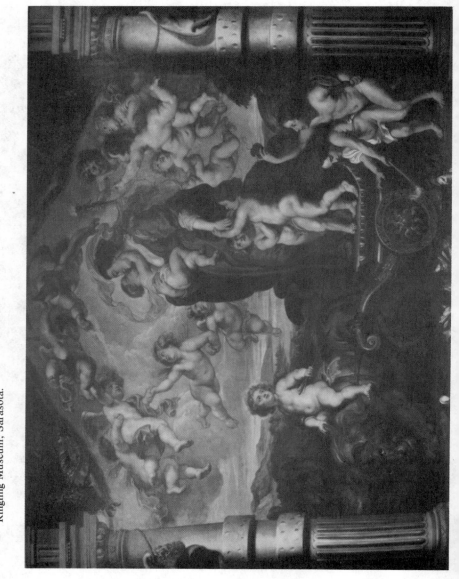

Fig. 22. Rubens and assistants, *The Triumph of Divine Love*, cartoon. Ringling Museum, Sarasota.

Fig. 23. Rubens, *The Triumph of the Church*, bozzetto. Fitzwilliam Museum, Cambridge.

Fig. 24.   Rubens, *The Triumph of the Church*, modello. Prado, Madrid.

Fig. 25. Rubens, *The Four Evangelists*, bozzetto. Fitzwilliam Museum, Cambridge.

Fig. 26.   Rubens, *The Four Evangelists*, modello.
Coll. Mrs. Dent-Brocklehurst, Sudeley Castle, Glos.

Fig. 27. Rubens and assistants, *The Four Evangelists*, cartoon.
Ringling Museum, Sarasota.

Fig. 28. Rubens, *Eucharistic Saints*, bozzetto.
Fitzwilliam Museum, Cambridge.

Fig. 29. Rubens, *Eucharistic Saints*, modello. Prado, Madrid.

Fig. 30.   Rubens and assistants, *Eucharistic Saints*, cartoon.
Ringling Museum, Sarasota.

Fig. 31. Rubens, *The Adoration of the Blessed Sacrament* (altar group), bozzetto.
The Art Institute, Chicago.

Fig. 32. Reconstruction of altar tapestries by Elias Tormo.

Fig. 33. Rubens, *The Adoration of the Sacrament by the Ecclesiastical Hierarchy*, modello. Speed Museum, Louisville.

Fig. 34. Rubens, *Musician Angels*, two modelli (joined as single painting).
Grosse Bildergalerie, Potsdam-Sanssouci.

Fig. 35.   Rubens, *King David Playing the Harp, Accompanied by Singing Angels*, modello.
Barnes Foundation, Merion, Pa.

Fig. 36. Rubens, *The Allegory of Apostolic Succession*, modello.
Fine Arts Gallery, San Diego.

Fig. 37. Rubens, *An Allegory of Charity*, modello.
Mead Art Building, Amherst College, Amherst.

Fig. 38. Rubens, *An Allegory of Divine Wisdom*, modello.
Formerly art market, Berlin (now lost).

Fig. 39.   Rubens, *The Triumph of Hope*, bozzetto.
Richard L. Feigen, Inc., New York.

Fig. 40.   Author's reconstruction.
Above: Rubens, *The Four Evangelists*, cartoon;
Below: Rubens, *Eucharistic Saints*, cartoon.

Fig. 41. Author's reconstruction.
Above: Rubens, *The Victory of the Sacrament over
Pagan Sacrifices*, modello;
Below: Rubens, *The Sacrifice of the Old Covenant*,
modello.

Fig. 42. Author's reconstruction.
Above: Rubens, *The Victory of Eucharistic Truth over Heresy*, modello;
Below: Rubens, *The Triumph of Faith*, modello.

Fig. 43. Descalzas Reales: interior of convent chapel, facing the high altar.

Fig. 44.   Author's reconstruction.
Above: Rubens, *The Victory of Eucharistic Truth over Heresy*, bozzetto;
Below: Rubens, *The Triumph of Faith*, bozzetto.

Fig. 45.   Rubens, *Abraham and Melchizedek*, final modello, *reversed*.

Fig. 46.   A. Lommelin, *High Altar of Antwerp Cathedral*,
          engraving.
          Printroom of the Royal Library Albert I, Brussels.

Fig. 47.   Jean Fouquet, *Pompey in the Temple of Jerusalem*, from
Les antiquités judaïques.
Bibliothèque Nationale, Paris.

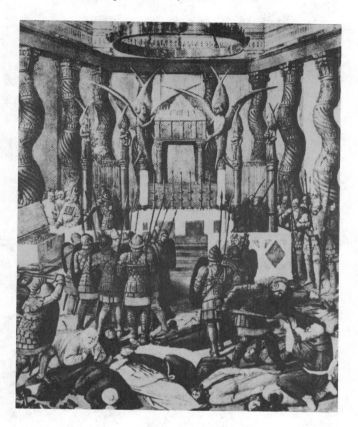

Fig. 48. Oratorio del Gonfalone, Rome: view of interior frescoes.

Fig. 49. Rubens, *Briseis Returned to Achilles*, oil sketch, Detroit Institute of Arts.

Fig. 50.   Theodor van Thulden, *The Stage of the Infanta*,
          etching after Rubens.

Notes

Chapter 1

1. This cycle was the subject of a doctoral dissertation by Micheline Moisan, entitled *"The History of Decius Mus by Peter Paul Rubens"* (Princeton University, 1975).

2. See J. S. Held, *The Oil Sketches of P. P. Rubens*, Princeton, 1980, 21f.

3. M. Rooses and C. Ruelens, *Correspondance de Rubens et documents epistolaires concernant sa vie et ses oeuvres*, II, Antwerp, 1898, 150. For an English translation, see R. S. Magurn, *The Letters of Peter Paul Rubens*, Cambridge, 1955, 63.

4. M. Rooses, *Rubens*, I, Philadelphia, 1904, 206.

5. See J. R. Martin, *Rubens: The Antwerp Altarpieces*, New York, 1969.

6. For further discussion of the contract and Rubens's relationship with tapestry weavers see J. S. Held, *Sketches*, 21f.

7. For Rubens's study of antiquity, see W. Stechow, *Rubens and the Classical Tradition*, Cambridge, 1968, 1-20.

8. See J. S. Held, *Rubens Selected Drawings*, 2 vols., London, 1959, pl. 94 (cat. no. 89).

9. The four modelli include *The Adlocution* (National Gallery, Washington, D.C.), *The Interpretation of the Victim* (Coll. O. Reinhart, Winterthur), *The Death of Decius* (Prado, Madrid), and *The Funeral* (Bayerische Staatsgemäldesammlungen, Aschaffenburg). See J. S. Held, *Sketches*, 25–30.

10. For Raphael's Sistine tapestries, see J. Shearman, *Raphael's Cartoons in the Collection of Her Majesty the Queen and the Tapestries for the Sistine Chapel*, London, 1972.

11. M. Rooses, *Rubens*, I, 270–71.

12. Translated by R. S. Magurn, *Letters*, 66.

13. For a study of this cycle, see D. Dubon, *The History of Constantine the Great, Designed by Peter Paul Rubens and Pietro da Cortona*, London, 1963.

14. See J. S. Held, *Sketches*, 65–70.

15. J. Coolidge, "Louis XIII and Rubens: the Story of the Constantine Tapestries," *Gazette des beaux-arts*, LXVII, 1966, 282–85.

16. Ibid., 283–84.

17. J. S. Held, "On the Date and Function of Some Allegorical Sketches by Rubens," *Journal of the Warburg and Courtauld Institutes*, XXXVIII, 1975, 225–27.

18. See J. S. Held, *Sketches*, 67.

19. J. R. Martin, *The Ceiling Paintings for the Jesuit Church in Antwerp, Corpus Rubenianum Ludwig Burchard*, I, London–New York, 1968.

20. Ibid., 38.

21. For a thorough study of the commission, see J. Müller Hofstede, "Zu Rubens' zweitem Altarwerk für Sta. Maria in Vallicella," *Nederlands Kunsthistorisch Jaarboek*, XVII, 1966, 1–78.

22. See J. Thuillier and J. Foucart, *Rubens' Life of Marie de' Medici*, New York, 1967.

23. J. S. Held, "Rubens' Designs for Sepulchral Monuments," *The Art Quarterly*, XXIII, 1960, 262.

24. J. R. Martin, *The Decorations for the Pompa Introitus Ferdinandi, Corpus Rubenianum Ludwig Burchard*, XVI, London–New York, 1972.

Chapter 2

1. M. Rooses, *L'oeuvre de P. P. Rubens*, I, Antwerp, 1886, 53f. For a compendium of all known documents concerning the tapestries, see N. de Poorter, *Eucharist*, 409f.

2. For a discussion of Rubens's diplomatic career, see F. Baudouin, *Rubens et son siècle*, Antwerp, 1972, 139–63.

3. For a summary of the convent's religious background, see E. Tormo, *En las Descalzas Reales de Madrid*, III, *Los tapices: La apoteosis eucaristica de Rubens*, Madrid, 1945, 9–10. See also N. de Poorter, *Eucharist*, 47f.

4. Although *discalced* ("shoeless"), the nuns are not Carmelites, as several writers have assumed, but Franciscans (Poor Clares). The order of Discalced Franciscans dates back to 1556 and was established by the Spanish mystic, St. Peter of Alcantara, who was a spiritual counselor of St. Theresa d'Avila. See A. G. Dickens, *The Counter Reformation*, New York, 1969, 72.

5. See D. Steadman, ed., *Selections from the Norton Simon, Inc., Museum of Art*, Princeton, 1972, 35–39.

6. E. Tormo, *Apoteosis*, 9–10.

7. E. Tormo, *En las Descalzas Reales*, I-IV, Madrid, 1944–1947. For further background on the convent, see N. de Poorter, *Eucharist*, 47f.

8. M. Rooses, *L'oeuvre*, I, 71f.

9. M. de Maeyer, *Albrecht en Isabella en de Schilderkunst*, Brussels, 1955, 383 (doc. 214).

10. J. S. Held, "Rubens' Triumph of the Eucharist and the *Modello* in Louisville," *J. B. Speed Art Museum Bulletin*, XXVI, 1968, 4. See also, Held, *The Oil Sketches of Peter Paul Rubens*, 2 vols., Princeton, 1980, 139f.

11. M. de Maeyer, *Albrecht*, 385 (doc. 219).

12. M. Rooses, *L'oeuvre*, I, 72.

13. M. de Maeyer, *Albrecht*, 387 (doc. 222).

14. J. S. Held, "Louisville," 6.

15. M. Rooses, *Rubens*, II, 427.

16. V. H. Elbern, "Die Rubensteppiche des Kölner Domes, ihre Geschichte und ihre Stellung im Zyklus 'Triumph der Eucharistie,' " *Kölner Domblatt*, X, 1955, 51. This article is an expansion of Dr. Elbern's catalogue for the exhibition of the Cologne tapestries at the Villa Hügel in Essen in the winter of 1954–1955.

17. R. S. Magurn, *The Letters of Peter Paul Rubens*, Cambridge, 1955, 110–12.

18. M. de Maeyer, *Albrecht*, 375 (doc. 199).

19. Rooses entitled the cycle *Le Triomphe et les Figures de l'Eucharistie* (*L'oeuvre*, I, 53) and thereafter it has usually been known as *The Triumph of the Eucharist*. Tormo, however, preferred the term *apotheosis* to triumph and consequently retitled the tapestries *La Apoteosis Eucaristica*, noting that the doctrine of transubstantiation, the theme of the cycle, is an apotheosis *par excellence*, the deification of bread and wine (*Apoteosis*, 8). Although Tormo's point is valid, the present writer prefers the more common title, for the word *triumph* best conveys the Counter-Reformational theme of Rubens's cycle.

20. E. Müller-Bochat, "Der allegorische Triumphzug, ein Motiv Petrarcas bei Lope de Vega and Rubens," *Schriften und Vorträge des Petrarca-Instituts Köln*, XI, Krefeld, 1957.

21. See J. S. Held, "Louisville," 6.

22. M. Rooses, *L'oeuvre*, I, 73. The Spanish text is quoted at the bottom of the page.

23. J. S. Held, "Louisville," 6.

24. E. Müller Hofstede, "Neue Ölskizzen von Rubens," *Städel-Jahrbuch*, II, 1969, 235, n. 61.

25. E. Tormo, *Apoteosis*, 21.

26. V. H. Elbern, "Rubensteppiche," 55.

27. E. Müller-Bochat, "Triumphzug," 15.

28. J. S. Held, "Louisville," 6.

29. J. Müller Hofstede, "Ölskizzen," 235, n. 61.

30. E. Tormo, *Apoteosis*, 20–23 and 52–54. N. de Poorter believes the tapestries were used *only* on Corpus Christi. See *Eucharist*, 53.

31. M. Rooses, *Rubens*, II, 432–33.

32. Ibid., 432–33.

33. E. Tormo, *Apoteosis*, 52–54.

34. J. S. Held, "Louisville," 8.

35. See J. S. Held, *Rubens Selected Drawings* 2 vols., London, 1959, I, 136, no. 102 (pl. 112).

36. H. Gerson and J. W. Goodison, *Fitzwilliam Museum Catalogue of Paintings*, I, Cambridge, 1960, 241–43, nos. 228–31.

37. Musée Bonnat, *Exposition d'oeuvres de Pierre Paul Rubens*, Bayonne, 1965, 9–10, cat. nos. 20–21.

38. J. Müller Hofstede, "Ölskizzen," 204. N. de Poorter, *Eucharist*, 84f., believes that the bozzetti were originally painted together on large panels and later cut up, but there is no evidence in support of this theory.

39. J.-A. Goris and J. S. Held, *Rubens in America*, New York, 1947, 34–35, no. 57.

40. [E. Haverkamp Begemann], *Olieverfschetsen van Rubens* (exhibition catalogue), Museum Boymans, Rotterdam, 1953, 84.

41. E. Tormo, *Apoteosis*, 27. N. de Poorter, *Eucharist*, 87, rejects the hypothesis that the bozzetti were intended to be shown to Rubens's patron, but the degree of detail, relative to other bozzetti by Rubens, remains a strong argument in favor of the hypothesis.

42. M. Rooses, *L'oeuvre*, I, 73–74.

43. V. H. Elbern, "Rubensteppiche," 53.

44. M. Rooses, *L'oeuvre*, I, 73.

45. Ibid., 74.

46. For a thorough history of the cartoons, see N. de Poorter, *Eucharist*, 149–60. This author is grateful to Pierre Rosenberg of the Louvre for permitting access to its files, which contain much useful information about the history of the cartoons.

47. E. Tormo, *Apoteosis*, 13–15. For more information on the tapestries themselves, and the workshops, see N. de Poorter, *Eucharist*, 161f.

48. V. H. Elbern, "Rubensteppiche," 64–69.

49. E. Tormo, *Apoteosis*, 6. A listing of prints and copies is included in N. de Poorter's *catalogue raisonné* (*Eucharist*, 257f).

50. W. Stechow, *Rubens*, 94. For a *catalogue raisonné* of the Eucharist cycle, see N. de Poorter, *Eucharist*, 257f. The best *catalogue raisonné* of the oil sketches is found in J. S. Held, *Sketches*, 143–66.

Chapter 3

1. E. Mâle, *L'art religieux après le Concile de Trente*, Paris, 1932, 337.

2. Ibid., 336–37.

3. J. R. Martin, *The Ceiling Paintings for the Jesuit Church in Antwerp, Corpus Rubenianum Ludwig Burchard*, I, London–New York, 1968, 195.

4. Ibid., 196.

5. E. Mâle, *Trente*, 339.

6. J. R. Martin, *Ceiling*, 196f.

7. See V. H. Elbern, "Addenda zum Zyklus 'Triumph der Eucharistie' von P. P. Rubens," *Kölner Domblatt*, XXI/XXII, 1963, 77f.

8. See E. Panofsky, *Early Netherlandish Painting*, Cambridge, 1953, *passim*.

9. See T. L. Glen, "*Rubens and the Counter-Reformation*" (Ph.D. dissertation, Princeton University, 1975).

10. I. Lavin, *Bernini and the Crossing of St. Peter's*, New York, 1968, 16–17. See also M. L. Chappell and C. W. Kirwin, "A Petrine Triumph: The Decoration of the Navi Piccole in San Pietro under Clement VIII," *Storia dell'arte*, XXI, 1974, 119–25.

11. E. Mâle, *Trente*, 340–41.

12. L. Réau, *Iconographie de l'art Chrétien*, II.1, Paris, 1956, 128.

13. J. R. Martin, *Ceiling*, 76f., cat. no. 7.

14. J. S. Held, "Rubens' Triumph of the Eucharist and the *Modello* in Louisville," *J. B. Speed Art Museum Bulletin*, XXVI, 1968, 15.

15. L. van Puyvelde, *Les esquisses de Rubens*, Bâle, 1940, 33.

16. J. R. Martin, *Ceiling*, 64.

17. See J. S. Held, "Le Roi à la Ciasse," *Art Bulletin*, XL, 1958, 146–47.

18. According to a letter (Louvre files) dated 12 January 1956 from Kenneth Donahue, curator of the Ringling Museum, to the curator of the Louvre. The alterations had been revealed by a recent cleaning.

19. L. van Puyvelde, "Projects de Rubens et de Van Dyck pour les tapissiers," *Gazette des beaux-arts*, LVII, 1961, 147–48.

20. E. Larsen, *P. P. Rubens, With a Complete Catalogue of His Works in America*, Antwerp, 1952, 172–74.

21. F. van den Wijngaert, *Inventaris der Rubeniaansche Prentkunst*, Antwerp, 1940, 76, no. 461.

22. J. Walker, *The National Gallery of Art, Washington, D.C.*, New York, n.d., 156 and 164.

23. L. van Puyvelde, "Projects," 146.

24. M. Trens, *La Eucaristía en el arte español*, Barcelona, 1952, 25.

25. V. H. Elbern, "Der Eucharistische Triumph, ergänzende Studien zum Zyklus des P. P. Rubens," *Kölner Domblatt*, XIV/XV, 1958, 136.

26. M. Jaffé, "Rediscovered Oil Sketches by Rubens—II," *The Burlington Magazine*, CXI, 1969, 534. See J. S. Held, *The Oil Sketches of Peter Paul Rubens*, 2 vols., Princeton, 1980, 634.

27. R. de Piles, "La vie de Rubens," in *Dissertation sur les ouvrages des plus fameux peintres*, Paris, 1681, 37.

28. The modello at some point had its architecture painted out and was enlarged by additional strips of wood so that the scene was set into an oval frame and decorated by sculpture and garlands of fruit and flowers. This painting hung in the Pacully Collection as a collaborative work by Rubens and Jan Brueghel. When the additions and overpainting were subsequently removed the original surface was abraded, as a comparison between photographs of the modello in its two states reveals. This author was fortunate to have found an old photograph of the painting (then in the Pacully Collection) in the Platt Collection at Princeton University.

29. See M. Rooses, *L'oeuvre* de P. P. Rubens, I–IV, Antwerp, 1886–92, V, 1892, 308; also, V. H. Elbern, "Die Rubensteppiche des Kölner Domes ihre Geschichte und ihre Stellung im Zyklus 'Triumph der Eucharistie,' " *Kölner Domblatt*, X, 1955, 74–75.

30. C. D. Cuttler, *Northern Painting from Pucelle to Brueghel*, New York, 1973, 142.

31. The location and provenance of the modello was established in a letter from Paul Bazé of the Musée Bonnat to Jacques Foucart of the Louvre, dated 14 August 1968. The painting was left to the Musée Bonnat in 1921 by the widow of General Derecagaix, whose family had inherited it from the Pastrana Collection. The Musée Bonnat is thus in the fortunate—and unique—position of owning both the bozzetto and the corresponding modello for one of the Eucharist tapestries. Once again, this author is grateful to the Louvre for access to its files.

32. J. Smith, *A Catalogue Raisonné of the Works of the Most Eminent Dutch, Flemish, and French Painters*, II, London, 1830, 278–79, no. 937. Smith explains the temple as "a liberty which the artist has taken" but makes no mention of David's absence from the scene.

33. As it was entitled in *Export of Works of Art: 1961–1962*, London, 7. The title was retained in the subsequent reproduction of the modello in [G. Agnew], *Agnew's 1817–1967*, London, 1967.

34. For the Solomonic column and its iconographic significance see Part III of this study. N. de Poorter (*Eucharist*, 310f.) prefers this interpretation of the subject.

35. M. Rooses, *L'oeuvre*, I, 64–65, no. 48. Rooses, however, adds that "ce groupe rappelle probablement le transfert de l'Arche sainte de la maison d'Obed-Edom au temple" (65).

36. Cf. E. Tormo, *Apoteosis*, 41. If, however, this tapestry alludes to the dedication of the original Tabernacle (Exodus, XL, 1–33) then the high priest must be identified as Aaron himself. In this case, Rubens's tapestry would be more closely related to the fourth subject (Aaron) of the Lateran sacrament altar (cf. page 34 *supra*, and notes 10 and 11).

37. See Part III of this study, p. 132. According to Villalpando's reconstruction of Solomon's Temple (see below, n. 38), the main interior supports were Solomonic columns (V. H. Elbern, "Rubensteppiche," 59).

38. Ibid., 59. For a discussion of Villalpando's significance for Rubens's altarpiece of *The Real Presence in the Holy Sacrament* (St. Paul, Antwerp, Fig. 68), see B. Fredlund, *Arkitektur i Rubens måleri, form och funktion*, Göteborgs, 1974, 47–48. For documentary evidence of Rubens's purchase of Villalpando's book from Balthasar Moretus, see M. Rooses, "Petrus-Paulus Rubens en Balthasar Moretus," (IV), *Rubens-Bulletijn*, II, Antwerp, 1885, 190. An excellent discussion of Villalpando's reconstruction and

theory is found in R. Taylor, "Hermetism and Mystical Architecture in the Society of Jesus," in *Baroque Art: the Jesuit Contribution*, (I. Jaffé and R. Wittkower, eds.,) New York, 1972, 63–97.

39. E. Mâle, *Trente*, 340–41.

40. N. Beets, "Het offer van het Oude Verbond door Rubens," *Oud-Holland*, LXIX, 1954, 31–42; M. Jaffé, review of V. H. Elbern's *Peter Paul Rubens: Triumph der Eucharistie* (Villa Hügel exhibition, 1954/1955), *The Burlington Magazine*, XCVIII, 1956, 133.

41. F. Basan, *Catalogue des estampes gravées d'après P. P. Rubens*, Paris, 1767, 6, cat. no. 20: "*Sacrifice de Samuel à l'occasion du recouvrement de l'Arche, qui avoit été enlevée par les Philistins. Cette pièce est en deux planches & très-mal gravée par Lommelin. 23po. 6 lig. de haut, sur 33 po. 5 lig. de large.*" For a later edition of this print, see N. de Poorter, *Eucharist*, 313, 317.

42. V. H. Elbern, "Addenda zum Zyklus 'Triumph der Eucharistie' von P. P. Rubens," *Kölner Domblatt*, XIV/XV, 1958, 77–78. Elbern is mistaken, however, in claiming that Réau failed to recognize the subject's typological connection with the Eucharist: see L. Réau, *Iconographie*, II.1, 353.

43. L. Réau, *Iconographie*, II.2, 425.

44. V. H. Elbern, "Addenda," 79.

45. This thoroughly Counter-Reformational idea—that Christ is recognized only in the Eucharist—was similarly exploited by Caravaggio in his first version of *The Supper at Emmaus* (National Gallery, London), painted ca. 1600. For a study of this unprecedented interpretation of the Biblical subject and its Catholic significance, see Charles Scribner III, "*In Alia Effigie*: Caravaggio's London *Supper at Emmaus*," *The Art Bulletin* (LIX, 1977).

46. V. H. Elbern, "Addenda," 79–80.

Chapter 4

1. J. R. Martin, *The Ceiling Paintings for the Jesuit Church in Antwerp, Corpus Rubenianum Ludwig Burchard*, I, London–New York, 1968, 188–89.

2. V. H. Elbern, "Die Rubensteppiche des Kölner Domes ihre Geschichte und ihre Stellung im Zyklus 'Triumph der Eucharistie,' " *Kölner Domblatt*, 1955, N. de Poorter (*Eucharist*, 65) also subscribes to Elbern's belief that Rubens succumbed to spatial ambiguity—a point of view I cannot share.

3. Elbern, "Rubensteppiche," 77.

4. E. Haverkamp Begemann, *Olieverfschetsen van Rubens*, catalogue of Museum Boymans exhibition, Rotterdam, 1953, 87–88. See J. S. Held, *The Oil Sketches of Peter Paul Rubens*, 2 vols., Princeton, 1980.

5. V. H. Elbern, "Rubensteppiche," 77.

6. A. A. Vasiliev, *History of the Byzantine Empire*, I, Madison, 1973, 74.

7. Ibid., 82.

8. Ibid., 83.

9. M. Rooses, *L'oeuvre de P. P. Rubens*, I–IV, Antwerp, 1886–92, I, 59.

10. J. Smith, *A Catalogue Raisonné of the Works of the Most Eminent Dutch, Flemish and French Painters*, II and IX, London, 1830 and 1842, II, 259.

11. E. Tormo, *Apoteosis*, 45.

12. See J. S. Held, *Sketches*, 576–77. See also below, n. 19, Chapter 6.

13. Luther's classic denial of the sacrificial efficacy of the Mass appears in his treatise *On the Babylonian Captivity of the Church*, issued in 1520. For a modern English translation see J. Dillenberger, *Martin Luther: Selections from His Writings*, Garden City, N.Y., 1961, 249–359, especially 286 for the denial itself.

14. A. M. Hind, *Catalogue of Drawings by Dutch and Flemish Artists in the British Museum*, II, London, 1923, 11–12, no. 19.

15. E. Haverkamp Begemann, *Olieverfschetsen*, 87.

16. F. Lugt, *Musée du Louvre: inventaire général des dessins des écoles du nord, école flamande*, II, Paris, 1949, 20, no. 1033.

17. E. Haverkamp Begemann, *Olieverfschetsen*, 87, considered one such copy to be autograph. L. van Puyvelde, *Rubens*, Paris–Brussels, 1952, 186, published another studio copy as an original. But neither is accepted today. See J. S. Held, *Sketches*, 152.

18. F. Saxl, "Veritas filia temporis," *Philosophy and History, Essays Presented to Ernst Cassirer*, Oxford, 1936, 197f.

19. Quoted in A. A. Vasiliev, *History*, 56.

20. D. Dubon, *Tapestries from the Samuel H. Kress Collection at the Philadelphia Museum of Art: The History of Constantine the Great, Designed by Peter Paul Rubens and Pietro da Cortona*, London, 1964, 33–38.

21. See above, n. 18. Illustrated in A. Blunt, *Nicholas Poussin*, Washington, 1967, pl. 142.

22. See R. Wittkower, *Gian Lorenzo Bernini, The Sculptor of the Roman Baroque*, London, 1966, 218–19, cat. no. 49, pls. 76, 77.

23. V. H. Elbern, "Addenda," 79.

Chapter 5

1. E. Panofsky, *Problems in Titian: Mostly Iconographic*, New York, 1969, 61–62.

2. Ibid., 62.

3. V. H. Elbern, "Die Rubensteppiche des Kölner Domes, ihre Geschichte und ihre Stellung im Zyklus 'Triumph der Eucharistie,' " *Kölner Domblatt*, X, 1955, 55.

4. E. Müller-Bochat, "Der allegorische Triumphzug, ein Motiv Petrarcas bei Lope de Vega und Rubens," *Schriften und Vorträge des Petrarca-Instituts Köln*, XI, Krefeld, 1957, 6.

5. E. Mâle, *L'art religieux de la fin du moyen âge en France*, Paris, 1925, 280.

6. Ibid., 281–82.

7. E. Panofsky, *Problems*, 62–63.

8. E. Mâle, *La fin*, 282–83.

9. Ibid., 283–84.

10. Ibid., 286.

11. See V. H. Elbern, "Rubensteppiche," 56–57. One set is preserved in the Prado, Madrid. This author is grateful to Professor Held for calling attention to this series which he, too, believes may have contributed to Rubens's compositions.

12. V. H. Elbern, "Rubensteppiche," 55.

13. E. Mâle, *La fin*, 285.

14. The full title of the series is "*Fundamenta et principia fidei et catholicae religionis in sex triumphales currus dispartita*": see V. H. Elbern, "Rubensteppiche," 56.

15. E. Müller-Bochat, "Triumphzug," *passim*.

16. J. R. Martin, *The Decorations for the Pompa Introitus Ferdinandi, Corpus Rubenianum Ludwig Burchard*, XVI, Brussels, 1972.

17. H. Trevor-Roper (ed.), *The Age of Expansion, Europe and the World 1559–1660*, London, 1968, 90.

18. For a good survey of this liturgical development, see M. Trens, *Eucaristia*, 146–58. The summary here is based primarily on Trens's study.

19. *Sessio XIII*, 11 October 1551: *Decretum de s.s. Eucharistia*, cap. 5: "*De cultu et veneratione huic ss. Sacramento exhibenda.*" For the original text of the Council's decree, see H. Denzinger, ed., *Enchiridion symbolorum definitionum et declarationum de rebus fidei et morum*, 33rd ed., Barcelona, 1965, 387.

20. M. Rooses, *L'oeuvre de P. P. Rubens,* I–IV, Antwerp, 1886–92, 56.

21. V. H. Elbern, "Rubensteppiche," 82. Cf. E. Tormo, *Apoteosis*, 38; M. Rooses, *L'oeuvre*, I, 56; and J. Smith, *Catalogue*, II, 140.

22. J. R. Martin, *Pompa*, 207.

23. G. de Tervarent, *Attributs et symboles dans l'art profane*, II, Geneva, 1959, cols. 363–64.

24. A. Scharf, "The Exhibition of Rubens's Sketches at Brussels," *Burlington Magazine*, LXXI, 1937, 188.

25. Ibid., 57. The tapestry is illustrated in *Jahrbuch der Kunsthistorischen Sammlungen*, I, Vienna, 1883, between 248 and 249. For more on this series, see below, p. 105.

26. E. Müller-Bochat, "Triumphzug," 20.

27. Title page for M. de Morgues, *Diverses pièces pour la défense de la Royne Mère*, Antwerp, 1637. See H. F. Bouchery and Fr. van den Wijngaert, *P. P. Rubens en het Plantijnsche Huis*, Antwerp, 1941, 143–44, fig. 87. The title page was engraved by Cornelis Galle I.

28. See M. Vloberg, *L'Eucharistie dans l'art*, Grenoble–Paris, 1946, 227.

29. See N. de Poorter, *The Eucharist Series* (Corpus Rubenianum Ludwig Burchard, II), 2 vols., London, 1978, 351f.

30. M. Dobroklonsky, "Einige Rubenszeichnungen in der Eremitage," *Zeitschrift für Bil-*

dende Kunst, LXIV, 1930–1931, 36. N. de Poorter, similarly, proposes a direct connection between this drawing and the tapestry (*Eucharist*, 348–49), but the argument is unconvincing.

31. For example, the title pages for the *Breviarium Romanum* (1614) and the *Summa conciliorum omnium* (1623): see H. F. Bouchery and Fr. van den Wijngaert, *Plantijnsche Huis*, figs. 33 and 60.

32. In Bolswert's engraving of this scene, however, the foremost virtue is shown carrying a sword, the attribute of Justice. Thus the engraver evidently interpreted the group as the cardinal virtues and added an extra attribute to facilitate their identification.

33. H. F. Bouchery and Fr. van den Wijngaert, *Plantijnsche Huis*, fig. 103.

34. The notion of the triumphal carriage running over the bodies of defeated personifications derives both from tapestries illustrating Petrarch's *Trionfi* and from the tapestry series of the *Seven Deadly Sins* by Van Aalst. See V. H. Elbern, "Rubensteppiche," 57. See also above, p. 67 and note 11, Chapter 5.

35. This author cannot agree with Irving Lavin that the former is a deliberate allusion to Socrates (and hence paganism) and the latter a reference to the Synagogue (hence Judaism): see I. Lavin, "Divine Inspiration in Caravaggio's Two *St. Matthews*," *The Art Bulletin*, LVI, 1974, 78–79. The personifications in Rubens's tapestry are both generalized and straightforward: e.g., Furor, Hate and Envy, to which Ignorance and Blindness make natural (if less malicious) companions. Rubens already included Socrates in his proper role as a philosopher in the preceding tapestry. If the features of Ignorance appear similar to those of Socrates, it is only because the philosopher was supposed to have resembled Silenus in his ugliness. That Rubens's personification of Ignorance derives from Silenus and not Socrates is confirmed by his painting (ca. 1618, Alte Pinakothek, Munich, *K.d.K.* 177) of *The Drunken Silenus*, who corresponds to Ignorance in pose as well as features.

36. J. R. Martin, *Pompa*, 43.

37. J. Burckhardt, *Recollections of Rubens*, tr. H. Gerson, London, 1950, 126.

38. E. Müller-Bochat, "Triumphzug," 7.

39. H. Gerson and J. W. Goodison, *Fitzwilliam*, I, 103.

40. V. H. Elbern, "Rubensteppiche," 85.

41. E. Müller-Bochat, "Triumphzug," 14.

42. Ibid., 18.

43. For a detailed critique of Müller-Bochat's argument and an analysis of the possible connections between Rubens's tapestries and Van Veen's paintings, see V. H. Elbern, "Der Eucharistische Triumph, ergänzende Studien zum Zyklus des P. P. Rubens," *Kölner Domblatt*, XIV/XV, 1958, 121–33. The conclusions here merely summarize Elbern's convincing treatment of this question of literary influences on Rubens.

Chapter 6

1. E. Müller-Bochat, "Der allegorische Triumphzug, ein Motiv Petrarcas bei Lope de Vega und Rubens," *Schriften und Vorträge des Petrarca - Instituts Köln*, XI, Krefeld, 1957, 15.

2. V. H. Elbern, "Der Eucharistische Triumph, ergänzende Studien zum Zyklus des P. P. Rubens," *Kölner Domblatt*, XIV/XV, 1958, 124–25, n. 11.

3. J. Müller Hofstede, "Neue Ölskizzen von Rubens," Städel-Jahrbuch, II, 1969, 235, n. 61.

4. E. Mâle, *L'art religieux après le Concile de Trente*, Paris, 1932, 339.

5. J. de Voragine, *The Golden Legend*, translated by G. Ryan and H. Ripperger, I, London, 1941, 61–62.

6. J. Smith, *Catalogue*, II, 141.

7. G. Waagen, *Treasures of Art in Great Britain*, London, 1854-1857, II, 261 and IV, 109-110.

8. J. Smith, *A Catalogue Raisonné of the Works of the Most Eminent Dutch, Flemish, and French Painters*, II and III, London, 1830 and 1842, II, 141.

9. M. Jaffé, "Rediscovered Oil Sketches by Rubens–II," *The Burlington Magazine*, CXI, 1969, 537–38.

10. Prado, no. 1702. See E. Tormo, *Apoteosis*, 49, and L. van Puyvelde, *Catalogus der tentoonstelling schetsen van Rubens*, exhibition catalogue, Musées royaux des beaux-arts, Brussels, 1937, 81–82, no. 79. However, Puyvelde later rejected the attribution (*Esquisses*, 32).

11. R. Oldenbourg, however, included it as an original (*K.d.K.* 298).

12. G. Waagen, *Treasures of Art in Great Britain*, I-IV, London, 1854–57, II, 163.

13. See M. Rooses, *L'oeuvre*, II, 193–94, no. 367; R. Oldenbourg, *K.d.K.* 68; and H. Vlieghe, *Saints* (I), *Corpus Rubenianum Ludwig Burchard*, VIII, London, 1973, 70-72, no. 54.

14. Cf. H. Vlieghe, *Saints*, I, 71. While recognizing the symbolic grouping of the synoptic authors, Vlieghe failed to note that only Matthew is shown writing.

15. I. Lavin, "Divine Inspiration in Caravaggio's Two *St. Matthews*," *Art Bulletin*, LXI, 1974, 62–66.

16. H. Vlieghe, *Saints*, I, 71.

17. M. Rooses, *L'oeuvre*, I, 68.

18. J.-A. Goris and J. S. Held, *Rubens in America*, 53. Held now considers Norbert the correct identification.

19. See above, n. 12, Chapter 4 Professor Held has pointed out to me that the statue itself has been incorrectly restored: St. Norbert now holds a chalice instead of his original monstrance. For a discussion and illustration of the statue, see I. Leyssens, "Hans van Mildert," *Gentsche Bijdragen tot de Kunstgeschiednis*, VII, 1941, 122–23.

20. J. R. Martin, *Ceiling*, 184, no. 39.

21. E. Tormo, *Apoteosis*, 51.

22. See M. Rooses, *L'oeuvre*, I, 68.

23. H. Vlieghe, *Saints*, I, 75.

Chapter 7

1. J. S. Held, "Rubens' Triumph of the Eucharist and the Modello in Louisville," *J. B. Speed Art Museum Bulletin*, 1968, 18.

2. E. Tormo, *Apoteosis*, 56.

3. The full text of St. Thomas's "*Lauda Sion*" is found under the feast of Corpus Christi in the *Missale Romanum*.

4. See M. Trens, *La eucharistía en el arte español*, Barcelona, 1952, 231–33.

5. M. Rooses, *Rubens*, 2 vols., London, 1904, II, 432–33.

6. E. Tormo, *Apoteosis*, 20–23.

7. Ibid., 52–54.

8. E. Tormo, *En las Descalzas Reales de Madrid*, IV, 38–44, fig. 157.

9. J.-A. Goris and J. S. Held, *Rubens in America*, 34, no. 57.

10. J. S. Held, "Louisville," 12.

11. Held, Ibid., 12, originally thought this area represented the empty tabernacle of Good Friday, but now agrees that the area is too large for such a representation.

12. Ibid., 16.

13. However, the cartoon—or a copy thereof—for *The Princes of the House of Austria in Adoration of the Eucharist*, painted on paper, is mentioned by Rooses (*L'oeuvre*, V, 308) as having been in the Van Spruyt sale, Ghent, 1815. According to J. S. Held, a similar cartoon (probably the same piece) was sold 5 April 1910 in Vienna from the collection of Dr. M. P.

14. J. S. Held, "Louisville," 16.

15. See H. G. Evers, *Rubens und sein Werk, neue Forschungen*, Brussels, 1943, 203–204, fig. 219; and J. S. Held, "Louisville," 22, n. 37.

16. The modello may be recorded in an engraving by J. J. van den Bergh, an example of which is preserved in the Teylers Foundation in Haarlem. The cartoon was in the collection of "Mr. Magnan, physician to the King" (of France). This information was provided by Professor Held. See also, N. de Poorter, *Eucharist*, 262–64.

17. J. S. Held, "Louisville," 18. In view of his other copies, on copper, of Rubens's bozzetti, in which the framing devices are similarly excluded, it is tempting to suggest Victor Wolfvoet as the possible author of the "Lemonnier copy." For Wolfvoet's collection, which included six Eucharist bozzetti, see J. Denucé, *Inventare von Kunstsammlungen zu Antwerpen im 16. u. 17. Jahrhundert*, Antwerp, 1932, 150.

18. See above, Part I, n. 21.

19. For proposed reconstructions of the altarpiece, see H. G. Evers, *Peter Paul Rubens*, Munich, 1942, 42–51, fig. 11; and F. Huemer, "Some Observations on Rubens' Mantua Altarpiece," *Art Bulletin*, XLVIII, 1966, 84–85, also 468–69 for letters by J. S. Held and Huemer.

Chapter 8

1. H. G. Evers, *Rubens und sein Werk, neue Forschungen*, Brussels, 1943, 202–3.

2. Examples of the print are preserved in the Metropolitan Museum, New York, and the Rijksmuseum, Amsterdam.

3. It was so titled at the Rubens exhibition in 1942, New York (see below, n. 5). This title is retained in the Fine Arts Gallery of San Diego *Catalogue* (San Diego, 1960, 38).

4. See V. H. Elbern, "Der Eucharistische Triumph, ergänzende Studien zum Zyklus des P. P. Rubens," Kölner Domblatt, XIV/XV, 1958, 127.

5. L. M. Nash, *Peter Paul Rubens: Loan Exhibition for the Benefit of the United Hospital Fund of New York*, exhibition catalogue, New York, 1942, no. 25.

6. E. Tormo, *Apoteosis*, 60–62.

7. M. Rooses, *L'oeuvre de P. P. Rubens, I-IV, Antwerp, 1886–92, I, 69.*

8. J. S. Held, *"Some Rubens Drawings—Unknown or Neglected," Master Drawings*, XII, 1974, 258, n. 11.

9. Ibid., 250.

10. Ibid., 251.

11. See V. H. Elbern, "Ergänzende," 127.

12. J. S. Held, "Rubens' Triumph of the Eucharist and the *Modello* in Louisville," *J.B. Speed Art Museum Bulletin*, XXVI, 1968, 8.

13. E. Tormo, *Apoteosis*, 63.

14. J. S. Held, "Louisville," 8.

15. E. Tormo, *Apoteosis*, 62.

16. J. Müller Hofstede, "Ölskizzen," 204.

17. J. S. Held, "Louisville," 8 and 21, n. 25.

18. Ibid., 13 and 21, n. 32.

19. I owe this observation to Professor Held.

Chapter 9

1. Sotheby's and Parke-Bernet, *Art at Auction: 1966–67*, New York, 1967, 28.

2. See M. Bernhart, *Handbuch zur Münzkunde der römischen Kaiserzeit*, II, Halle, 1926, pl. 17, nos. 1–4.

3. E. Mâle, *La fin du moyen age*, 309–28.

4. For a discussion of the new iconography of *Spes*, see I. Bergström, "The Iconological Origins of *Spes* by Pieter Brueghel the Elder," *Nederlands Kunsthistorisch Jaarboek*, VII, 1956, 53–63.

5. See J. Müller Hofstede, "Ölskizzen," 202–3.

6. See N. I. Romanov, "The Flemish Tapestry of 'Spes' in the Moscow Museum of Fine Arts," *Art in America*, XVII, 1929, 223f., fig. 1.

7. Ibid., 232.

8. This point was first brought to the attention of this writer by Professor Held in a lecture delivered at Princeton University on 13 November 1973. See J. S. Held, *Sketches*, 118.

9. J. Müller Hofstede, "Ölskizzen," 203.

10. J. S. Held, "Louisville," 13.

11. J. Müller Hofstede, "Ölskizzen," 203.

12. Ibid., 204. N. de Poorter, *Eucharist*, 209, believes that Rubens never intended to depict the three virtues *per se*—or even two, for that matter—a view that runs counter to all the visual evidence (i.e., the three bozzetti and their iconographic identifications), as well as to the iconographic precedents.

Chapter 10

1. See J. Q. van R. Altena, "Rubens as a Draughtsman, I—Relations to Italian Art," *Burlington Magazine*, LXXVI, 1940, 199.

2. See *Palazzi antichi di Genova raccolti e designati da Pietro Paolo Rubens*, Antwerp, 1622, Figura 56. The columns flank the main entrance of the Palazzo Giorgio Doria.

3. E. Tormo, *Apoteosis*, 52–54, 66–70, and 78.

4. Ibid., 67.

5. Ibid., 70.

6. Ibid., 78.

7. V. H. Elbern, "Die Rubensteppiche des Kölner Domes, ihre Geschichte und ihre Stellung im Zyklus 'Triumph der Eucharistie,' " *Kölner Domblatt*, X, 1955, 60–61.

8. For the various linear arrangements that have been proposed, see above, Part I of this study, p. 20.

9. The Cologne set is illustrated in V. H. Elbern, "Rubensteppiche," figs. 23, 25, 27, 30, 37, 41, 43, 45.

10. R. S. Magurn, *The Letters of Peter Paul Rubens*, Cambridge, 1955, 56–57.

11. For a condensed version of the following proposed reconstruction and analysis of the cycle, see my article: "Sacred Architecture: Rubens's *Eucharist* Tapestries," *Art Bulletin*, LVII, 1975, 519–28. N. de Poorter, *Eucharist*, 47f., subsequently arrived at the same conclusions.

12. Approximately 4.8–4.9 meters. See illustrations in E. Tormo, *Apoteosis*, for calculations of the various dimensions.

13. Six are lit from the upper left, five from the right.

14. See above, Part II, p. 81.

15. If the lower tapestry does illustrate the exterior of the Temple of Solomon, this inten-

tional pairing of architectural elements may account for the absence of Solomonic columns.

16. Again, the Chicago sketch may be cited as evidence that not every tapestry was designed to have an identical counterpart.

17. See E. Tormo, *En las Descalzas Reales*, IV, 27f. N. de Poorter, *Eucharist*, 95f., reached no new conclusions about the reconstruction of the tapestries.

18. Tormo, 13f. For a survey of Spanish architecture, see G. Kubler and M. Soria, *Art and Architecture in Spain and Portugal, 1500–1800*, Baltimore, 1959, *passim*. See also N. de Poorter, *Eucharist*, 55f. for a discussion of the original chapel.

19. See J. S. Held, "Rubens's Glynde Sketch and the Installation of the Whitehall Ceiling," *Burlington Magazine*, CXII, 1970, 274f.

20. J. White and J. Shearman, "Raphael's Tapestries and Their Cartoons," *Art Bulletin*, XL, 1958, 193–221; see especially 201–2.

21. V. H. Elbern, "Ergänzende Studien," *Kölner Domblatt*, XIV/XV, 1958, 135.

Chapter 11

1. U. Reinhardt, "La tapisserie feinte: un genre de décoration du maniérisme romain au XVIᵉ siècle," *Gazette des beaux-arts*, LXXXIV, 1974, 285f.

2. J. R. Martin and C. L. Bruno, "Rubens's *Cupid Supplicating Jupiter*," in J. R. Martin (ed.), *Rubens Before 1620*, Princeton, 1972, 4f.

3. See above, n. 1, Chapter 10.

4. U. Reinhardt, "Tapisserie," 286–87 and 295.

5. Ibid., 292. For the contract, see H. Hibbard, *Carlo Maderno*, University Park and London, 1971, 113. The contract was signed on 26 June 1598 and the nave frescoes were finished by September, 1600.

6. See U. Reinhardt, "Tapisserie," 291. For a thorough discussion of the commission and frescoes, see M. L. Chappell and C. W. Kirwin, "A Petrine Triumph: The Decoration of the Navi Piccole in San Pietro under Clement VIII," *Storia dell'arte*, XXI, 1974, 119–25. Particularly illuminating is their analysis of the Counter-Reformational significance of these frescoes.

7. U. Reinhardt, "Tapisserie," 292.

8. G. R. Kernodle, *From Art to Theatre, Form and Convention in the Renaissance*, Chicago, 1944, 105.

9. H. Gerson briefly notes in passing this formal connection between the altarpiece and the Eucharist tapestries: see H. Gerson and E. H. ter Kuile, *Art and Architecture in Belgium 1600–1800*, Baltimore, 1960, 93. But he offers no iconological interpretation of this "entirely new way of giving realistic expression to a spiritual concept" (75).

10. Quoted in E. G. Holt, *A Documentary History of Art*, II, Garden City (N.Y.), 1958, 63–64.

11. See L. Steinberg, "Observations in the Cerasi Chapel," *Art Bulletin*, XLI, 1959, 185.

12. See D. Posner, *Annibale Carracci*, II, London, 1971, 57–58, cat. no. 130, pls. 130 (a–d).

13. See F. Baudouin, "Altars and Altarpieces before 1620," in J. R. Martin, ed., *Rubens before 1620*, 73.

14. M. Rooses, *Rubens*, I, 130.

15. See I. Leyssens, "Hans van Mildert," *Gentsche Bijdragen tot de Kunstgeschiednis*, VII, 1941, 117–18.

16. K. Fremantle, *The Baroque Town Hall of Amsterdam*, Utrecht, 1959, 127–28. Quoted in F. Baudouin, "Altarpieces," 82 and 85.

17. See R. Wittkower, *Art and Architecture in Italy 1600–1750*, Baltimore, 1973, 180–81, figs. 100–1.

18. V. H. Elbern, "Rubensteppiche," 58.

19. J. Müller Hofstede, "Ölskizzen," 204–5. N. de Poorter, *Eucharist*, 185–7, arbitrarily rejects Müller Hofstede's important insight.

20. J. B. Ward Perkins, "The Shrine of St. Peter and Its Twelve Spiral Columns," *Journal of Roman Studies*, XLII, 1952, 21f.

21. Quoted in I. Lavin, *Bernini and the Crossing of St. Peter's*, New York, 1968, 15.

22. Ibid., 22, note 107. See also K. Perls, *Jean Fouquet*, Paris, 1940, 215.

23. I. Lavin, *Crossing*, 22.

24. Ibid., 35.

25. Ibid., 33–34.

26. Ibid., 34.

27. Ibid., 34–35.

28. Cf. G. Cadioli, *Descrizione delle pitture, sculture et architetture che si osservano nella Citta di Mantova*, Mantua, 1773, 42: in this early description of the altarpiece the architecture was interpreted as the Temple of the Holy Trinity ("il Tempio della SS. Trinità"). H. G. Evers (*Rubens*, 50) understood the architecture as part of the "fast religiöse Ordnung." Most recently, F. Huemer ("Observations," 85) proposed that the altarpiece originally contained twelve such columns as a deliberate "reference to those of St. Peter's, as a holy temple." My interpretation (which does not depend upon the assumption that there were originally twelve columns) need not preclude any of the above, but attempts to define Rubens's architectural reference more precisely and in conjunction with the tapestry device.

29. See G. Smith, "Rubens' Altargemälde des Hl. Ignatius von Loyola und des Hl. Franz Xaver für die Jesuitenkirche in Antwerpen," *Jahrbuch der Kunsthistorischen Sammlungen in Wien*, LXV (N.F. XXIX), 1969, 45. See also B. Fredlund, *Arkitektur*, 184–86 (English summary). Fredlund believes that in the preliminary modello Rubens "not only intended to *allude* to St. Peter's but actually to let the event *take place* in that church" (185). Surprisingly, Fredlund's study of architecture in Rubens's works ignores the Eucharist cycle.

30. For a brief discussion of the Jesuit altar, see F. Baudouin, "Altarpieces," 85–91.

31. See P. Jean de la Croix, O.C.D., "La Glorification de l'Eucharistie de Rubens et les Carmes," *Metropolitan Museum Journal*, II, 1969, 168. The altar and church have been demolished.

32. I. Lavin, *Crossing*, 30.

33. Ibid., 16, n. 72.

34. See M. Rooses, *L'oeuvre*, II, 47f., no. 265. Rooses describes the columns as "*corinthiennes*" (48), and, to be sure, on first glance they may appear straight. But on close inspection we find pentimenti which indicate that the columns were originally Solomonic (with vine-scroll reliefs). Significantly, the reproductive engraving by Boethius a Bolswert, which Rooses himself illustrates (plate 91), reveals Solomonic columns. The Brera painting appears to have suffered from subsequent repainting in this area.

35. See I. Lavin, *Crossing*, 15.

Epilogue

1. E. Haverkamp Begemann, *The Achilles Series, Corpus Rubenianum Ludwig Burchard*, X, Brussels, 1975, 15–19.

2. Ibid., 39.

3. Ibid., 40.

4. Ibid., 41.

5. Ibid., 41.

6. J. R. Martin, *The Decorations for the Pompa Introitus Ferdinandi, Corpus Rubenianum Ludwig Burchard*, XVI, Brussels, 1972, 43, cat. no. 1a.

7. Ibid., 131f., cat. no. 34.

Bibliography

[Agnew, G.,] *Agnew's 1817–1967*, London, 1967.

Altena, J. Q. van R., "Rubens as a Draughtsman, I—Relations to Italian Art," *The Burlington Magazine*, LXXVI, 1940, 194f.

Basan, F., *Catalogue des estampes gravées d'après P. P. Rubens*, Paris, 1767.

Baudouin, F., "Altars and Altarpieces before 1620," in *Rubens before 1620*, J. R. Martin, ed., Princeton, 1972, 45–91.

————, *Rubens et son siècle*, Antwerp, 1972.

Beets, N., "Het offer van het Oude Verbond door Rubens, een gewassen pentekening van de Meester Ontwerp voor één der tapisserieën uit de serie: De triomf der Eucharistie," *Oude-Holland*, LXIX, 1954, 31f.

Bergström, I., "The Iconological Origins of *Spes* by Pieter Brueghel the Elder," *Nederlands Kunsthistorisch Jaarboek*, VII, 1956, 53f.

Bernhart, M., *Handbuch zur Münzkunde der römischen Kaiserzeit*, I–II, Halle, 1926.

Birk, E. R. von, "Inventar der im Besitze des Allerhöchsten Kaiserhauses befindlichen Niederländer Tapeten und Gobelins," *Jahrbuch der Kunsthistorischen Sammlungen des Allerhöchsten Kaiserhauses*, I, Vienna, 1883, 213f.

Blunt, A., *Nicolas Poussin*, Washington, 1967.

Bouchery, H. F. and Wijngaert, F. van den, *P. P. Rubens en het Plantijnsche Huis*, Antwerp, 1941.

Burchard, L., "On a Rubens Drawing after Mantegna," *The Burlington Magazine*, XCVIII, 1956, 415.

Burchard, L., and d'Hulst, R.-A., *Rubens Drawings*, 2 vols., Brussels, 1963.

Burckhardt, J., *Recollections of Rubens*, tr. H. Gerson, London, 1950.

Cabanne, P., *Rubens*, New York, 1967.

Cadioli, G., *Descrizione delle pitture, sculture et architetture che si osservano nella Citta di Mantova*, Mantua, 1773.

Cahier, C., *Caracteristiques des saints dans l'art populaire*, Brussels, 1966.

Carandente, G., *I trionfi nel primo rinascimento*, Edizioni Rai Radiotelevisione Italiana, 1963.

Chappell, M. L. and Kirwin, C. W., "A Petrine Triumph: The Decoration of the Navi Piccole in San Pietro under Clement VIII," *Storia dell'arte*, XXI, 1974, 119f.

Coolidge, J., "Louis XIII and Rubens: the Story of the Constantine Tapestries," *Gazette des beaux-arts*, LXVII, 1966, 271f.

————, "Rubens and the Decoration of French Royal Galleries," *The Art Bulletin*, XLVIII, 1966, 67f.

Cuttler, C. D., *Northern Painting from Pucelle to Brueghel*, New York, 1973.

Denucé, J., *Inventare von Kunstsammlungen zu Antwerpen im 16. u. 17. Jahrhundert*, Antwerp, 1932.

Denzinger, H., ed., *Enchiridion symbolorum definitionum et declarationum de rebus fidei et morum*, 33rd ed., Barcelona, 1965.

Dickens, A. G., *The Counter Reformation*, New York, 1969.

Dillenberger, J., *Martin Luther: Selections from His Writings*, Garden City (N.Y.), 1961.

Dobroklonsky, M., "Einige Rubenszeichnungen in der Eremitage," *Zeitschrift für Bildende Kunst*, LXIV, 1930/31, 31f.

Dubon, D., *Tapestries from the Samuel H. Kress Collection at the Philadelphia Museum of Art: The History of Constantine the Great, Designed by Peter Paul Rubens and Pietro da Cortona*, London, 1964.

Elbern, V. H., "Addenda zum Zyklus 'Triumph der Eucharistie' von P. P. Rubens," *Kölner Domblatt*, XXI/XXII, 1963, 77f.

_____, "Der Eucharistische Triumph, ergänzende Studien zum Zyklus des P. P. Rubens," *Kölner Domblatt*, XIV/XV, 1958, 121f.

_____, *Peter Paul Rubens, Triumph der Eucharistie*, Wandteppiche aus dem Kölner Dom, catalogue of Villa Hügel exhibition, Essen, 1954–1955.

_____, "Die Rubensteppiche des Kölner Domes, ihre Geschichte und ihre Stellung im Zyklus 'Triumph der Eucharistie,' " *Kölner Domblatt*, X, 1955, 43f.

Evers, H. G., *Peter Paul Rubens*, Munich, 1942.

_____, *Rubens und sein Werk, neue Forschungen*, Brussels, 1943.

Fredlund, B., *Arkitektur i Rubens måleri, form och funktion*, Göteborgs, 1974.

Fremantle, K., *The Baroque Town Hall of Amsterdam*, Utrecht, 1959.

Gaya-Nuño, J. A., *Pintura europea perdida por España de Van Eyck a Tiépolo*, Madrid, 1964.

Gerson, H. and Goodison, J. W., *Fitzwilliam Museum Catalogue of Paintings, Vol. I: Dutch and Flemish*, Cambridge, 1960.

Gerson, H. and ter Kuile, E. H., *Art and Architecture in Belgium, 1600–1800*, Baltimore, 1960.

Glen, T. L., "Rubens and the Counter-Reformation: Studies in his Religious Paintings between 1609 and 1620," Ph.D. dissertation, Princeton University, 1975.

Glück, G. and Haberditzl, F. M., *Die Handzeichnungen von Peter Paul Rubens*, Berlin, 1928.

Göbel, H., *Tapestries of the Lowlands*, New York, 1924.

_____, *Wandteppiche*, 2 vols., Leipzig, 1923.

Goris, J.-A., and Held, J. S., *Rubens in America*, New York, 1947.

Hartt, F., *Giulio Romano*, 2 vols., New Haven, 1958.

[Haverkamp Begemann, E.,] *Olieverfschetsen van Rubens*, Catalogue of Museum Boymans exhibition, Rotterdam, 1953.

Haverkamp Begemann, E., "Rubens Schetsen," *Bulletin Museum Boymans, Rotterdam*, V, 1954, 2f.

_____, *The Achilles Series, Corpus Rubenianum Ludwig Burchard*, X, Brussels, 1975.

Held, J. S., "Le Roi à la Ciasse," *Art Bulletin*, XL, 1958, 139f.

_____, *The Oil Sketches of Peter Paul Rubens*, 2 vols., Princeton, 1980.

_____, "On the Date and Function of Some Allegorical Sketches by Rubens," *Journal of the Warburg and Courtauld Institutes*, XXXVIII, 1975, 218f.

_____, "Rubens' Designs for Sepulchral Monuments," *Art Quarterly*, XXIII, 1960, 247f.

_____, "Rubens's Glynde Sketch and the Installation of the Whitehall Ceiling," *Burlington Magazine*, CXII, 1970, 274f.

————, *Rubens Selected Drawings*, 2 vols., London, 1959.

————, "Rubens' Triumph of the Eucharist and the *Modello* in Louisville," *J. B. Speed Art Museum Bulletin*, XXVI, 1968, 2f.

————, "Some Rubens Drawings—Unknown or Neglected," *Master Drawings*, XII, 1974, 249f.

Hibbard, H., *Bernini*, Baltimore, 1965.

————, *Carlo Maderno*, University Park and London, 1971.

Hind, A. M., *Catalogue of Drawings by Dutch and Flemish Artists in the British Museum*, II, London, 1923.

Holt, E. G., *A Documentary History of Art*, II, Garden City (N.Y.), 1958.

Huemer, F., "Some Observations on Rubens' Mantua Altarpiece," *Art Bulletin*, XLVIII, 1966, 84–85.

Hulst, R.-A. d', *Tapisseries flamandes du XIVe au XVIIIe siècle*, Brussels, 1960.

Jaffé, M., "Peter Paul Rubens and the Oratorian Fathers," *Proporzioni*, IV, 1963, 209f.

————, "Rediscovered Oil Sketches by Rubens—II," *The Burlington Magazine*, CXI, 1969, 529f.

————, Review of V. H. Elbern's catalogue *Peter Paul Rubens, Triumph der Eucharistie* (Villa Hügel exhibition, Essen, 1954–55), *The Burlington Magazine*, XCVIII, 1956, 133.

————, "Rubens' Sketching in Paint," *Art News*, LII, 1953, 34f.

Jean de la Croix, P., "La Glorification de l'Eucharistie de Rubens et les Carmes," *Metropolitan Museum Journal*, II, 1969, 179f.

Kernodle, G. R., *From Art to Theatre, Form and Convention in the Renaissance*, Chicago, 1944.

Kitlitschka, W., "Rubens und die Bildhauerei, Die Einwirkung der Plastik auf sein Werk und Rubens' Auswirkung auf die Bildhauer des 17. Jahrhunderts," unpublished Ph.D. dissertation, Vienna, 1963.

Knipping, B., *De Iconografie van de Contra-Reformatie in de Nederlanden*, 2 vols, Hilversum, 1939.

Kubler, G. and Soria, M., *Art and Architecture in Spain and Portugal, 1500–1800*, Baltimore, 1959.

Larsen, E., *P. P. Rubens, With a Complete Catalogue of His Works in America*, Antwerp, 1952.

Lavin, I., *Bernini and the Crossing of St. Peter's*, New York, 1968.

————, "Divine Inspiration in Caravaggio's Two *St. Matthews*," *Art Bulletin*, LVI, 1974, 59f.

Lemoine, J. G., *Exposition d'oeuvres de Pierre Paul Rubens*, Catalogue of Musée Bonnat exhibition, Bayonne, 1965.

Leyssens, I., "Hans van Mildert," *Gentsche Bijdragen tot de Kunstgeschiednis*, VII, 1941, 73f.

Los Angeles County Museum of Art Bulletin, Annual Report, XIX, 1967–68, 12f.

Lugt, F., *Musée du Louvre: Inventaire général des dessins des écoles du nord, Ecole flamande*, II, Paris, 1949.

Maeyer, M. de, *Albrecht en Isabella en de Schilderkunst*, Brussels, 1955.

Magurn, R. S., *The Letters of Peter Paul Rubens*, Cambridge, 1955.

Mâle, E., *L'art religieux après le Concile de Trente*, Paris, 1932.

————, *L'art religieux de la fin du moyen age en France*, Paris, 1925.

Martin, J. R., *Rubens: The Antwerp Altarpieces*, New York, 1969.

————, *The Ceiling Paintings for the Jesuit Church in Antwerp, Corpus Rubenianum Ludwig Burchard*, I, London–New York, 1968.

_____ , *The Decorations for the Pompa Introitus Ferdinandi, Corpus Rubenianum Ludwig Burchard*, XVI, Brussels, 1972.

_____ , *The Farnese Gallery*, Princeton, 1965.

_____ (ed.), *Rubens Before 1620*, Princeton, 1972.

Martin, J. R. and Bruno, C. L., "Rubens's *Cupid Supplicating Jupiter*," in *Rubens Before 1620*, 3f.

Michel, E., *Rubens: His Life, His Work, and His Time*, I–II, London, 1899.

Moisan, M., "The History of Decius Mus by Peter Paul Rubens," Ph.D. dissertation, Princeton University, 1975.

Molfino, A., *L'oratorio del Gonfalone*, Rome, 1964.

Mongan, A., *Drawings and Oil-Sketches by P. P. Rubens from American Collections*, catalogue of Fogg Art Museum and Pierpont Morgan Library exhibition, Cambridge–New York, 1956.

Müller-Bochat, E., "Der allegorische Triumphzug, ein Motiv Petrarcas bei Lope de Vega und Rubens," *Schriften und Vorträge des Petrarca-Instituts Köln*, XI, Krefeld, 1957.

Müller Hofstede, J., "Neue Ölskizzen von Rubens," *Städel-Jahrbuch*, II, 1969, 189f.

_____ , "Rubens in Rom 1601–1602, die Altargemälde für Sta. Croce in Gerusalemme," *Jahrbuch der Berliner Museen*, XII, 1970, 61f.

_____ , "Zu Rubens' zweitem Altarwerk für Sta. Maria in Vallicella," *Nederlands Kunsthistorisch Jaarboek*, XVII, 1966, 1–78.

Nash, L., *Peter Paul Rubens: Loan Exhibition for the Benefit of the United Hospital Fund of New York*, catalogue of Schaeffer & Brandt, Inc. exhibition, New York, 1942.

Oldenbourg, R., *P. P. Rubens, des Meisters Gemälde (Klassiker der Kunst)*, Berlin–Leipzig, 1921.

Oppé, A. P., *Raphael*, New York, 1970.

_____ , "Right and Left in Raphael's Cartoons," *Journal of the Warburg and Courtauld Institutes*, VII, 1944, 85f.

Panofsky, E., *Early Netherlandish Painting*, Cambridge, 1953.

Panofsky, E., "Good Government or Fortune?," *Gazette des beaux-arts*, LXVIII, 1966, 305f.

_____ , *Problems in Titian: Mostly Iconographic*, New York, 1969.

Perls, K., *Jean Fouquet*, Paris, 1940.

Pigler, A., *Barockthemen*, I, Berlin, 1956.

Piles, R. de, *Dissertation sur les ouvrages des plus fameux peintres*, Paris, 1681.

Poorter, N. de, *The Eucharist Series* (Corpus Rubenianum Ludwig Burchard, II), 2 vols., London, 1978.

Posner, D., *Annibale Carracci*, 2 vols., London, 1971.

[Prado,] *Museo del Prado, Catálogo de las pinturas*, Madrid, 1972.

Puyvelde, L. van, *Catalogus der tentoonstelling Schetsen van Rubens*, exhibition catalogue, Musées royaux des beaux-arts, Brussels, 1937.

_____ , *Les esquisses de Rubens*, Bâle, 1940.

_____ , "On Rubens Drawings," *The Burlington Magazine*, LXXVII, 1940, 123f.

_____ , "Projets de Rubens et de Van Dyck pour les tapissiers," *Gazette des beaux-arts*, LVII, 1961, 143f.

_____ , *Rubens*, Paris–Brussels, 1952.

Réau, L., *Iconographie de l'art Chrétien*, 6 vols., Paris, 1955–1959.

Reinhardt, U., "La tapisserie feinte: un genre de décoration du maniérisme romain au XVIe siècle," *Gazette des beaux-arts*, LXXXIV, 1974, 285f.

Ripa, C., *Iconologia*, 1603 ed. republished, Hildesheim-New York, 1970.

Romanov, N. I., "The Flemish Tapestry of 'Spes' in the Moscow Museum of Fine Arts," *Art in America*, XVII, 1929, 223f.

Rooses, M., *L'oeuvre de P. P. Rubens*, I–IV, Antwerp, 1886–92.

————, "Petrus-Paulus Rubens en Balthasar Moretus (I)," IV, *Rubens-Bulletijn*, II, Antwerp, 1885, 176f.

————, *Rubens*, 2 vols., London, 1904.

Rooses, M. and Ruelens, C., *Correspondance de Rubens et documents epistolaires concernant sa vie et ses oeuvres*, 6 vols., Antwerp, 1887–1909.

[Rubens, P. P., ed.,] *Palazzi di Genova*, Antwerp, 1622.

[San Diego], *Fine Arts Gallery of San Diego Catalogue*, San Diego, 1960.

Saxl, F., "Pagan Sacrifice in the Italian Renaissance," *Journal of the Warburg Institute*, II, 1939, 346f.

————, "Veritas filia temporis," in *Philosophy and History, Essays Presented to Ernst Cassirer*, Oxford, 1936, 197f.

Scharf, A., "The Exhibition of Rubens' Sketches at Brussels," *The Burlington Magazine*, LXXI, 1937, 187f.

Scribner, C. III, "Sacred Architecture: Rubens's *Eucharist* Tapestries," *Art Bulletin*, LVII, 1975, 519f.

————, Review of N. de Poorter, *The Eucharist Series*, in *The Burlington Magazine*, Nov. 1980, 772–73.

Shearman, J., *Raphael's Cartoons in the Collection of Her Majesty the Queen and the Tapestries for the Sistine Chapel*, London, 1972.

Smith, G., "Rubens' Altargemälde des Hl. Ignatius von Loyola und des Hl. Franz Xaver für die Jesuitenkirche in Antwerpen," *Jahrbuch der Kunsthistorischen Sammlungen in Wien*, LXV, 1969, 39f.

Smith, J., *A Catalogue Raisonné of the Works of the Most Eminent Dutch, Flemish, and French Painters*, II and IX, London, 1830 and 1842.

Sotheby's and Parke-Bernet, *Art at Auction: the Year at Sotheby's and Parke-Bernet*, 1966–67, New York, 1967.

Steadman, D. (ed.), *Selections from the Norton Simon, Inc., Museum of Art*, Princeton, 1972.

Stechow, W., *Rubens and the Classical Tradition*, Cambridge, 1968.

Steinberg, L., "Observations in the Cerasi Chapel," *Art Bulletin*, XLI, 1959, 183f.

Stevenson, S. W., *A Dictionary of Roman Coins, Republican and Imperial*, London, 1889.

Suida, W., *A Catalogue of Paintings in the John and Mable Ringling Museum of Art*, Sarasota, 1949.

Tervarent, G. de, *Attributs et symboles dans l'art profane 1450–1600*, 2 vols., Geneva, 1958–59.

Thuillier, J. and Foucart, J., *Rubens' Life of Marie de' Medici*, New York, 1967.

Tormo, E., *En las Descalzas Reales de Madrid: Los Tapices: La Apoteosis Eucaristica de Rubens*, Madrid, 1945.

————, "La Apoteosis Eucaristica de Rubens: Los tapices de las Descalzas Reales de Madrid," *Archivo Español de Arte*, XV, 1942, 1–26, 117–31, 291–315.

Trens, M., *La eucaristía en el arte español*, Barcelona, 1952.

Trevor-Roper, H. (ed.), *The Age of Expansion, Europe and the World 1559–1660*, London, 1968.

Valentiner, W. R., "Rubens' Paintings in America," *The Art Quarterly*, IX, 1946, 153f.

Vasiliev, A. A., *History of the Byzantine Empire*, I, Madison, 1973.

Vlieghe, H., *Saints, Corpus Rubenianum Ludwig Burchard VIII*, 2 vols., London, 1973.

Vloberg, M., *L'Eucharistie dans l'art*, Grenoble–Paris, 1946.

Voorhelm Schneevoogt, C. G., *Catalogue des estampes gravées d'après P. P. Rubens*, Haarlem, 1873.

Voragine, J. de, *The Golden Legend*, tr. G. Ryan and H. Ripperger, I, London, 1941.

Waagen, G., *Treasures of Art in Great Britain*, I–IV, London, 1854–57.

Walker, J., *The National Gallery of Art, Washington, D.C.*, New York, [n.d.].

Ward Perkins, J. B., "The Shrine of St. Peter and Its Twelve Spiral Columns," *Journal of Roman Studies*, XLII, 1952, 21f.

Wehle, H., "The Triumph of Henri IV by Rubens," *Metropolitan Museum of Art Bulletin*, N.S. I, 1943, 213f.

Weisbach, W., *Der Baroch als Kunst der Gegenreformation*, Berlin, 1921.

————, *Trionfi*, Berlin, 1919.

White, C., *Rubens and his World*, London, 1968.

White, J. and Shearman, J., "Raphael's Tapestries and Their Cartoons," *The Art Bulletin*, XL, 1958, 193f.

Wijngaert, F. van den, *Inventaris der Rubeniaansche Prentkunst*, Antwerp, 1940.

Wittkower, R., *Art and Architecture in Italy 1600–1750*, Baltimore, 1973.

————, *Gian Lorenzo Bernini, The Sculptor of the Roman Baroque*, London, 1966.

Wittkower, R. and Jaffé, I. B., eds., *Baroque Art: The Jesuit Contribution*, New York, 1972.

Index